'*Accidence Will Happen* is a unique and indispensable guide to usage. It's distinguished by the author's keen discernment, his reliance on scholarship rather than dogma and superstition, and an ability to cite literary examples of contested constructions that is literally (yes, literally) awesome (yes, awesome)'   Steven Pinker

'*Accidence Will Happen* is an immensely intelligent and playful polemic, cheeky and erudite by turns ... Like the best things, it is about much more than it at first might appear to be about. If nothing else, you'll be able to go out and about, head held high, saving your stranded prepositions from harm and scooping up all your dangling modifiers from danger'   Roger Lewis, *The Times*

'This is the most intelligent and entertaining book about the English language I've ever read, one that has transformed how I think about usage. It should be required reading for anyone who loves the language, especially those entrusted to teach it. Pedants are going to hate this book – and quietly take its lessons to heart'   James Shapiro

'The English language is not your enemy and Oliver Kamm is your best friend to help you navigate it. Never has a book on language been so illuminating and funny'   Agnès Poirier

'*Accidence Will Happen* is a joyous and joyously liberating assault on the "rules" of grammar ... It is the most sensible style guide I have read, not least because Kamm always puts clarity first. I have only had *Accidence Will Happen* for a week, and have already referred to it dozens of times. If this book is a bestseller, as it may well be, its monument will be the liberated prose of the writers Kamm has freed'   Nick Cohen, *Spectator*

Accidence
Will Happen

Accidence
Will Happen

A Recovering Pedant's Guide to
English Language and Style

Oliver Kamm

PEGASUS BOOKS
NEW YORK LONDON

To the memory of my father, Anthony Kamm.

—◊—

ACCIDENCE WILL HAPPEN

Pegasus Books Ltd.
148 W 37 Street, 13th Floor
New York, NY 10018

First Pegasus Books hardcover edition July 2016

ISBN: 978-1-68177-147-2

10 9 8 7 6 5 4 3 2 1

Printed in the United States of America
Distributed by W. W. Norton & Company, Inc.

Contents

Introduction

Many people are passionate about language. I'm one of them. For some years I've written a weekly column for *The Times* about questions of English usage. The column is prescriptive. It gives the best advice I can devise on what constructions are possible in Standard English, and how to write stylishly and grammatically.

Opinions on usage have to be based on something if they're to be anything more than prejudices. My columns and this book invoke the evidence of how English is used. That's the only standard we can employ for what the English language (or rather, the various dialects that make up English) consists of. I'm interested in how English is spoken and written. I'm much more interested in those mechanics than I am in complaining about how native English speakers use their own language.

Perhaps you grimace at the phrase *between you and I* (instead of *between you and me*), or *bored of* (instead of *bored with* or *bored by*), or *different to* (instead of *different from*), or *very unique* (instead of just *unique*), or *less than ten items* (instead of *fewer than ten items*). I get many letters on these and other alleged errors of English usage, seeking my support in banishing them from public life. Yet constructions like these are used by native English speakers every day. All of them are common and none are (note that I say *none are*, even though some people will tell you that you must say *none is*) ungrammatical.

Looking at the way language is used gives you some perspective on a subject that recurs in, and even dominates, public debate about English. Pedants are loud, numerous and indignant. They are convinced that standards in English usage are falling, and they blame schools and the media for tolerating this alleged deterioration. The outcome, so these purists maintain, is linguistic barbarism, in which slang, sloppiness and text-speak supplant English grammar.

Don't believe it. If there is one language that isn't endangered, it's English. The language is changing because that's what a living language does. Linguistic change is not decline. Change is always bounded by the need to be understood. People can make mistakes in English but the grammar of the language never breaks down.

The abbreviations and symbols that make up text-speak follow grammatical rules. Text-speak wouldn't be usable otherwise. Perhaps it blurs the gap between spoken and written English but that's no bad thing.

If you worry that English is changing so radically that our cultural heritage of language and literature will be lost to our descendants, your concerns are well intentioned but groundless. The prophets of decline have been around for a long time. They appear in every generation and they are always mistaken. This book explains how and why they're wrong. More broadly, it offers guidance and reassurance on the range of possibilities in English usage.

From fearing for the future of English it's a short step to worrying about the way we ourselves use language. It's natural and proper to do this. The task of being expressive is worth thinking about and taking time over. Many articulate people, fluent in the spoken and written word, take this apprehension a stage further, however. How many times have you met people who diffidently, even apologetically, explain that they were never taught grammar? It happens to me often.

Opposite me at *The Times* sits one of Britain's leading political commentators. Prime ministers seek his advice. Television inter-viewers vie for his opinions. He is a brilliant conversationalist, columnist, debater and public speaker. Yet scarcely a day passes when he doesn't look up from his desk to ask me if a particular construction in English is grammatical, or to check his spelling and punctuation. Is it possible to say *the best candidate* if there are only two of them, or must it be *the better candidate*? Should the word *data* be singular or plural? Is it illogical to say *a friend of mine*, when *a friend of me* should be sufficient?

Almost invariably, I tell him to go with his instinct. Yet I can't shift him from his conviction that he doesn't know the structure of his own language.

My friend is wrong about the state of his linguistic knowledge. In that respect, he is like many *Times* readers who write to me on questions of usage. They are intelligent and use language well, yet are convinced that their English is sub-standard. Their eloquence proves that they're mistaken.

Perhaps the generation educated since the 1960s is particularly prone to such worries because, for them, instruction in English grammar became quite rare. My impression is that many older people too doubt their abilities in English.

The purpose of this book is to offer advice on usage, and I hope it does so entertainingly and reliably, but it's also to argue that the prospects for the English language are bright. Standards of English are not declining; *your* standards of English are likely to be high. If you're among these worriers, I recommend you stop now and embrace the language that you already speak and write, in all its sophistication and complexity.

The title of this book encapsulates my reasoning. It's taken from the English edition of *Asterix the Gaul*. The indomitable Gaul has just bashed some Roman legionaries. One of the Romans says, dazedly: 'Vae victo, vae victis.' Another observes: 'We decline.' The caption above this scene of destruction reads: 'Accidence will happen.'

You have to believe me that this is funny. The first legionary's Latin phrase means: 'Woe to the one who has been vanquished, woe to those who have been vanquished.' The scene is a riff on grammar. It was made up by Anthea Bell, the English translator of the Asterix books. She is my mother and I have stolen her joke. I'll render it leaden by explaining why it appeals to me. *Victo* is the dative singular and *victis* is the dative plural. The legionary is literally declining, in the grammatical sense. The aspect of grammar that deals with declension and conjugation is called accidence.

One of the most remarkable characteristics of English usage is this: if you are a native speaker, you already know its grammar. The same is true of the vast numbers of non-native English speakers whose command of the language is indistinguishable from that of articulate native speakers.

The grammar that you use may not be that of Standard English – though the fact that you're reading this book, which is written in Standard English, suggests that it probably is. It will be one variant of English among others. You have already acquired a mastery of complex grammatical constructions. We have all done this, through an instinct by which we can learn a set of rules. Those rules, once learnt at a very young age, stay with us. We know, for example, that a plural noun in Standard English is usually formed by adding -*s* or -*es* to a noun stem. We also know the exceptions (*aircraft, children, feet, oxen, sheep, teeth* and so on) to this rule and don't have to learn them afresh.

That's a very simple rule. There are many rules that are less obvious but that we also unfailingly follow. How about the fact that we know *John admires himself* is fine but that *John thinks Mary admires himself* isn't? We know that *John likes him* is about two people whereas *John thinks he's clever* may be about only one. We know that *read* is pronounced like *reed* in *give me a book to read* but like *red* in *I've now read the book*. We know that *house* ends with an *s* sound in *they made the council house immaculate* but with a *z* sound in *they made the council house the family*.

I'm not suggesting you grant yourself credit for an achievement that is common to everyone. Learning rules of language is part of what it is to be human. By some instinct, we have the ability to learn and apply those rules. (Not everyone has the same set of rules, of course. The instinct is universal but languages differ. Which language, or languages, you speak as a native depends on the environment in which you grew up. A German toddler doesn't have a biological instinct to learn German grammar, nor does a Japanese toddler have an instinct to learn Japanese grammar. But all toddlers have an instinct to learn some set of rules.)

However, there's no need either to scold yourself for being bad at grammar, because you're not. Granted that the ability to write fluently and speak articulately is precious and there is no easy route to it. It requires practice and a good ear for language. The tools are already with you, though. It's not conscious knowledge but, believe me, you do know your own language. You know English intimately. You probably know Standard English thoroughly even if you use a different dialect of the language in everyday life. You don't need manuals to tell you how English grammar goes. You've grasped it already.

Why, then, do people use style manuals? And what, given my conviction that you're already a master of English grammar, is the point of this one?

There is a good reason and a bad reason for style manuals. Unsurprisingly, I consider that the good reason is behind this volume. It's that there are many decisions about usage that are not obvious. Some of these decisions are about tacit conventions rather than rules of grammar. Conventions change, and so indeed can rules of grammar.

Every writer of English needs to make judgments, every day, about such issues as the case of pronouns, agreement in number of subjects and verbs, vocabulary and many others. Should it be *it's I* or *it's me*? When should you use the verbs *deny*, *refute* and *rebut*, or are they so alike in meaning that it doesn't matter which you choose?

Careful writers (the phrase is a cliché beloved of usage commentators, but I like it and it's accurate) also need to make judgments about how to communicate in different contexts. Linguists use the term *register* to distinguish between these different styles of prose, such as casual or formal.

We all adapt our style of prose according to our audience. We use intimate terms (and perhaps a private vocabulary) with a loved one, casual language with friends, and varying degrees of more formal language in our dealings with strangers, experts or figures in authority. Adopting different registers is known as *code switching*. Good style depends far more on picking the right register for the occasion – on a decision about code switching – than it does on footling rules such as the precise difference between *less* and *fewer*.

Not all conventions of usage will be common to all forms of English, and I'm restricting myself here to the conventions of Standard English. If we know these conventions, and if we internalise them so that we don't have to think about them, it saves us time and gains us credibility with listeners or readers whose attention we want to secure.

Those are important gains. Children (and adults) ought to understand that if they are familiar with conventions of usage in

Standard English they will be quicker in writing and more likely to gain a hearing for anything they want to say. Not every opinion is worth a hearing, but any opinion will be at a disadvantage in the public square if it does not adhere to the social contract under which words are given meanings and fitted together in certain ways to form sentences.

The bad reason is to believe that the benefits of internalising conventions of usage amount to learning 'proper English', and that a style manual will teach it to us. There is not proper English and sub-standard English. There are *Englishes*, all of which conform to grammatical rules. Standard English is one form of the language. Its conventions are vital to know, and for children to be schooled in, as a means of gaining fluency in a recognised and universally recognisable form of the language.

By the use of the word and the sentence we have a near-infinite range of expressiveness. Dismayingly, pedants aren't much interested in this potential. The aspect of language that most exercises them is not what we can do with it but what we can prohibit. In the media, popular books and public life, arguments rage about split infinitives, when to say *hanged* rather than *hung*, and the true meanings of words such as *disinterested* and *decimate*.

I want to convince you that the English language has never been more popular or in better health. You should be far more relaxed about modern usage than the pedants are. Language is a richer subject than these purported purists imagine.

Modern English, so far from being embattled and denigrated, is powerful and vital. Pedants mistake linguistic change for impoverishment. Yet the conventions of Standard English aren't objective and eternal truths. Instead, they are tacit agreements that in a small but not trivial way aid communication. These implicit understandings are in operation now but may not have been in the past. We don't know if they'll hold in the future. We can say confidently that the language will follow rules of grammar and have conventions of usage but we don't know which rules and conventions that make up Standard English will be superseded twenty, fifty or a hundred years from now. Nor is it always clear whether we're dealing with a genuine rule of grammar or a looser convention of usage. Scholars of language spend much of their time trying to work out the rules of grammar from the evidence of how native speakers use the language. It's not an easy task and it can't be done in advance of looking at the evidence.

We don't know, because there is no one in charge of the language. No one, that is, apart from us, the users of English. In the apt phrase of Steven Pinker, of whom we shall hear more, the lunatics are in charge of the asylum. This is a difficult truth for language purists to accept.

An autobiographical note: I am a reformed stickler. I was a reasonably moderate one, in that I'd happily disregard edicts that I thought made no sense and that had no effect on fluency except to undermine it. I would split infinitives and use stranded prepositions, and sometimes say *who* where pedants would insist on *whom*. But for a long time I did hold that a word such as *disinterested* or *enormity* had a specific meaning and that treating variant uses as legitimate would erode its nuance. In reality, language is stronger than that.

I'm much influenced by the argument of Noam Chomsky, the seminal scholar of linguistics, that language is the realisation of an innate human faculty. We use it for communication, and if our meaning is obscure then we recast it till it isn't. Whatever changes happen to a language, it still has a complex structure that allows the expression of a full range of meanings. Its grammar has rules and we follow them.

Above all, language is interesting. Pedantry isn't. The sticklers can pursue their obsessions in private if they wish, but their voice in public debate is loud and lamentable and it ought to be accorded the disrespect it deserves.[1] Contrary to the pedants, I don't insist that a form of words that's alien to the way native speakers use the language must be correct. If it isn't used, it isn't English.

Apart from code switching and convention, there's another sense in which expressive users of English are constantly making judgments about language. Though I reject the notion that there is a 'correct' form of English that stands apart from the way people use the language, it's not *mandatory* to adopt in your speech and writing whatever is in general use. Nor is it illegitimate to criticise other people's use of language.

Consider the way that terms such as *chairman* and *fireman* have been increasingly supplanted in the past 40 years by non-gendered alternatives (*chair* and *firefighter*), or *handicapped* has been replaced with *disabled*. Racial epithets that were once common even on primetime television as recently as the 1970s have all but disappeared from public life through the force of social disapproval. One or two of my recommendations in this book (for example, my advice to avoid the word *authoress*, even in jest) are based on similar judgments about what's appropriate to modern mores.

Those are important changes in the way language is used. They aren't arguments about what constitutes 'proper English', however. They are choices.[2] By dispensing with the notion that there is a 'proper English' that stands apart from the users of the language, we can better appreciate the range of expressive possibilities that are open to us. This book argues that the choices open to good stylists of English prose are far more expansive than most style manuals conceive of.

Oliver Kamm, August 2014

Author's Note

This book is a source of advice and an argument about language. In Part 1, I outline my view of English usage. There are genuine rules of grammar, there are conventions of usage and then there are the superstitions of the sticklers. Those superstitions have bedevilled debates on language. I then dissect the principal fallacies in the pedants' case and their indifference to modern studies of language. Last, I identify where these superstitions come from. The pedants themselves generally don't know. Their bizarre notions of correct English aren't principles of logic, nor have they been conveyed across the generations by guardians of the language. They're just a bunch of shibboleths dreamt up by some eighteenth-century (or later) amateur enthusiasts, whose present-day equivalents are determined not to examine evidence.

In Part 2, I set out a long but far from comprehensive list of disputed usages, with my recommendations on whether to observe or (more usually) ignore them, along with advice on a number of more general subjects that writers do need to pay attention to, such as style, sentences and punctuation.

Though the book is about usage, and has many quotations, I've tried not to litter the text unduly with quotation marks. Hence, for a word or phrase that I discuss, I use italics. Likewise for definitions. For a direct quotation, I use quotation marks and cite the source, with the exception of quotations from two particular newspapers.

Where I produce a quotation in bold type, and without a source, it is taken from a recent (that is, twenty-first-century) edition of *The Times* of London or its sister newspaper, the *Sunday Times*. These quotations appear mainly in the compendium of disputed usages and other practical issues in Part 2. Where a word or phrase is given in italics and upper-case letters, it has its own entry in this compendium.

Part One

The State of the Language

In considering the use of grammar as a corrective of what are called 'ungrammatical' expressions, it must be borne in mind that the rules of grammar have no value except as statements of facts: whatever is in general use in a language is for that reason grammatically correct.

Henry Sweet, *New English Grammar*, Vol. 1, 1892, p. 5

Principles of English usage

Language is distinctively human. It differentiates us from every other species. All human societies have language, in immense grammatical complexity. The ability to speak language emerges in very young children, who can form words and combine them into sentences according to complex rules. Language ensures that societies can replicate ideas and inventions rather than have to create or discover them anew in every generation.

This book is about one language, English, and one form of it, Standard English. And it discusses just one aspect of Standard English, namely the way it's used in the modern world.

Many books of advice on usage exist. The typical style manual makes judgments on what is proper English usage and what isn't. I argue instead that many of the purported rules of English grammar should be ignored. Those rules (more accurately, superstitions or shibboleths) are really just stylistic preferences. They should be considered on their merits, which are more commonly demerits. There is no literate purpose in avoiding prepositions at the end of sentences or insisting that *between* can apply to only two things rather than three or more. Sticking to pointless stipulations in the mistaken belief that they're grammatically required clogs up prose and makes it sound stilted.

Nor is that the only problem with traditionalist books on usage. Worse, they miss what is really interesting about language: that it's always in flux but never loses its structure. Constant invention is intrinsic to the use of language, yet the requirement that the speaker or writer be understood imposes constraints. Usage is always changing, and grammar can change too, yet it remains consistently bound by a set of rules.

Those rules aren't the ones that pedants fuss about, such as whether it's permissible to use the adverb *hopefully* to modify an entire sentence (as most native speakers in Britain and North America habitually do, and as you assuredly can), or begin a sentence with *because* (you can), or use *they* as a singular as well as a plural pronoun (again, you can). They're ones that ensure that subjects, objects, verbs, adjectives, adverbs and other parts of speech conform to a certain structure. We learn these rules as children. An instinct for language allows a child to acquire an appropriate set of rules and then apply them.

This book has three main arguments. First, you are already a master of grammar. Trust me on this. You became one when, as a young child, you acquired a set of rules – whether of Standard English, or another variety of English, or another language. Second, there's no cause for alarm about the state of the English language, which is in excellent health and can look after itself.

Third, if you use English, it's useful to know the conventions of Standard English.

These premises seem to me unspectacular, even obvious. Yet public debate over language typically ignores the first, denies the second and misrepresents the third. Let's examine them in reverse order.

Conventions are convenient

The reasons for adopting a particular convention are not logic and consistency, for language operates by its own rules. The reasons are instead convenience, concision and fluency.

It's helpful to know the conventions of usage as you make your way in life, education, work and leisure. They put you on the same level as everyone else in being listened to. Adopting conventions of usage may not guarantee a hearing for your own voice with any audience but at least you won't be instantly dismissed for some perceived solecism. Everyone's language offends someone sometimes and there is no shortage of (incompatible) advice on what is proper usage. In this book, I describe conventions that currently exist, while stressing that conventions shift and may be supplanted by others. The death of a convention isn't a sign of decline, only of change.

The beginning of wisdom in English usage is to realise that there are many right ways of saying things. Imagine the position of a schoolchild who uses a FLAT ADVERB (that is, an adverb that takes the same form as its related adjective, such as *quick* or *wrong*) and gets penalised for it on the grounds that an adverb should end with *-ly*.

It happens. I've come across it. Faced with a sentence like *I flew direct to New York*, many adults (including some English teachers) will instinctively 'correct' *direct* to *directly*, not realising that this adverbial use of *direct* is Standard English. What will happen if children get marked down for using this type of completely legitimate construction in an essay? They'll be deterred ever after from writing something that's fluent and idiomatic, and perhaps in later life they'll misguidedly 'correct' others who do the same.

I'm an enthusiast, even a zealot, for teaching English grammar in schools, and on the whole the subject is taught well. The purpose of grammar teaching, however, is not to instil rules that have no better grounding than a teacher's idiosyncrasies or insecurities. It's irksome to be accused (as I often am) of arguing that 'anything goes' in language, because that isn't even a parody of the view that linguists hold and that I present in my columns. There are right and wrong ways of using commas, for example, but there are also many permissible variations in the conventions of usage.

A further stage in enlightenment is to realise that many stubbornly held and vigorously expounded but utterly worthless linguistic superstitions, which pedants remorselessly cite, should be junked. Berating people on arbitrary stylistic grounds for not adhering to rules is worse than self-defeating. It undermines the cause of clear writing and damages appreciation of the real study of language.

The pedants are not necessarily wrong on every particular recommendation. The problem with their case is that it's false from the outset. They believe that linguistic usage should accord with an external standard of correct English, of which they are the arbiters. This is the premise of almost all usage guides. The more thoughtful guides are prepared to make pragmatic concessions to the way the language is spoken and written, but even these go astray if they treat general usage as somehow linguistically deficient.

You can be wrong and I can be wrong in our grammar, spelling and punctuation. But, as Henry Sweet argued (in the formulation quoted at the head of this chapter, with which all academic linguists known to me would agree), it's not possible for everyone, or for the majority of educated users of the language, to be wrong. The only evidence we have of what makes up the English language is how people write and speak it. If an 'incorrect' form is more widely understood than an alternative construction, it isn't incorrect. It's what the language is.[1]

Amateur grammarians who insist otherwise are a menace. What drives them is not a feel for language but more often a superstition that English must fit certain patterns. These patterns are not, as their advocates maintain, rules of logic. They are more usually an irrational belief that English should follow Latin in certain ways. These stifle prose and bore an audience. The greatest writers in the language, including Chaucer, Shakespeare, Jane Austen and Dickens, have used constructions that breach the sticklers' notion of correct English. You're free to do it too. In Part 2, I discuss some of these mistaken notions, which you can follow if you like but that you can also violate without hesitation or embarrassment.

Standards aren't falling

As well as mistaking convention for correctness, pedants inaccurately see an English language in crisis.

'Acceptance of popular low standards undermines the glories of our unique linguistic heritage,' declares a writer to *The Times*.

'Everywhere one looks, there are signs of ignorance and

indifference,' laments Lynne Truss, author of a bestselling guide advocating a 'zero-tolerance approach to punctuation'.[2]

Surveys of literacy don't support this gloomy view.[3] They show a stubborn problem (not a new one) that some adults can't read and write well enough but that isn't the same thing.

Every generation believes that standards of English are deteriorating and seeks to fix the language in a state that will stop further damage. Defoe and Dryden sounded the alarm, as did Samuel Johnson before investing formidable industry and intellect in compiling his *Dictionary of the English Language*.

That chronology should tell you something. Even great writers are liable to confuse linguistic change with decline. Yet people carry on speaking, writing and understanding English, and the expressive power of the word is undiminished.

It's odd. Most language pundits won't acknowledge that English is in a good state. The more typical message is a lament for a lost age of linguistic standards.

I spoke in a debate in London in March 2014 under the title 'Between You and I: the English Language is Going to the Dogs'. The proposers of the motion were two eminent journalists, John Humphrys and Simon Heffer, who maintain that failing to distinguish FLAUNT from FLOUT or DISINTERESTED from UNINTERESTED is a threat to critical thinking and therefore civilisation itself. I'm not misrepresenting their view.[4] It's wrong – as is the alarmist claim, implied by the debate's title, that the common phrase BETWEEN YOU AND I is a mark of illiteracy.

Most media commentary on language is of the Heffer/Humphrys school. It regrets the decline of formal grammar teaching in schools when the subject is in fact being taught better than ever, and far more thoroughly and usefully than it was to generations of schoolchildren who were taught bogus, pointless and manufactured rules that have nothing to do with the effective and fluent use of language.

The notion that the English language is going to the dogs is false and ugly. It's false because it misunderstands the way language works. It's ugly because it evinces suspicion of, even contempt for, modern culture. To the purist, the way people speak and write is an opportunity to find fault rather than listen. Even in the case of simple error (say, a common spelling mistake, such as *accomodate* for *accommodate*, or a misunderstanding of the meaning of a word due to a phonetic confusion, such as the difference between MITIGATE and MILITATE), they will see evidence of cultural decline. Their critiques are loaded with words such as ignorance, atrocity, illiteracy, vandalism and the like, yet what they're railing against is either remediable and limited, or not an error at all. Their complaint is not with illiteracy but with the perplexing circumstance that not enough people speak like them (or, as they would doubtless prefer to say, *speak as they do*). Sometimes they don't really know how they use language and complain about people doing things that they also do themselves. Sometimes they complain about things that aren't even there.[5]

You can recognise these people by their rhetoric and also by their technique, for no amount of evidence of usage will change their mind about language. As a shorthand term I've called them purists but theirs is not a pure form of English. No such thing exists. If you want a 'pure' English, you'll need to go back at least to Old English before the Normans invaded. The purists' English is nothing like that. It's a dialect specific to a time and place: the English that emerged in the dominant part of England, primarily London and its environs, in the modern era. My preferred term for these purists is sticklers or pedants, and collectively the sticklocracy. I mean to imply by that name a fastidiousness, a fussing, about things that don't matter.

If you fear that your standards of spoken and written English are deficient, you're far from alone. But you've probably arrived at this nagging doubt because you've been bamboozled into it. Generations of schoolchildren grew up having English grammar beaten into them (sometimes literally). Some grammar instruction of this bygone age was useful but much of it was junk, derived unquestioningly from the prejudices of eighteenth-century grammarians.[6]

Children (and adults) need to know how to write well, and spell and punctuate. That's not in dispute. That end is being overlooked in the current educational fad of grammar testing in schools. There is dispiriting evidence that children are being marked down by nervous examiners for not following some of the misguided rules that I outline in this book: things like the THAT, WHICH rule or the prohibition on SPLIT INFINITIVES. Those rules are of no use to anyone and shouldn't be inculcated in a new generation.

Rules, usage and superstition

None of this means that writing good English is easy, only that a lot of what passes for linguistic advice is beside the point. In language, there are rules, there is usage and then there are superstitions. These shouldn't be confused.

Rules are the patterns that underlie our use of words, phrases, clauses and sentences. Different varieties of English may have different rules. For example, the rules of Standard English would permit a construction like *I didn't see anybody* but proscribe *I didn't* *see nobody*. The rules of other varieties of English might allow both constructions. There is no inherent logic that makes one set of rules right and another wrong.

Usage is a set of implicit agreements about how language ought to be used. Again, these will differ according to the variety of the language used.

Superstitions (also known as fetishes and shibboleths) are a subset of usage. These are a set of judgments on what constitutes correct English that have no justification and are best ignored.

These first two categories correspond to what are often called descriptive and prescriptive rules. The descriptive rules are observations about how people do in fact use English. Linguists record and examine these rules, which by definition are already followed by English speakers, and try to account for them. This book is not about rules in that sense. It is instead about the conventions of usage – how people ought to speak and write.

Here is an example of the third category: a superstition.

Early in my first job, as a junior analyst at the Bank of England, I wrote a report on financial markets that was sent to a rather grand executive director. He returned it to my manager with the comment that it included a split infinitive. The experience has stayed with me. I was grateful that the director had read my note but perplexed that this was his sole observation, especially as I did not (and certainly don't now) consider that I had committed any offence against grammar. If there is an objection to split infinitives at all, it's solely aesthetic, not grammatical, and even then applies only under some circumstances. The split infinitive *to boldly go* is excellent English, as it puts the stress in the right place.

Guides to English usage don't usually object to split infinitives but they do often make judgments that have no better grounding in any reasonable conception of grammar or style. They repeat purported rules that, to the extent that they have any use, are merely expedients to avoid ambiguity. Frequently those rules lack even that justification. If adopted, they make prose clumsy or opaque. They should be ignored. Prohibitions on the passive voice, on conjunctions at the beginning of sentences, on prepositions at the end of them and on much else besides have nothing to do with good grammar.

The sense in which we can genuinely talk about rules of grammar is that all languages have the same type of machinery. This involves putting words together in certain ways to yield meanings. The wonder is that the rules whereby verbs, nouns and other parts of speech are combined are common to everyone who speaks a particular language variety. Linguists since the 1950s have generally (though not unanimously) inferred from this remarkable fact that the facility for language is innate rather than a cultural invention. Even small children understand how words are combined and inflected (that is, their endings are changed) in some ways, which are permissible, and not others. The sentence *I want an ice-cream* is a complex combination of subject pronoun, present-tense verb in the first person and indicative mood, indefinite article and noun, in which the noun-phrase *an ice-cream* serves as the object. Any parent or grandparent of a child who has reached the age of three has heard it flawlessly expressed, many times. (Next time you hear it, check your irritation long enough to marvel at the sophisticated syntax.)[7]

Public commentary about the use of language rarely touches any of this. Pundits instead spend their time decrying a supposed decline in standards of written and spoken English, especially in education. Some make this complaint as part of a jeremiad about the state of society generally. Melanie Phillips, the conservative commentator, asserted in a polemic in the 1990s against progressive education: 'The revolt against teaching the rules of grammar became part of the wider repudiation of external forms of authority.'[8]

One reason for these conflicting accounts is that, when referring to the rules of grammar, the linguists and the purists are talking about different things. The purists mean not the observed regularities of language but a much smaller category of usages. These are prescriptive rules on such matters as the meanings of words and the cases of pronouns (for example, when to use *who* and *whom*). The rules of language as the concept is understood by linguists are patterns acquired by natural processes, such as knowing that some word orders make sense (*I want an ice-cream*) and others don't (*an want ice-cream I*). The rules of language as understood by the pedants – prescriptive rules of the type that most people understand as 'grammar' – are acquired not that way but through explicit teaching. When people confess to having 'bad grammar', they generally mean that they haven't had that sort of explicit instruction.

Yet the prescriptive stipulations are made up. They come from culture rather than biology. Agreement on usage is necessary because standardisation in language makes it easier for the writer to be understood and the reader to understand the writer. But the agreement is tacit. No one legislated these usages. They can change. Nor is there any moral element to them.

Usage isn't anarchy

Usage is the criterion of English, but that doesn't mean that *any* usage is legitimate. The usage that I refer to is *general* usage. The majority of writers of Standard English cannot be mistaken on the same linguistic question at the same time. You don't need to believe that the language is constantly improving to scorn the sticklers' efforts. You just need a sense of proportion and an appreciation of what language is.

Language isn't a delicate artefact of civilisation but something we're programmed to do. Standards aren't in danger from barbarian hordes and undereducated youth. They're maintained by the need to communicate. English isn't tarnished by new usages that differ from what words and phrases once meant. The language is constantly replenished. Once you grasp that the sky is not falling and that English belongs to its speakers rather than its self-appointed guardians, questions of usage become far more interesting than the complaints of the grammar sticklers.

Even in a short time, a convention about language may become obsolete. As a reformed stickler, I recall arguing that it helped if the pace of change were not so rapid that the literature of previous generations became obscure. Modern readers are fortunate in being able to easily make sense of Shakespeare, because our conventions have enough in common with his. But developments in language are far from impoverishing. Standardised spelling and conventions of punctuation postdate Shakespeare. Conversely, a non-Standard construction such as the double negative (*I didn't see nothing*) has been used for centuries despite being deplored as illogical by the pedants.

A sense of history will indicate why laments about linguistic and cultural decline tend to be overwrought. Language is part of human nature. If there is a need for a word or a shade of meaning, the human mind will devise it. It always has done. This may seem obvious but it isn't. It's certainly lost on the sticklers.

Take N. M. Gwynne, author of a slight and perplexingly popular volume with the alluringly modest title *Gwynne's Grammar: The Ultimate Introduction to Grammar and the Writing of Good English*, published in 2013. The author wrote in a newspaper article: 'For five decades and more I have been complaining, with dismay and disgust, about the abolition of the formal study of grammar which took place without warning or any sort of serious consultation with parents in the 1960s... Learning grammar does not just happen; it is not just picked up.'[9]

He is exactly wrong. Learning grammar does just happen and it is just picked up. That is a precise description of how infants become masters of complex grammatical constructions. The grammar may not be that of Standard English but it is a grammar of some variety of English (or of another language). Recall the contention of modern linguistics that the faculty for language is innate. Language is not a cultural construction but part of the makeup of the human brain. Language instruction has the important but specific task of making native speakers fluent, in writing as well as speech, rather than merely intelligible, and in different registers: a letter is different from an essay, which is different from a sonnet. Language instruction also enables people who aren't speakers of Standard English to become familiar with the rules of this form of the language (so that they know, for example, that it's Standard English to say *I didn't see anything* rather than *I didn't see nothing*).[10]

We all have an informal language that combines casual speech and jargon. There's nothing wrong with this. It's often expressive and economical, and by no means necessarily ungrammatical.

But beyond close acquaintances (or, in the case of jargon, other specialists in the relevant subject), that variety of speech may not be readily comprehensible.

Every user of English, every day, makes many judgments about the right word or phrase, and chooses among different forms of usage. By recognising the conventions of disputed usages and particular choices of word, we save time and gain fluency. The difficulty lies in distinguishing genuine grammatical questions from whimsy. But once grasped, the conventions of language enable you to talk to any audience without being dismissed or patronised because of the way you write or speak. Fluency secures credibility. Practical advice on style, provided it is founded in the way the language is used rather than on a self-appointed authority's whim, can help you gain a hearing for your ideas, allowing them to be judged on their merits.

That philosophy of usage is different from the one advanced by Kingsley Amis some years ago: 'This book is founded on a principle taken for granted by most writers and readers since time immemorial: that there is a right way of using words and constructing sentences and plenty of wrong ways.'[11] Wrong, wrong, wrong. There are conventions about the use of language and the meaning of words that are never settled and constantly argued about. It's valuable to know those conventions and their history, not least because it gives you a sound basis for disregarding ones that make little or no sense. But there are many legitimate ways of using language. Even within Standard English there are numerous variant usages, spellings and constructions that nothing but a commentator's caprice would object to.

Linguists describe the structure of language rather than intervene in the comparatively trivial task of, say, adjudicating on the cases of pronouns. That doesn't mean that prescription is absent from their work. There is a sense in which prescription is integral to what they do. When they describe some aspect of Standard English, they are committed to the idea that that's how you need to speak if you want to be considered a fluent speaker of Standard English. But they are also committed to similar prescriptions when they describe some aspect of non-Standard English. Their task is not to judge Standard English correct and non-Standard English wrong (or illiterate, or barbaric). That's just not what the study of language is about. Yet an appreciation of what linguists do is essential to usage pundits. The distinction between description of language and prescription in usage is cogently described by Steven Pinker, the cognitive scientist: 'The rules people learn (or, more likely, fail to learn) are called *prescriptive* rules, prescribing how one "ought" to talk. Scientists studying language propose *descriptive* rules, describing how people *do* talk. They are completely different things, and there is a good reason that scientists focus on descriptive rules.'[12]

The reason, says Pinker, is that many prescriptive rules about language are merely bits of self-perpetuating folklore. They are at best irrelevant and often insensitive to the texture of language; the very fact that they need to be learnt by rote shows that they are alien to how language naturally works. An example is that question of the use of pronouns. One prescriptive rule is that, where a phrase is the object of a verb and requires an object case, every word in that phrase is an object that requires an object case. Pinker points to the ease with which intelligent people say things like *give Al Gore and I a chance* whereas they would never say *give I a chance* (Pinker is quoting a statement by Bill Clinton). The implication is that proponents of the prescriptive rule misunderstand English grammar and the structure of language.

People who believe that split infinitives are always wrong

or that you can't end a sentence with a preposition are indeed repeating bits of inconsequential folklore. Prescriptive rules can be loosened and eventually dissolved. Others will then take their place. It's possible to make your meaning plain while paying little attention to these 'rules' of language, and if enough people make what is counted a mistake in Standard English it will eventually cease to be a mistake and become accepted usage. The rules of grammar will survive this process because the faculty for language is an instinct rather than an acquired skill.

The limited sense in which there is a role for a prescriptive rule is that at any moment English usage will have points of dispute and matters of decision, and users of language will wonder about them. They will in particular wonder how to use words to gain the attention of readers. That is where advice on grammar, spelling, punctuation and style can help. Pinker isn't being hypocritical in writing his books in lucid prose that adheres to the conventions of Standard English. The cover of the volume of Pinker's that I've quoted carries an endorsement by Chomsky, the theoretical linguist famous for his conclusion on the innateness of language, that it is 'very well written'. Pinker has gained a huge readership by expressing his ideas that way. He writes in the form demanded by the situation.

For a radical overstatement of the role of linguistic conventions, by contrast, consider the view of Roger Scruton, the philosopher and critic: 'Language is the *sine qua non*, without which there cannot be a national identity or culture. It is the fundamental stratum of the collective consciousness, and its influence is reflected in all the institutions and customs of society.'[13]

I'm less concerned than Scruton with language as a means of creating national identity. I just want English speakers to be able to communicate clearly and expressively and not to needlessly hold themselves back. That's a practical observation, not a moral stricture. When we speak or write, we instantly lay ourselves open to judgment. That may be unfair but its inevitability was acknowledged by the actor Emma Thompson on a widely reported visit to her old school. Urging pupils to avoid slang words such as *like* (as in *I was, like…*) and *innit*, she concluded for her teenaged audience: 'Just don't do it. Because it makes you sound stupid and you're not stupid.'[14]

This was wise advice proffered for the right reason. Thompson was distinguishing between different registers: the language used in any official capacity and the language teenagers use among their friends. The reason for speaking and writing fluently in Standard forms isn't to show refinement; it is to make us at home in the world. Slang makes us at home in a likeminded group. That isn't wrong but it is limiting.

Slang is a mode of expression that works with people we know or people we are like. Standard English works with a wider audience. That's its merit: not correctness but usefulness. Standard English is more useful than any non-Standard variety because it can be used in more contexts. That is much like saying that it's more useful to know English around the world than it is to know Welsh, Danish or Dutch. It's more useful to know Spanish than it is to know Catalan. We need to know what sort of audience we're addressing to judge how best to address them. In debates on English usage, that question is far more important than the issues that the pedants obsess about.

Likewise, argots and how they develop are a field of study in their own right but they are specific to time and place. There was a short-lived and unfortunate educational controversy some years ago when a California school board passed a resolution on what's known as African American English (AAE) – a vernacular spoken

by many but far from all Americans of African descent. A popular
and misleading term for AAE is Ebonics, which wrongly suggests
that a form of language coincides with skin colour. In fact, AAE
shares many features, such as the DOUBLE NEGATIVE (*don't know
nothing*), with the dialects of Southern states in the United States.
It has grammar and conventions of usage. It's neither a separate
language nor slang: it's a non-Standard form of English.

The school board was denounced by politicians and pundits for
recognising black slang as a language of its own. 'The very idea
that African American language is a language separate and apart is
very threatening,' declared Maya Angelou, the poet, 'because it can
encourage young men and women not to learn Standard English.'[15]

Yet the board did no such thing. All it did was to consider,
temperately and reasonably, whether to contrast Standard English
with AAE in language classes, as a teaching aid. The proposal was
swiftly abandoned amid the controversy. It might have been justified or it might not. The answer would have depended on evidence. But the intention would have been clear: to teach Standard
English. As Chomsky observed, including AAE in the curriculum
for young black Americans would have the same purpose that
'Standard English is taught to unintelligible white kids in eastern
Tennessee – as a means of making them fluent'.[16]

Making them fluent, that is, in Standard English. There's no
point in teaching students to be fluent in AAE if it's their native
dialect. If it's their native dialect then, by definition, they already
speak it.[17]

Teenagers may be highly intelligent and also habitual users of
slang and non-Standard forms; but if all they use is slang or non-
Standard English, then their intelligence will not be recognised
and their abilities will be needlessly constrained. That isn't culture:
it's confinement. Fluency in Standard English offers a means of

escape and enrichment. It just so happens that the sticklers don't help them gain fluency; instead, they muddy the issue altogether. They are a liability to the teaching of language.

Fluency and the sticklers' failures

Emma Thompson's advice was sadly misunderstood by politicians. Michael Gove, who was then the Education Secretary, approvingly cited her views. Alluding ironically to the slang that Thompson had criticised, Gove told the Conservative Party conference: 'I am bovvered by the fact that our English language, our birthright, the language that Shakespeare used, is not being passed on to the next generation in all its beauty and its clarity.'[18]

The language that Shakespeare used is indeed not being passed on to the next generation. But it isn't being used by Gove's and my generation either. How could it be? Shakespeare's influence on the development of the language is immense, but that development is unplanned. Consider vocabulary. Many words now in common use have their first recorded instance in the works of Shakespeare. But many of his neologisms (that is, a newly coined word or phrase; see INVENTED WORDS) failed to survive. For example, Othello declares: 'I shall turn the business of my soul / To such exsufflicate and blown surmises.' It's possible to guess from the context what Shakespeare meant by *exsufflicate* and to admire his inventiveness. But it isn't a word used by anyone else, including the former Secretary of State for Education.

There are big differences between Shakespeare's English and modern English in grammar as well as vocabulary. Shakespeare's characters use such constructions as 'What sayst thou?' (Olivia in *Twelfth Night*) and 'I know not where to hide my head' (Trinculo in

The Tempest). No one would say these things now. We'd say instead *What do you say?* and *I don't know where to hide my head.*

Gove's point is rhetorical. Depressingly, he is echoing the long-standing complaint of pedants. There are always people who decry declining standards of English. Many of them assume that other dialects of English are themselves instances of linguistic decline. An extreme case is Alfred Knox, a Conservative MP of the 1930s, when moving pictures had recently acquired sound. Knox urged the Board of Trade to restrict the number of imported films from America, as they spread a dialect and accents that were 'perfectly disgusting, and there can be no doubt that such films are an evil influence on our language'.[19]

It's easy to laugh at such fastidiousness but Knox has many imitators who don't grasp the nature of linguistic change. The English language is not static, nor are its boundaries clear. Nor is it a language tied to the British Isles. English is a river. Its content is always changing and it has many tributaries. Its characteristics include impermanence. Indeed, there can be no single definition of the English language.

This conclusion applies across history and across countries. It's not only the language that's different now. So are its speakers. In the middle of the last century, around 400 million people spoke English. The total is now 1.5 billion, while the proportion of them living in Britain, North America and Australasia has declined. There is no historical parallel for this growth in English usage and the shift in the language's centre of gravity. English has become a global language not through any inherent virtues but because of the political and economic power of successively the British Empire and the United States.

Amid this ferment, if not cacophony, of different variants of the language, it's hard to make generalisations about what English consists of or what its prospects are. The most sensible conclusion is that it isn't possible to define English apart from how its speakers use the language. Usage is not just usage: it's what the language is.

Not everyone understands this. Many supposed rules of grammar were formulated by autodidacts in the eighteenth century, a time of particular worry about the state of the English language. By the end of the eighteenth century, more than 250 handbooks of grammar and twenty dictionaries had been published, some of them in several imprints. As there was no such thing as English grammar taught in schools and universities of the time, these early codifications reflected the biases of their creators, who were drawn from a narrow social and geographical circle and believed that English should accord with Latin and Greek syntactical patterns. Thus was born the notion that the language was crucial to the moral character of English-speaking peoples. It was famously espoused much later by Winston Churchill, who insisted on pronouncing *Nazi* as *Nar-zee*, as if it were an English rather than a German word.

Standard and non-Standard, not right and wrong

Linguists are loath to judge that a construction is incorrect rather than non-Standard. It depends on context. The issues that style manuals typically argue about (often with passion) are not rules of logic but conventions of usage that may hold at one time but aren't a permanent feature of the language. These are perpetually in dispute: if they weren't, there'd be no need for the manual.

Concern for language shouldn't be like that. Let me give an autobiographical example. I gained appreciation at an early age of authors who used language fluently, through the school stories of P. G. Wodehouse. From those stories (I particularly enjoyed *Mike and Psmith*, in which cricket plays a large part) I graduated to his other comic creations. Wodehouse's protagonists may be hapless but they always use language discriminatingly, as in Bertie Wooster's observation of the mood of Bingo Little: 'The brow was furrowed, the eye lacked that hearty sparkle, and the general bearing and demeanour were those of a body discovered after being several days in water.' It is a pleasure and not a pedagogical chore to observe here the difference between imagery and cliché.

In this respect alone, I agree with Scruton: a society lacking a sense of its literary and linguistic inheritance is diminished. Language evolves. The orthodox view is that language change is primarily the result of new generations of speakers developing grammars that are slightly different from those of earlier generations. Knowing the linguistic conventions that have been superseded ensures that the literature of the past remains open to us. Observing the conventions that now apply, provided they are useful, will help preserve and spread today's culture. Disregarding conventions that aren't useful, but merely come out of a stickler's imagination, will also help preserve and spread culture, by speeding their demise.

Unfortunately, the pedants have an unhealthy influence on the question. As even Amis acknowledged, in his bizarre guide to modern usage, *The King's English*: 'I would guess that for every acquaintance of mine who looks on me as some sort of authority on correct usage or pronunciation there is at least one who sees me as an officious neurotic who sets right venial blunders uninvited.'[20]

Pedantry is weak scholarship, bad tactics and poor manners. It doesn't aid good prose. To gain a sense of the richness of the language and the range of possible ways of using it, it helps to have a sense of the poverty of the pedantic imagination.

The Errors of Pedantry

And the Gileadites took the passages of Jordan before the Ephraimites: and it was so, that when those Ephraimites which were escaped said, Let me go over; that the men of Gilead said unto him, Art thou an Ephraimite? If he said, Nay; Then said they unto him, Say now Shibboleth: and he said Sibboleth: for he could not frame to pronounce it right. Then they took him, and slew him at the passages of Jordan: and there fell at that time of the Ephraimites forty and two thousand.

(Judges 12:5–6)

Sticklers' shibboleths

The Book of Judges records that two tribes, the Gileadites and the Ephraimites, fought a battle in which the Ephraimites were defeated. The Gileadites mounted a blockade on the River Jordan to prevent the flight of their enemies. The sentries who guarded it asked those who wished to cross to say *shibboleth* – a word meaning *ear of grain* in ancient Hebrew. It was a means of identifying who was part of the 'in' group and who wasn't. The Ephraimites, who had no *sh* sound in their dialect, pronounced it with an *s* sound.

By the way they spoke, they gave themselves away as being part of the excluded group, and were slaughtered.

The penalties may be milder but linguistic shibboleths still work in the same way. The subjects that exercise the sticklers, the pedants, the purists, the zealots and the dogmatists are only tangentially, if at all, about the rules of grammar. Some are not about grammar at all but concern disputed meanings of particular words. In aggregate, they are a tiny subset of usages. The fervour with which these are prosecuted and insisted on has little to do with the virtues of clarity and expressiveness. These usages serve merely to denote who is part of a charmed circle of discourse and who is outside it.

Lest you think this unfair, consider the history of debates over usage. For centuries, people have been bemoaning declining standards in English. Eminent writers and pundits have sought to reverse this purported decline by expounding rules, proposing official bodies and publishing style guides. The effort has apparently been unavailing. If the pedants are to be credited, native English speakers still don't know their own language.

That view is mistaken but the problem is not just with the diagnosis. The pedants treat these issues as a mark of civilisation. Gwynne says: 'If enough societies in the world crumble as a result of bad decisions taken because of bad thinking, yes, the whole of world civilisation faces collapse, with consequences for each individual that are literally incalculable.'

Gwynne represents an extreme point on the spectrum of silliness. Even so, his views are worth considering because, while a caricature, they exemplify where the sticklers' assumptions eventually and disastrously get you. Gwynne's premise is shared by all the pedants, however learned and ostensibly moderate, in varying degrees. They believe that usage should be determined by some external standard of what is correct English.

Prescriptivists are all alike: moralisers

The difference between an informed prescriptivist such as H. W. Fowler and a dogmatic one such as Gwynne is immense. But these authors hold that assumption in common. Fowler's recommendations are tempered by pragmatic adjustments to current usage and a feel for language, but he was still an 'instinctive grammatical moraliser'.[1]

That phrase was applied to Fowler by Otto Jespersen, the great Danish scholar of English grammar, and Fowler welcomed it. He maintained that the purpose of a grammarian was 'to tell the people not what they do and how they came to do it, but what they ought to do for the future'.[2] Fowler's approach has many flaws. The main one is that it doesn't work. If it did, there wouldn't be a need for more manuals on usage. One manual would be enough to establish correct English. Language isn't like that. Modern studies of language aren't a branch of ethics: they're a branch of science. They don't assess language against some external measure of correctness: they study the way language is used.

I adopt the approach of modern linguistics. I am not a linguist but a writer and commentator. I aim to inform general readers about choices in their use of language. In that sense, there is an inevitable element of prescription in this book and in my columns on language. But the criterion for judging a particular point of usage is not some ideal standard: it's instead the evidence of how English is spoken and written.

That's the raw material of research in linguistics. So far from believing that 'anything goes', linguists love rules. They spend much of their time trying to formulate rules that distinguish between what is and what is not grammatically possible (and it's a tough job).

What's not possible? Here's an example, not in grammar but in meaning. If I want to say that my mood on finishing writing a book is *ebullient*, yet owing to a misapprehension because of the phonetic similarity of these words, I say instead that it's *emollient*, I've made an error. I've assumed that a word means something that it doesn't. I'd be grateful if, in that case, some learned colleague corrected me.

If I demand a source for the correction, the colleague will point me to a dictionary. The dictionary will give a definition (or a range of definitions). Its source will be the evidence of how a word is used. Recommendations on language have to be based on that evidence. They can't be driven by some external notion of correctness, otherwise they'll be irrelevant at best and in fact misconceived. At every stage in my compendium of usage conundrums, in Part 2, I've therefore appealed to historical, linguistic and literary evidence to demonstrate the record of usage.

The sticklers do it differently. Gwynne insists (emphasis in original): 'The rules always have a *logic* underpinning them.' In my experience, people who assert a correspondence of grammar with logic usually lack training in either field. What drives them is instead a superstition that English must fit certain Latin syntactical patterns. These aren't rules of logic at all. They're just the way that Latin worked.[3]

There are broad generalisations about the syntax of any language, but there is nothing logical about these generalisations, and different languages have different generalisations. For example, English normally has subject–verb–object order, but Welsh has verb–subject–object order, and Japanese has subject–object–verb order. Moreover there are always exceptions to the generalisations (*'Hello,' said John* has object–verb–subject order).

Gwynne's argument is admittedly such an outlier that it's a caricature of the pedants' position. Yet the point of caricatures is that they have a kernel of truth in them: otherwise they wouldn't work. President de Gaulle really did have a big nose; cartoonists therefore exaggerated this characteristic rather than invented it. And Gwynne is expressing a view that some great minds too have advanced in linking grammar and logic. John Stuart Mill declared in his Inaugural Address to the University of St Andrews in 1867: 'The principles and rules of grammar are the means by which forms of language are made to correspond with the universal forms of thought... The structure of every sentence is a lesson in logic.'[4]

Assuming that there is a universal standard of good usage, the pedants reduce language to a tiny set of issues – in fact, a tiny collection of disputed usages. The answers they come to and argue for *may* be defensible on the standard I've set, namely the record of actual usage, but they more usually aren't and they're derived in the wrong way. Sticklers ignore usage and go by instinct and dogma. What they end up with is shibboleths. Let's consider the ten major errors of their approach to language.

Error 1: Sticklers are confused about what grammar is

Sticklers are worried about grammar. So they say. Yet many of their most fervent complaints are not about grammar at all and they don't realise it.

Linguists have a precise definition of grammar. (When speaking of linguists, I mean people who study language, not people who speak languages. The one term serves to describe both types, but it's the scientists of language that I'm concerned with here.) They mean *syntax*, which is the way words fit together to form clauses and sentences; *morphology*, which is the way words are formed; and *phonology*, which is the system of sounds that a language has.

Pedants are barely interested in any of this. They worry instead about meanings of words, and about spelling and punctuation. Spelling and punctuation are known as orthography. Meaning is known as semantics. When sticklers lament that some public figure doesn't know the difference between *imply* and *infer*, their complaint has nothing to do with grammar. It's about what words mean. When sticklers condemn someone for illiteracy for confusing *it's* (contraction of *it is*) and *its* (possessive adjective) their complaint is again not about grammar. It's about orthography.

Is this not just a trivial distinction? The pedants are, after all, complaining about *something* to do with language.

No, it's important. Grammar has rules. They are fundamental to the way we speak and write and they are instinctive. Nobody needs to be told that *trashed reviewer book the the* doesn't conform to grammatical rules whereas *the reviewer trashed the book* does. When a new word enters the language, the forms it takes aren't arbitrary. How it's used depends on the part of speech that it is (a noun, a verb or whatever) and its complements. It follows the forms a native speaker would expect for that part of speech, such as (usually) adding *-s* or *-es* to a noun stem to make it plural. The rules aren't a branch of logic, as Mill claimed: they *exhibit* a logic. For example, most words' meanings have no connection with their sounds. That doesn't make language chaotic. Language has a logic of its own.

The stipulations of the pedants aren't that type of rule. Pedants insist that standards of English depend on people observing pre-scriptive rules that are often arbitrary. For example, it would be logical if the possessive *its* did have an apostrophe, to make it align with *Mother's* or *the Prime Minister's*. But when the apostrophe entered the language, the conventions for its use took a long time to form and even then weren't necessarily regular.

The apostrophe was introduced into English print quite late in the development of the language – not till Early Modern English in the sixteenth century. Its original purpose was to denote an elision or contracted form. That practice continues to this day in such formulations as *can't*, *haven't* and *it's*. The usage didn't trouble grammarians when it was adopted from French as a print-ers' convenience.

In the seventeenth century use of the apostrophe was extended to denote singular possession, but it took a while. Some writers in the late sixteenth century started using this practice but they were far outnumbered by uses of the *his*-genitive form (such as *the King his men* for *the King's men*). It took a century more for the editors of the greatest writer in the language to consistently adopt the apostrophe marking singular possession (in the Fourth Folio of Shakespeare, published in 1685). Yet even so, grammar manuals of that time still omitted mention of the genitive apostrophe. And only in the eighteenth century were the apostrophe's uses extended to denote plural possession.

That may sound a logical, step-wise progression but it's not hard to show how arbitrary the standards were. The use of the apostrophe for a singular noun was rationalised as marking an elision of the *his*-genitive form (for example, in the phrase *the man's journey*, the apostrophe was there, so it was said, to represent a missing possessive *his*). But the extension of the apostrophe to plural possession provoked much wondering. As Elizabeth Sklar, an academic linguist, notes: 'By the middle of the eighteenth century grammarians agreed, by and large, about the use of the apostrophe in the genitive singular, and had more or less willingly extended it to include irregularly formed plurals as well (*women's, children's*). But the propriety of extending the apostrophic genitive to nouns forming their plurals in *s* was an issue that troubled theorists until the end of the century.'[5]

It's only because we're now familiar with the convention for plural genitive marking that we mistake it as a rule of grammar rather than a contingency of history. If you try and think yourself into the position of an eighteenth-century grammarian, you may be able to see the reason for wonderment. Why would a phrase such as *the printers' decisions* have an apostrophe, when there was no elision – no letter or word had been removed?

It was because the original use of the apostrophe was to denote elision that we have one of the most confounding aspects of punctuation today: why the possessive adjective *its* has no apostrophe. Sticklers are ferocious when confronted with a confusion of *its* and *it's*. Truss extends zero tolerance to such malefactors (emphasis in original):[6]

> If the word does not stand for 'it is' or 'it has' then what you require is 'its'. *This is extremely easy to grasp*. Getting your itses mixed up is the greatest solecism in the world of punctuation. No matter that you have a PhD and have read all of Henry James twice. If you still persist in writing, 'Good food at it's best', you deserve to be struck by lightning, hacked up on the spot and buried in an unmarked grave.

For what? It's an accident of the history of printing that this problem exists at all. When the printing conventions for the use of the apostrophe were established, the construction *it's* was already in use. It denoted the elision in *it is*. Or maybe the printers just didn't anticipate the problem. They certainly would have had no notion of the nightmares they would give generations of schoolchildren thereafter, castigated by their teachers for stupidity when making the completely reasonable supposition that, because an apostrophe marks possession, *it's* should denote a neuter possessive.

Indeed, *it's* was a possessive until the nineteenth century. And even the so-called greengrocer's apostrophe, in which an apostrophe is added to simple plurals such as *tomato's* and *potato's*, has historical warrant. Through the magic of the internet, I come across a digital transcription of an early eighteenth-century volume entitled *Handel's Opera's for the Flute*. That's not an error. It was orthographical convention of the time to add an apostrophe to plurals when the singular noun ended in a sibilant (so *genius* became *genius's*, rather than *geniuses*) or a vowel (hence *idea's, toga's, folio's, quarto's*).[7]

Words in English that end in a vowel are unusual. They are often borrowed from other languages. It makes intuitive sense to mark this unusual ending by inserting an apostrophe. Even Truss grants that there is some reasonableness in the assumption, though she prefaces her admission with a comment of condescension characteristic of the sticklocracy:[8]

> The only illiteracy with apostrophes that stirs any sympathy in me is the greengrocer's variety. First, because greengrocers are self-evidently horny-thumbed people who do not live by words. And second, because I agree with them that something rather troubling and unsatisfactory happens to words ending in vowels when you just plonk an 's' on the end.

Did you detect the note of scorn? Use of the apostrophe divides the literate from the rest, the in-crowd from the unruly. And because greengrocers are engaged in trade rather than more elevated pursuits, they can be excused from the obligation to know about this quality of refinement. Truss even acknowledges that the greengrocer's apostrophe was once Standard usage for a plural of a foreign word ending in a vowel, yet she adds this unwittingly revealing observation: 'As Professor Loreto Todd tartly remarks in her excellent *Cassell's Guide to Punctuation* (1995), "This usage was correct once, just as it was once considered correct to drink tea from a saucer."'[9] So to this way of thinking, it's not just an error of orthography but an error of manners to insert a greengrocer's apostrophe.

In fact, the apostrophe isn't a rule (and, contrary to Truss, it certainly isn't a virtue) but a convention. It doesn't exist in speech at all, being a characteristic purely of the written language, yet speech is perfectly comprehensible without it. (Consider that *the cat's bowl* and *the cats' bowl* have the same pronunciation.) There are huge advantages to having standardised conventions, which is why they need to be taught and children (and adults) should know them. But conventions are what they are; they're not a defining feature of civilisation. And they change, as do rules of grammar. Again, Truss undermines the assurance of her case by noting correctly that it's customary in American publications to use an apostrophe when referring to decades (such as 'the 1960's'), which some people in Britain consider a barbarism whereas it's just a convention.

Or take the rules of spelling. It's essential for children and adults to know how to spell correctly; doing so makes it easier for their prose to be read and for them to be taken seriously in employment and in life. But English spelling isn't a grand and immutable structure. It's a continuous historical collection of improvised standards and foreign borrowings.

English spelling isn't a branch of logic either. Like punctuation, it's a set of conventions, which have been shaped by accidents of history. Here's a small example. In *Paradise Lost*, Milton refers to 'The Serpent suttlest Beast of all the Field'. It's our word *subtlest*. Milton spells it without the silent *b* (and likewise refers to 'his wit and native suttletie'). How come? Well, the word was spelt that way before the eighteenth century. At some point thereafter, the word came to have its silent *b* to reflect its Latin root. There was no phonetic reason that *subtle* should be modelled after the Latin *subtilis*; but it happened because of a concern to signal Latin derivations and shared meanings.

There were attempts at comprehensive spelling reform long before Milton. Simon Horobin, in his illuminating *Does Spelling Matter?* (2013), provides a valuable succinct summary of these doomed ventures. Among the earliest such reformers was Sir John Cheke, a Cambridge classicist, who in the 1530s sought to reform spelling in line with English sounds. He was supported by another Cambridge scholar, Sir Thomas Smith, who proposed that the number of letters in English orthography be the same as the number of 'voyces or breathes in speaking and no more' (which necessitated inventing new letters, some of which he took from Greek). They in turn influenced John Hart, of Chester, who wrote successive works nonetheless differing from these authors in the matter of pronunciation. Hart's volume, revealingly entitled *The Opening of the Unreasonable Writing of our Inglish Toung* (though unpublished in his lifetime), attempted to tidy up the messiness of spelling and the 'vices and corruptions' of the language. It was at this time that reformers attempted to change spellings to show the Latin origins of words. This was when *debt* (then variously spelt *det*, *dett* or *dette*, from the French *dette*) acquired its silent *b*, to indicate its derivation from the Latin *debitum*. It was also when *people* acquired its silent *o* to indicate its derivation from the Latin *populum*. Odd as it may seem, spelling reformers considered that linking English spellings more closely to Latin roots would make them more comprehensible and easier to learn.

Horobin notes that sometimes the etymology was wildly awry. Reformers reworked the Middle English word *iland* as *island* on the premise that it was comparable to the French word *isle*, derived from the Latin *insula*. Yet it wasn't a French borrowing at all; and we've been stuck with it ever since.

The attempt at standardisation failed for a predictable reason. There was more than one scheme for spelling reform, and these were not compatible. The resulting inconsistencies were early evidence of a characteristic of the language that still infuriates the sticklers: no one is in charge of it. It just happens. Shakespeare later satirised the pedant as Holofernes in *Love's Labours Lost* ('he draweth out the thread of his verbositie...').

This sort of linguistic adaptation, mostly by unplanned development and occasionally by fiat, has happened frequently in English spelling, and while you can see the process at work in many individual words, the overall result is quite inconsistent on any measure. Take the word *receipt*, which has a silent *p* indicating its association with the noun *receptacle*. You would imagine that logic would require that *deceit* also have a silent *p*, as the word is related to *deception*. And, of course, it doesn't. English spelling doesn't lend itself to that sort of logical scheme. You just have to know the words.[10]

This doesn't make spelling arbitrary. Part of the reason that English words are often not spelt phonetically is that there are consistent spellings for particular recognisable morphemes. (A morpheme is the smallest unit of speech that can distinguish one word from another. The word *pins*, for example, contains two morphemes: *pin* and the plural suffix -*s*.) The usual past-tense ending in English is -*ed*. But this ending isn't pronounced consistently across all words. In *forged* or *fitted* or *lunged*, for example, it has a *d* sound. In *lacked*, it has a *t* sound. Yet regardless of the variant pronunciations the morpheme -*ed* in the past tense of most English verbs is spelt the same way. (Note, however, that some verbs can take the *t* ending; I've just given *spelt*, and there is also *learnt*, *dreamt*, *burnt*, *leapt*, *spoilt*, *leant* ...)

But while spelling has regularities, it doesn't have any underlying scheme to it. It is what it is through evolution rather than Intelligent Design. It can't be anything other than an approximation to the patterns of speech. There are only five vowels in the Roman alphabet yet the number of vowel sounds that English makes is far greater. Consider the different pronunciations of *pat*, *pet*, *part*, *peat*, *put*, *putt*, *pit*, *pot*, *port*, *pert*, *pate* ... The way letters can be put together to form words that represent speech-sounds has to be approximate. And many inconsistencies result.[11]

There's scant evidence, by the way, that the idiosyncrasies of English spelling are a barrier to literacy but they have prompted numerous modern proposals for reform, despite the mixed results of their sixteenth-century counterparts. George Bernard Shaw is among the most famous evangelists for spelling reform. He wrote to *The Times* in 1941 with this complaint: 'It may interest you to learn that your leading article contains 2,761 letters. As these letters represent only 2,311 sounds, 450 of them are superfluous and could have been saved had we a British alphabet.'

Phonetic spelling, so that the words on the page approximate the sounds that are uttered, has appeal to the logical mind but language has an infuriating habit of not conforming to these constraints. English has become the lingua franca of the digital age, yet it has never been spelt phonetically. Admittedly, some languages have more phonetic spelling systems than others but no language, from Egyptian hieroglyphs to the present, has ever been spelt strictly phonetically.

Our system of standardised spelling today reflects contingent historical circumstances. One of the most important is printing, and especially its mechanisation in the nineteenth century. Jane Austen's manuscripts, for example, were characterised by poor spelling, crossings-out and blots. A news story in 2010 quoting Professor Kathryn Sutherland of Oxford University, who had examined the unpublished manuscripts, prompted much excited comment about how a great writer could have been so lax in what sticklers now insist are objective standards of literacy. Professor Sutherland speculated that Austen may have had an expert editor. But in fact it's not so surprising that even a great writer would have been unconcerned about strict accuracy in her spelling, because the division of labour relieved her of that responsibility. It was a standard practice that the printers would set the spelling. And it was printing conventions that made English orthography standardised in a way that it had never been before.

The system of spelling that we have now was largely formalised by around 1800 but there are numerous spelling variants. Most obviously, the dominant English-speaking country of today, the United States, has a different system of orthography from that of the United Kingdom. This is partly due to the efforts of the only truly successful spelling reformer the English language has ever had: Noah Webster, who in the nineteenth century devised a dictionary (which still bears the Webster name) and specific spelling variants for an American tongue. I say more about Webster in the next chapter, on the history of the usage debate. His views on language were generally more enlightened than those that held sway in England at the time.

American orthography also differs in punctuation; if there are quotation marks in a sentence, for example, a full stop will fall within rather than outside them, even if the quotation is a fragment rather than a full sentence, 'like this.'

Orthographical variants are not only national, however. There simply is no right answer to whether *ageing* or *aging* is the spelling you should adopt, or whether you should use an apostrophe to denote the plural of an abbreviation (*MP's* or *MPs*, to denote two or more Members of Parliament). And as publishing becomes more diverse in the digital age, with self-publishing becoming much more common than in the days of the printed and spoken word alone, variant spellings are likely to expand. Before printing, writers often used their own private spellings. That is likely to become more common as the barriers to entry in publishing are now so low. The sticklers will have still more material with which to decry the decline of standards of modern English, and the world will go on as before.

In short, the pedants' complaint is wrong from the outset. Their jeremiads about the decline of grammar typically have little or nothing to do with grammar. They focus on other aspects of language instead, usually spelling, punctuation and the definitions of words. These are not inviolable rules but conventions, which have developed not arbitrarily but with a good deal of historical contingency. Learning these conventions is a boon to users of English and to their listeners and readers. But the virtue lies not in the conventions themselves; it's because standardisation helps comprehension. Note that it helps: it isn't essential, otherwise the varied spellings that writers used even for their own names before around 1800 would have rendered communication impossible. In fact, they were fully consistent with some of the greatest fruits of English literature, including Chaucer and Shakespeare – whose grammar, never mind spelling and punctuation, would horrify today's sticklers if they stopped to consider it.

Error 2: Sticklers confuse their stylistic preferences with correct English

After their confusion about what grammar is, the pedants' most destructive myth is that their own stylistic preferences are the test of proper English. They aren't. They're just preferences.

A strident example of this confusion is offered by Carol Sarler, a columnist for several national newspapers:

> Confession: I actually do it anyway. I correct people by reflex; to the immense embarrassment of my family I have been known to do it to adults I hardly know. It's like a nervous tick.
>
> If someone says, 'I had less than eight hours sleep' – and if my daughter isn't near enough or fast enough to kick me – out it pops: 'Fewer!' I cannot tolerate 'different to' in place of 'different from' (although if the speaker is American I will allow 'different than'. Nice of me, don't you think?)... Extreme, you say? Potty, perhaps? You might be right yet I remain unrepentant.[12]

Not potty, just ill-informed and lacking a feel for language. *Less than eight hours* is idiomatic English. It's what I would say, and if Sarler 'corrected' me on it, I'd explain that I was using *hours* not as a count noun but in the same way that I would judge Brighton to be less than 100 miles from London. I'd add that my own use of *fewer* rather than *less* for count nouns was a stylistic preference that had nothing to do with the rules of grammar. I'd also assume, but not say, that Sarler had absorbed the purported rule about *less* and *fewer* at an early stage in her education and never thought about it again. It's her prerogative to use the words in the way she's chosen, but it's no more than that.

Show me a style guide and I'll show you preferences smuggled in and depicted as rules. The very existence of numerous style guides shows how wide the spectrum of legitimate difference is. Every publishing house and every newspaper has its own style guide because the conventions of usage are not fixed.

Do you treat *data* as singular or plural? My own newspaper, *The Times*, treats it as singular, and we periodically get letters from readers castigating us for our illiteracy on this. If you want to use *data* as a plural noun, I won't criticise you, let alone try to stop you. But yours is only a preference. It's no good telling me that *data* is a Latin plural: I know that. The origins of a word don't determine the way it's used.

You criticise me for using a SPLIT INFINITIVE? That's up to you, but English doesn't strictly even have an infinitive form and what's commonly but inaccurately known as a split infinitive breaks no genuine grammatical rule. In a column I once used the phrase *to legislatively protect people*, which some readers took exception to. I explained that, as the adverb *legislatively* modified the verb *protect* and not the noun *people*, I didn't want to say *to protect people legislatively*. That would be to split the adverb from the verb, which struck me as poor style – and a greater transgression than a split infinitive, which is not grammatically a transgression at all. I convinced most readers but not a gentleman who insisted that my wording was 'extremely ugly'. That's progress in a sense. I have no objection to pedants expressing their aesthetic views on the use of language, so long as they don't mistake them for rules of grammar.

There are many questions about usage that can't be reduced to a rule. We looked at orthography in the context of the pedants' first error, and it's a subject that is freighted with choices. The conventions of punctuation are many and varied, and some don't have definitive answers even under the pedants' own edicts.

Do you use an Oxford comma? This is a *COMMA* that precedes *and* at the end of a list, like this: *I wrote two letters, a newspaper column, and a magazine essay.*

It isn't necessary to use an Oxford comma (so called because it's a stylistic choice of Oxford University Press), as the conjunction *and* will distinguish and link the last two items in the list. But some people prefer it as a guard against possible ambiguity. I sometimes use it but not religiously. It isn't an issue about a rule; it's just a stylistic preference.

On other issues of punctuation I'm firmer. Do you use a comma splice? This is a comma used between two clauses, each of which could stand as a sentence on its own, like this: *I got to the theatre early, I had to stand outside until the doors opened.*

That, to me, is poor style. The comma in a comma splice ought to be a semi-colon or a full stop, because the break in the diction is too long for just a comma. But people use it. Orthographical convention favoured it 200 years ago. Some modern novelists employ it effectively in dialogue. My own contributions to the *Times* style guide oppose it and I have to explain it as a preference for a mark that signals a pause, not just an intake of breath.

Style varies from generation to generation, and publication to publication, and it's the mark of the pedant to imagine that there is only one answer and that it is known. Take the example of how you enumerate a list of points, which I discuss in Part 2 as *FIRST*,

SECOND, THIRD. The ultra-stickler Gwynne insists that this must (not may) go *first*, *secondly*, *thirdly* and so on. He urges his readers to 'join the fight against firstly'.

What? How to enumerate points in a list is a question of usage where different sticklers have their own preferences disguised as instructions. Some insist that you must be consistent in your usage, so say *firstly*, *secondly*, *thirdly* and so on. Others insist on consistency in another way, with *first*, *second*, *third*. Gwynne throws in a variant about which he's equally adamant – and which doesn't matter.

Error 3: Sticklers think there is correct English and the rest

There is no single standard for what counts as good English. Sticklers go wrong in thinking that there is correct English and then every other variety. In reality, how you should speak and write depends on who you're talking to.

Note that I didn't say *to whom you're talking*. That's because the writing style I normally adopt as a newspaper commentator, and in this book, is intended to be more conversational than formal. I write columns and essays, not treatises. Using language effectively requires adapting it to the circumstances. It is far more important to be able to judge the appropriate register than it is to know when you should choose the subject or the object case of a personal pronoun. Really.

If I read the words *you asked Giles and I to help in the office over Christmas*, I'm not going to scream in indignation. *Giles and I* is the object of the clause, and the object case of the first-person singular personal pronoun is *me*, not *I*. But a very large number of native speakers put the pronoun in the subject case after the coordinator *and*. Shakespeare was among them (see BETWEEN YOU AND I). That isn't wrong. It doesn't violate logical relations. Just because the verb *asked* takes a direct object, which is *Giles and I*, it doesn't mean that every word in the phrase needs to be in the object case. It's convention alone that requires that they be written that way. It's the difference between Standard and non-Standard English, not correct English and illiteracy.

But if you adopt a register out of keeping with the requirements of the situation you're in, you've made an error. A ceremony of commemoration of the Srebrenica massacre needs a highly formal register; a sports commentary needs a more conversational one. Mix them up, and you've failed not only in standards of behaviour but also in language.

The task of instruction in English should be to instil the conventions of fluent communication, not shibboleths. Linguistic superstitions don't matter. Tacit conventions that make up Standard English do, because they enable you to get listened to without prejudice. But most of all, choosing the right form of language, the right register for the situation, matters. If you have something to say, you'll wish to say it in the way that is most apt as well as pleasing.

You want evidence of the sticklers' incomprehension? The *Daily Telegraph* published a 'good grammar quiz'. It was devised by Gwynne, and it revealed more about his and the newspaper's approach to the language than either intended. Here's one of the questions:

'Which of these sentences is grammatically correct? A) 'Do you see who I see?' or B) 'Do you see whom I see?'

The right answer, according to the *Telegraph*, is B.

No, it isn't.

Or rather, I could have guessed that they'd count it the right answer but it isn't what I would ever say. No native speaker with a respect for the conventions of usage would say it either. The question is direct speech. It sounds prissy to use the object case *whom* in that context. Not many people use it in prose; no one except the insufferably pedantic uses it in speech. The question (or rather, the answer) is not relevant to the conventions of English usage. That point is not lost on the pedants and they draw exactly the wrong conclusion. They believe that the fault lies not with their rules but with speakers of English who, in vast numbers, fail to abide by them.

This defies common sense as well as scholarly inquiry into what language is. More lamentably still, it diverts attention from the real test of fluency, which is knowing how to speak and write. If every stipulation of the sticklers were adopted universally, from the 'correct' use of DISINTERESTED to the prohibition on the use of HOPEFULLY as a sentence adverb, it would not in any respect improve public standards of literacy. If, however, children are taught the importance of the right register, that will help them and people who hear them in years to come.

Fortunately, that is in fact how language has been taught in schools since the reintroduction of grammar lessons at the end of the 1990s. As Gwynne ostentatiously laments, what passed for grammar stopped being taught in schools in the 1960s. That suspension wasn't a revolt against authority. To an extent, it was another type of traditionalism, stressing the qualities of literature, that contributed to this decline. Anything that smacked of science (and studying language and grammar is a science) was suspect.

That was a mistake – and in that sense Gwynne does have a point. He doesn't recognise how much better things are now, though. Children are being taught about the nature of language and ways of using it. Generally, this is being done well and effectively. This is the area where, unlike the irrational pedantry that this book criticises, prescriptions and guidance do work. Talking to an audience is different from asking a friend *do you see who[m] I see?* Writing an opinion column for a newspaper is different from writing an email and both are different from writing an academic paper. They require different registers. Let's take just the form of writing I'm most familiar with.

I'm a pundit. Every day, the Comment desk of a newspaper receives unsolicited articles for publication. Lots of them. Vanishingly few are of publishable quality, however great the knowledge of the aspiring contributor. The principal reason is that they just don't read fluently. They're verbose, and not only in being typically far longer than any newspaper could publish. They lack structure and argument, being mainly a series of assertions and unrelated digressions. And the most besetting problem is that they are dull.

It's as if the writer, aware of the responsibility of addressing the public, can't talk naturally but adopts a tone of affected gravity. You can tell that from the first paragraph and sometimes from the first sentence. I'm less hostile to the cliché *it goes without saying that* than the sticklers who typically deride it (*if it goes without saying, why say it? Hahahahahaha...*). It's an idiom. But it's a terrible way to start the argument of a case. And if you make it through to the end, you'll generally find an equally feeble conclusion, along the lines of: *Will X happen or will Y? Only time will tell...* There is no 'peg' for the article – a piece of news or an insight that would allow the reader to catch quickly the flow of the argument. There is no arresting metaphor or perception. It's like reading the transcript of an accountants' convention.

This isn't how people naturally talk. It's merely how they think they ought to write for a serious audience. The condition carries over to public speaking. People who are unused to giving a speech often write it out beforehand, peppering it with phrases that they believe convey seriousness but are merely dull and hackneyed.

It's a problem with a history. Even in the Renaissance, when there was a determined attempt to return English to its Latin roots, the wrong register laid a writer open to mockery. Thomas Wilson, the sixteenth-century critic, publicly derided a letter written by a parson to a patron. The parson wanted to make a show of his qualifications for a parish: 'I doubt not but you will *adjuvate* such poore *adnichilate* orphans as were *condisciples* with you and of *antique* familiarity in Yorkshire ... I *obtestate* your *clemencie* to *invigilate* thus much for me, but now I relinquish to *fatigate* your intelligence.'[13]

To say the least, the register is wrong. It's wordy and pretentious. The modern examples of writing an opinion piece for a general readership and speaking to an audience are one side of a conversation. They're not a dirge. And they are acquired skills. Not many people ever exercise them but everyone needs to know how to address an audience appropriately. Following the edicts of the pedants doesn't help in that. The task is far more important.

Error 4: Sticklers insist: 'That's not a real word/noun/verb ...'

Perhaps the most surprising stickler superstition is the insistence that a word is not a word. A variant of this objection is to insist that a word recognised as a noun can't be a verb, or vice versa.

Take IRREGARDLESS, which is caught (I note, having typed it) by software spellcheckers. Yes, it's a word. I can prove it. It's in the dictionary. And by the dictionary, I mean the principal lexicographical sources in the language, including the *Oxford English Dictionary* (*OED*). Whether a word is a word depends on whether it's used. *Irregardless* is used. Whether its derivation is through accident or deliberate levity is immaterial; it's entered the language.

That a word exists is no necessary reason for adopting it. No one is asking you to. I won't be using *irregardless* outside discussions about language because it's non-Standard and unnecessary (I prefer *regardless*). But that's my choice.

What the sticklers mean by the complaint is not that the word doesn't exist but that they don't recognise its legitimacy. That's a futile protest at best, for there is no central authority regulating the legitimacy of existing words and vetting the introduction of new ones. Such an authority does purportedly exist for some languages – French has the venerable Académie Française, a decorative irrelevance since 1635 – but exactly the same condition holds. No one can put up protectionist barriers against words; they enter the language anyway. As I was writing this chapter, the Académie issued a ruling against *ASAP*, which they described as 'modern junk'; they advised instead using *dès que possible*. It will have no effect.

Whenever a usage is coined, you will find some commentators (not all of them professional sticklers) wincing. Reflect, the next time you see this, not on these exaggerated sensibilities but on the ability of the English language to constantly replenish itself through adaptation and invention. The practice of 'verbing', or turning nouns into verbs, has a long history in English.

Take the sentence *I hosted a dinner party*. Go to some usage guides and you find that this sense is disputed – because, you see, *host* is a noun and not a verb. It came into vogue in the 1960s and is a useful term. You'd have to be a peculiarly obtuse stickler to object to it, yet the notion that *host* is not a real verb persists. And like so many usages that pedants decry, this one has a much longer history than they grant. The *OED* cites Spenser's *Faerie Queene* from 1596: 'Such was that Hag, unmeet to host such guests.'

Revisions to dictionaries are always happening. Oxford Dictionaries announces a 'word of the year' (in 2013 it was *selfie*, for a self-portrait photograph) to some pained media commentary, in which I've sometimes taken part. They mean to note a word that has either been coined in the previous year or gained notable popularity during it. You don't have to use neologisms but you should admire the inventiveness of them: *chav, retweeting, twerking, omnishambles* . . .

Some will perish; others will become entrenched in the language. What the sticklers overlook in their complaints is that the dictionaries are recording what is already out there. The words exist and they've entered public consciousness. The dictionaries formalise what has already happened.

Error 5: Sticklers think a word's origins tell us what it means

Who decides what a word means? The answer is that we do, collectively: the speakers of English. That isn't the view of the sticklers, however. If you use *decimate* to mean anything other than *reduce by a tenth*, they'll be after you. I know this from experience, having had an online argument with a noted historian, Professor Gary Sheffield, who condemned my *Times* columns for countenancing the 'incorrect' uses of that word and others. His argument (and I do him no disservice of parody) was that words mean what their roots tell us they mean, and that I was wrong and encouraging 'dumbing down'.

Linguists know this position as the etymological fallacy. And fallacy it is. It's fascinating to know the origins of a word and how meanings have changed through centuries, decades or even a few years (how, for example, did the adjective *wicked* come to have a favourable connotation in modern slang?). No native English speaker, however, consistently uses words in their original sense, even supposing these were recoverable. Consider the adjective *nice*. Philologists believe that it comes from two Indo-European roots: *skei*, meaning *cut*, and *ne*, meaning *not*. These eventually made up the Latin verb *nescire*, meaning *to be ignorant of*.[14]

No one uses *nice* to mean *not cutting*. Nor is it open to even the most determined of sticklers to do so. It would be a kind of private language. It's not open to us individually to decide what a word or phrase means if we wish to be understood.

Many arguments over usage are driven by the etymological fallacy – such as the pedantic insistence that there can be only one ALTERNATIVE to a course of action, not two or three, because the word *alternative* derives from the Latin *alter*, meaning *second*. The argument takes the same form each time. Pedants insist that a word means what it traditionally means, and other definitions are wrong. A letter in *The Times* in 2013 criticised usage that is 'ignorant of the true derivation [of words]' and lamented the fact that my language columns defended such usage.

No living language is immutable. The grammar and vocabulary of Latin may be capable of being defined and recorded completely. That isn't true of English. As one reader's reply to the *Times* letter pointedly noted: 'If we were to pay too much attention to "the true derivation" of words or phrases we might still be sounding the "k" in knee.'

The stickler objection is wrong in principle because it doesn't acknowledge that English lacks fixed boundaries. Its body of rules and definitions changes constantly. The objection doesn't take account of the history of a word. Take a usage that particularly irks the sticklers: the noun ENORMITY meaning *the quality of enormous size*. If you consult the dictionary, you find that this *was* the early definition of the word when it entered the language. Words go through shades and shifts of meaning. Sometimes the shift is slight and incremental, and you can see the link to the etymology. Sometimes it's radical and abrupt. It makes no difference to the outcome. The meaning of the word is not fixed by its origins.

Yet pedants tend not to consult dictionaries, or indeed reputable grammars. There's the oddity. While claiming to care about language, to the extent that they depict themselves as its embattled defenders, they seem curiously disinterested (all right, *uninterested*) in it. It's a sort of faith-based approach, analogous to biblical fundamentalism. The truth about language is not, in this view, established by inquiry and evidence but by revelation. The difference is that, in language, the revelation is the mythology passed from one stickler to the next, often through ill-informed newspaper commentary, rather than through a holy book. After all, the great written authorities on language – the dictionaries – provide a thorough refutation of the notion that a living language has some eternal essence of meaning.

I'd extend the analogy this way: the surest way to be convinced of the inerrancy of Scripture is not to read it; and the same is true, in reverse, of maintaining the fallibility of modern theories and observations of language. Just don't consult a dictionary, for you'll thereby remain in happy ignorance of the way language has constantly diverged from its origins.

Error 6: Sticklers ignore usage

This is the most fundamental of all the errors of pedantry about language. From it come many others, such as the etymological fallacy. Sticklers like to consider that they respect tradition and deplore innovation that is ignorant of history. In reality, they are radical social engineers. This argument has been going on for centuries and has involved eminent figures in English letters. Daniel Defoe proposed (in *An Essay Upon Projects* in 1697) the creation of an official body that would 'advance the so much neglected Faculty of Correct Language, to establish Purity and Propriety of Stile, and to purge it from all the Irregular Additions that Ignorance and Affectation have introduc'd'.

A few years later Jonathan Swift published *A Proposal for Correcting, Improving and Ascertaining the English Tongue*, which lamented that the language's 'daily Improvements are by no means in proportion to its daily Corruptions'.

Modern sticklers behave the same way. They don't take the language as it is: they want to wrench it into what they believe it ought to be. Yet their schemes, even if successful (which they couldn't be), wouldn't recreate some pristine and purer form of English as it was once known and taught. They would establish instead an artificial form of English, heedless of the language's traditions. English has evolved. The analogy with the natural world is close. By natural selection and random mutation, the extraordinary varieties of language in general and the dialects of English in particular have come to be. Sticklers seek to replace that with their own experiment, which ignores the only real evidence we have for what the language is: the evidence of usage.

Sticklers dictate. Linguists and lexicographers listen. Though the sticklers may claim either respect for or independence from modern studies of language, they don't really know how to respond. Their methods were tried in classrooms from around 1800 to the 1960s, and retain a prolonged afterlife in the books and columns of prescriptivist punditry, but they don't take account of the actual linguistic evidence provided by dictionaries. There is a gulf between the sticklers' insistence that usage needs to be evaluated and the lexicographers' concern that it be recorded. The division has been evident since Samuel Johnson's *Dictionary of the English Language*. And if you want to see the futility of the sticklers' case that there are standards of English independent of usage, consider any dictionary since.

Style guides make recommendations (or, more often, issue debatable or even completely unfounded edicts). Dictionaries record the evidence of language as it is used. Their purpose is not to select usages they approve of and exclude others they don't. Take the term AIN'T, which illustrates the problem. It's not Standard English. Parents chide their children for using it. There is, though, no inherent reason to do with the principles of English for treating it as incorrect. It has a literary pedigree too; it was used by Swift, among others, but fell out of use in Standard English in the nineteenth century.

Consider too the construction *aren't I?*, as in the columnist's perpetual lament: *I'm late with my copy again, aren't I?* Now, that is Standard, if informal, English. Yet the *aren't I?* construction was once also condemned as ungrammatical. You can see why by contrasting it with *I am*.

It's examples like these that make lexicographers reluctant to judge that a construction is incorrect rather than non-Standard. It depends on context. The issues that style manuals typically argue about (often with passion) are not rules of logic but conventions of usage. These are perpetually in dispute: if they weren't, there'd be no need for the manual. Pedants have it the wrong way round. It's the users of English who tell the lexicographers what words mean and how they are put together to form clauses and sentences. The lexicographers in turn tell us.

Pedants have no conception of the importance of usage. Gwynne declares airily of his absurd volume: 'As an argument for the usefulness of this little book, all of that [the salvation of civilisation, no less] is dramatic and far-reaching indeed. And the logic supporting the case is sufficiently clear-cut to be its own authority. After all, what is demonstrably true is true even if no one believes it. Truth is not decided by majority vote, nor even by unanimous vote, nor even by the majority or unanimous vote of experts.'

More sensible prescriptivists might object that such a determined disregard for linguistic inquiry hardly does justice to their case. But even the wisest of them all, H. W. Fowler, merely made pragmatic (and often sensible and sensitive) accommodations to the evidence of how the language is used. Sticklers do not give usage the respect it merits. The overriding characteristic of a living language is that no one has property rights to it. If you learnt certain rules of English at a young age and have carried them around with you ever since, it's natural that you'll judge other usages as just not good English. But they are. They have rules of grammar and conventions of usage. To call them illiterate and barbaric, as sticklers do, is tone-deaf.

Error 7: Sticklers believe that good grammar is essential to communication

In fact, I understate the sticklers' claims here. The most extreme of them maintain that good grammar, as they understand it, is essential to civilisation. Here, I'll deal with the more moderate claim that good grammar is essential to critical thinking and communication, for that isn't true either.

Gwynne again states his case with directness and a total absence of evidence. 'For thinking and reasoning we need words,' he writes. Does he never think in images? He adds: 'Learning grammar does not just happen; it is not just picked up.' On the contrary, and as we've noted, that's exactly what happens. Language is not a cultural construction but, as Pinker puts it, 'a distinct piece of the biological makeup of our brains'.

These objections may appear pedantic but they're fundamental. Sticklers profoundly misjudge human capabilities. Any small child is, without conscious effort, a master of complex grammatical constructions. The sticklers can't begin to imagine the power of this. So, for example, Humphrys can declare himself opposed to 'hoisting the white flag and surrendering to linguistic anarchy. A degree of discipline is not a constraint: it is a liberation. The more clearly we are able to express ourselves, the less room there is for ambiguity. The more elaborate and the more precise our vocabulary, the greater the scope for thought and expression.'[15]

This sounds good until you stop to think about it. Language is essential to verbal communication, by definition, but it's not essential to thought. Pinker makes a cogent case that we think not in the words of our language but in a separate system of symbols that he terms a universal mentalese. He defines this as a 'hypothetical representation of concepts and propositions in the brain'. There is a big scientific literature on this and other theories of cognition. Humphrys doesn't examine any of it.

Consider, too, the way a translator renders an idea from one language to another. An effective translation needs to read naturally in the second language, which a literal translation (even where one is possible) rarely achieves. Somewhere between the two languages, the translator has the thought before settling on words to express it. The concept exists as a mental construct rather than a form of words. The thought precedes the language.

Language instruction should teach thoroughly the structure and conventions of the dialect known as Standard English. That's not disputed by any linguist. It's an essential part of the argument of this book. It isn't necessary, though, to make exaggerated claims about the importance of good grammar for thought and communication. Doing so has two damaging side-effects.

First, it distracts attention from the really interesting aspects of language, such as how rules are learnt and faultlessly recalled. By rules, I mean *real* rules: things like word order or inflection for number (singular and plural) and tense. Sticklers focus instead on a tedious and hoary list of superstitions.

Second, it castigates dialects as bad grammar, when they are in fact fully expressive and merely non-Standard. And it anathematises non-Standard usages that are idiomatic and widely used, especially informally.

There is a famous essay by William Labov called 'The Logic of Nonstandard English' (1972), in a branch of linguistics known as sociolinguistics. Labov responds to a claim that black American children embark on pre-school years with no language at all. He demonstrates that in fact these children speak a sophisticated dialect of English that allows them to formulate complex logical arguments. His research is especially relevant to my argument here in that it demonstrates that Standard English can be used badly and non-Standard English well.

For example, take the sentence: *There's new neighbours we have to say hello to.* The use of *there's* with a plural noun often appears in spoken English and is in no respect ambiguous. Does this non-Standard construction diminish the capacity for thought and communication? It doesn't: it's just a phrase, expressing a relation that is clear to the utterer and to the listener. Indeed, users of Standard English would often say *there's a cat and a dog in the garden* even though the phrase *a cat and a dog* is plural.

Take also the tag-word *innit*, characteristic of some London dialects (and referred to by Emma Thompson correctly as slang). It's not Standard English but it's no more destructive of communication than the tag-phrase *n'est-ce pas?* in French, which is similarly invariant to tense. You just need to know when it's appropriate and when it isn't.

Error 8: Sticklers lack a sense of proportion

Having completely misunderstood the case for teaching the conventions of Standard English, the pedants can't help themselves from forecasting apocalypse. The language they use is extreme. They see barbarism, anarchy, solecism and illiteracy, and prescribe zero tolerance and capital punishment. Yes, I know it's hyperbolic, and I know what hyperbole is; but the violence of the language betrays a zeal that is out of place. Non-Standard usages aren't barbaric; they're testament to other ways of realising the language instinct than Standard English. They just happened not to be lucky enough to be incorporated into a particular dialect.

Some inadvertent blame for this error lies with George Orwell, and his conceit in *Nineteen Eighty-Four* that control of language grants control of the past and the future. The excision of words from the language has, in the novel, the aim and effect of making subversive thoughts literally unthinkable. If I'm being generous, I'd say that, from this brilliantly imaginative literary premise founded on Orwell's aversion to apologetics for tyranny, the sticklers are worrying about the capability of despotic governments to control the minds as well as the actions of their subjects by the control of language.

Even on this generous interpretation of their case, the pedants are still wrong. Language is constantly inventive because so is the human mind. If there is a need for a word, it will be coined. Because the mind can discriminate shades of meaning, it will be able to understand even the same word in directly opposed senses. The notion advanced by the sticklers that if we permit a disputed definition of a word (say, INFER to mean IMPLY) it will destroy the 'true' meaning is unsupported by the evidence of usage. Indeed, it's contradicted by the evidence. The phrase *that'll learn you* is non-Standard but it is part of many English dialects, and it uses what linguists call a converse term. *Learn* is the converse of *teach*, yet *teach* is what the verb in the phrase means. And there is no confusion of meaning in the phrase.

Sticklers ignore the context of language and the mind's capacity to grasp complex shades of meaning that might even appear contradictory. And on this concatenation of error, they construct a fantasy in which the forces of civilisation are threatened by cultural nihilism. It skews their judgment, as when Truss writes that 'we [sticklers] got very worked up after 9/11 not because of Osama bin Laden but because people on the radio kept saying "enormity" when they meant "magnitude", and we really hate that'.[16] Yes, I realise it's a witticism. It's one that a writer whose sense of taste has been supplanted by misplaced pedantry would make.

Error 9: Sticklers aren't interested in language

This may seem a surprising assertion yet it's rare to find a language pundit who has read about inquiry into language. This is true of highly intelligent pedants as well as determinedly obtuse ones. Michael Dummett was among the most eminent philosophers of the past century, who made outstanding contributions to the philosophy of language among other fields, but when it came to writing about grammar and style, in his slim usage guide, he was a rank amateur. In his discussion of gerunds and the need (as he argued) to precede them with possessives, he was explicitly unfamiliar with the research and evidence published by Otto Jespersen several decades previously (see FUSED PARTICIPLE).

Modern linguistics is often a formidably abstruse subject. The same is true of any scholarly discipline. A non-specialist would struggle with a technical paper in chemistry or physics too. Yet there is a lot of highly accessible writing on language, just as there is excellent popular writing on the solar system, the chemical elements or evolution. Intelligent general readers will have no trouble understanding the writings of David Crystal, for example. Usage pundits tend not to cite scholars of language, though. Here's an unintentionally revealing comment by Kingsley Amis from his *The King's English*: 'As I explain elsewhere, I am not a professional or even a trained linguist or linguistician, but I have found some linguistic terms and procedures useful. For this purpose I have many times consulted a volume inherited from my youth, *Language*, by Leonard Bloomfield (1st edn., 1933).'

Gwynne even makes a virtue of his own hostility to learning. In recommending two books by a nineteenth-century grammarian, he says: 'Not surprisingly given that both are more than a hundred years old, they can be recommended as free from even the most insignificant errors...'

The study of language is a scientific inquiry. Bloomfield is an essential name in its history and his work remains instructive and valuable. Yet it's odd to hold up writings of fifty, sixty, a hundred years ago as guides to the subject as if they were the last word. They may be great or even historic works (I have prefaced my opening chapter with a quotation from a grammar book of the nineteenth century, to show that Gwynne's prejudices were outdated even then) but the subject didn't stop there. Most linguists now would regard Bloomfield's methodology as not entirely satisfactory. Its weaknesses were a central theme in Chomsky's early work. Bloomfield and his followers sought to develop a set of mechanical procedures for deriving analyses from data, and Chomsky argued that this was unrealistic. Chomsky is far from definitive either; science doesn't work like that. Physicists don't rely on Newton's *Principia* and biologists don't treat Darwin's *Origin of Species* as the last word on evolution.

The usage pundits are, as Amis acknowledges of himself, not linguists but that makes their determined omissions still more deplorable. Subjects of universal human interest are the preserve of everyone. But the democratic approach to knowledge asserts that no one can claim the last word on grounds of authority, not that everyone's word is equally valuable. If I want a medical opinion, I seek a medical specialist, not a homeopath or other dilettante. Language is fascinating. You'd expect pundits who write about it to want to know more. Yet they give scant sign of it.

Heffer covers himself by declaring that he 'recognises the

scholarly value of descriptive linguistics' but he shows no evidence of this recognition. How could he? His aim is to instruct 'people who wish to speak or write English to a high standard of precision and without illogicality or solecisms', when descriptive linguistics rejects the notion that there is an inherent standard of correctness, or that you can judge the standards of one language by another (so the pedants' typical appeal to Latin grammar is entirely beside the point).

Scientific study of language can provide answers, or at least clues, to the most distinctive feature of the human species: that we have the faculty of language and that therefore ideas don't need to be reinvented across villages, nations, peoples and epochs. If the sticklers were interested in language they'd read research on (to name but a few) the grammar of English and other tongues; neuroscience and psychology, to illuminate how the brain processes the written word; computer science, to understand the use of artificial intelligence in simulating language; anthropology, to understand how languages develop across cultures; and philosophy, to understand the link between language and logical thought. Instead their mental universe is populated with instances of a small phonetic confusion between the words EFFECT and AFFECT, or a purportedly (though not actually) incorrect use of INFER. It's not only the pedants' lack of linguistic inquisitiveness that's dispiriting: it's the smallness of their world.

Error 10: Sticklers assume that other languages are not as expressive as their own

Pedants may be fluent in other languages and dialects without necessarily acknowledging that these are just as expressive as their native tongue. I once reviewed a book by Daniel Hannan, a Conservative politician, arguing that the idea of liberty was a specifically Anglo-American creation, which has thence been bestowed on the rest of the world. The historical and political argument doesn't concern me here, though it's rubbish. Of more direct relevance to my point is that Hannan, who speaks fluent French and Spanish, maintains that working in Strasbourg as a European Member of Parliament 'has convinced me that there are intrinsic properties in English that favour the expression of empirical, down-to-earth, practical ideas'.[17]

Consider how Hannan's judgment rests on nothing but an intuition. Other nationalities are susceptible to the same type of thinking. There is a long tradition of French sticklers, for example, who maintain that theirs is a uniquely logical language. The patriarch of French purists, Claude Favre de Vaugelas, referred in 1647 to 'clarity of language, the which property French possesses over all other languages in the world'. This notion is embedded in the French popular psyche to modern times. President Mitterrand referred in almost mystical tones to the subtlety and richness of the language, and sticklers throughout the centuries have worried at the popular dilution of the purity of French.[18]

How is French so peerlessly logical and pellucid a language? If the French sticklers are to be believed, it's because of word order: French syntax follows logic. It's a huge non sequitur. Ask anyone whether their own language is a natural vehicle for the transmission of thoughts and they'll reply that it is. Of course they will, for if the word or phrase for a particular object or concept is not readily available, one will be substituted or invented. Languages have different vocabularies but there is nothing inherent in any language that prevents it from acquiring words either through borrowing or through its own internal development. English, after all, had no language to deal with quantum mechanics or financial derivatives when Shakespeare was writing. It has developed that language and those terms. It will develop in future. There is nothing like a perfect state of the language – or of any language.[19]

It's infuriating to a linguist to suggest that there are intrinsic qualities of empiricism to English or of logic to French, or indeed intrinsic properties of anything to any language. Any language can express any concept. Clarity depends on the speaker's use of language, not the language itself.[20]

But if pedants overestimate the distinctiveness of their own language relative to others, they are equally uncomprehending of the role of dialect. Among the most durable of complaints about language is the supposed harm inflicted by American dialects on English, not only in Britain but wherever English is spoken – which is pretty much everywhere.

Prince Charles expresses this prejudice particularly brutally. He can afford to, being accorded a deference that largely insulates him from criticism. He declared to a British Council audience in 1995 that the American way of speaking was 'very corrupting'. How so? Well, 'people tend to invent all sorts of nouns and verbs and make words that shouldn't be'. The Prince urged his audience: 'We must act now to ensure that English – and that, to my way of thinking, means English English – maintains its position as the world language well into the next century.'

This is a very common view and is historically perverse. It identifies English with a particular country, and indeed with a particular region of a particular country, and assumes other influences are debased imitators against which barriers need to be arrayed.[21]

But the way that the English language has developed in North America is not corrupting at all. Both American English and the dialect of English that Prince Charles speaks are descendants of a common ancestor. Neither of these dialects is the type of English spoken by Shakespeare and his contemporaries. In some respects, as far as we know, American dialects are closer to that ancestor. The *r* sound in the name *Shakespeare* has been lost in the dialect of South-East England, but retained in American speech and many other accents and dialects of English (such as Scottish enunciation).

Prince Charles appears a model of temperate internationalism compared with some other sticklers, however. Dummett's attack on Americanisms verges on the xenophobic. He laments the now standard use in Britain of *billion* to mean a thousand million rather than a million million, and attributes it to an American documentary series shown on the BBC in the 1970s. He doesn't just dislike it or (which may have been true initially) count it potentially ambiguous; he calls it a 'minor piece of cultural rape'.

The interplay and exchange of different dialects of English is the same process as the borrowing of words and phrases from other lands that has gone on throughout the centuries. It extends meanings and adds new words, in unexpected ways. This isn't cultural impoverishment, let alone catastrophe. It's how the English language has always developed.

Norma Loquendi, the custom of speaking

Underlying this hair-raising combination of prejudice, ethnocentrism, ignorance, insularity and fallacy is the failure to acknowledge that English doesn't belong to anyone. It's what users make of it: not any user, anywhere, but the generally accepted customs of usage among native speakers.

Contrary to the sticklers' pretence of being defenders of Western civilisation and history, there is a literally ancient lineage to this notion. What standards of language people should adopt was considered by Horace, the Roman poet. He gave a wise answer in his poem *Ars Poetica* ('The Art of Poetry') in 18 BCE, which considers the varying fortunes and use of Latin words:

> *Multa renascentur quae iam cecidere, cadentque*
> *quae nunc sunt in honore vocabula (si volet usus,*
> *quem penes arbitrium est et ius et norma loquendi).*

Roughly:

> Many words that are now unused will be revived, and many now in vogue will be forgotten, if usage wills it, to whom belongs the choice and the right to lay down the law of language.

The poem was the most influential work of literary criticism in the Middle Ages. It deserves to be cited in every modern debate about standards of English. Horace understood what modern pedants don't: that the use of language is directed by custom, not dictated by committee. And nobody has control of it.[22]

It's an unfamiliar thought and an unsettling one to pedants. Whenever I present it to an audience where sticklers are well represented, they misinterpret the notion of custom as acceptance of any usage at all, in contrast to their own appreciation of language. Take an example. When R. W. Burchfield's third revised edition of *Fowler's Modern English Usage* was published in the 1990s, John Simon, a peculiarly vitriolic American usage pundit, reviewed it for the magazine *New Criterion*, whose customary line is both to lament and to forecast the collapse of culture and morals. Considering Burchfield's sensible and informed comments about the varying uses through the centuries of the verb *infer* used in the sense of *imply*, Simon commented:

> This raises an interesting question: who exactly is a reliable witness, giving excellent rather than less impressive evidence? On this rock much – if not all – linguistics comes to grief. Excellent evidence is usually construed as coming from reputed writers and reputable publications. But are writers, even great ones, above solecism? If famous writers are caught in error, as they often are, why should they be invoked as arbiters? Or is an error that can be found, let's say, in Alexander Pope and the present pope (quite a writer, he!), and in both Powells, Anthony and Dawn, *ipso facto* no longer an error? Does its occurrence in the *Times* – either the London or the New York variety, or both – absolve it from guilt? I think not. It was as fine a writer as Dickens who entitled one of his novels erroneously, and mistakes in large type hurt more than those in fine print.[23]

(The Dickens novel that supposedly carries an erroneous title is *Our Mutual Friend*. Sticklers complain that it should be *Our Common Friend*.)

It is quite some claim to suggest that a question wrecks 'much – if not all – linguistics'. The fatuousness of that assertion is where you end up if you refuse to consider even the type of evidence that a discipline considers, let alone the body of evidence itself.

I write daily for *The Times* of London, and am as aware as anyone of the capacity of a newspaper on a tight deadline to make mistakes. But no linguistic authority claims that what appears in *The Times* – anything at all, including typographical errors and flagrant misprints – any more than what emerges from the mouth of President George W. Bush, is by definition the content of the language. It's custom that establishes usage, and it's usage that defines the language.

How do we recognise custom? We read and listen. That's what lexicographers do and it's what linguists do. This isn't some esoteric fad of modern linguistics. It's what Johnson did in compiling his *Dictionary of the English Language*. Whereas the Académie Française ruled on what was and was not a proper French word (and has ever after provided other nationalities with unintended comic material for its sense of unreality), Johnson had no such body to appeal to. Instead he came to the right answer, as the French authorities had come to the wrong one. Meaning isn't decided by fiat: it's decided by the way the language is used. Hence Jespersen was able to write, 200 years later:

> In spite of the efforts of several authors of high standing, the English have never suffered an Academy to be instituted among them like the French or Italian academies, which had as one of their chief tasks the regulation of the vocabulary so that every word not found in their Dictionaries was blamed as unworthy of literary use or distinction. In England every writer is, and always has been, free to take his words where he chooses, whether from the ordinary stock of everyday words, from native dialects, from old authors, or from other languages, dead or living.[24]

The brilliance of Johnson's *Dictionary*, and its value even today beyond its historical importance, lies in its evidence as much as its definitions. For Johnson read. His knowledge of literature was vast. He was able to substantiate his definitions with evidence of how words had been used by writers throughout the history of the language. What does a word mean? It means what users of the language say it means. What is good English? It's English used according to the custom of those who know it.

The sticklers insist that good English is instead a body of rules to be adhered to. They typically make two assumptions. First, usage accords with principles of reason; second, the usage of the best writers is good because, and to the extent that, it accords with those principles of reasoning. They're wrong on both counts. The usage of the best writers, and innumerable others too, establishes what the conventions of language are. Yet these two assumptions have historically bedevilled the study and teaching of grammar.

William Ward, an eighteenth-century grammarian, was an early proponent of this stickler fallacy. In his book *A Grammar of the English Language* (1765), he started from the right premise – the importance of custom – but then came to a mistaken view of how custom arose:

Use and Custom are considered as the only Rules by which to judge of what is right or wrong in Process. But is the Custom which is observed in the Application of any Language the Effect of Chance? Is not such a Custom a consistent Plan of communicating the Conceptions and rational discursive Operations of one Man to another? And who will maintain, that this is, or can be, the Effect of unmeaning Accident? If then it be not so, it must be the Effect of the Reason of Man, adjusting certain means to a certain End: And it is the Business of Speculative or Rational Grammar to explain the Nature of the Means, and to show how they are applied to accomplish the End proposed. If this can be done with sufficient Evidence, the most simple of the Elements of Logic will become familiar to those who engage in a Course of Grammar, and Reason will go Hand in Hand with Practice.[25]

It is a fond belief that custom is formed by logical principles. You can find an echo in the satisfied reflections of modern pedants that the English language incorporates rules of logic. See, for example, Dummett's belief that the treatment of FEWER, LESS in English observes logical principles, and Gwynne's insistence that the rules – his rules – always have an underlying logic to them. But it's not true. Philologists (people who study the way the words are formed and what they are made of) have shown there is very little connection between grammar and logic.

Jespersen came to a nuanced conclusion from the standpoint of the study of language:

> Most linguists are against any attempt to apply a logical stand-ard to language. Language, they say, is psychology, not logic; or language is neither logical nor illogical, but a-logical. That is to say, language has nothing to do with logic. To many philologists the very word, logic, is like a red rag to a bull... It would be surprising however if language which serves to express thoughts should be quite independent of laws of correct thinking.[26]

That open-ended conclusion isn't, however, what modern pedants set out to show. Instead they insist that certain constructions are the correct ones, and the sole correct ones, mainly because they fit certain patterns that they think logical.

Take the so-called rule in English that after a linking verb a predicate must be in the same case as the subject. I explain this in Part 2, under IT'S I/ME but I will refer to it here too. It requires a little digression on verbs.

Some verbs are transitive and some are intransitive. Transitive verbs require an object. An example is the verb *to buy*. Intransitive verbs cannot take a direct object. An example is the verb *to despair*.

There are also some verbs that require not a direct object but a complement. These are, in effect, linking verbs (which grammarians call copular verbs). Examples are the verbs *to be* and *to become*. A complement is a part of a sentence that gives the reader more information about the subject or object.

I like to think that I have a reasonable sense of humour, but it is not so pronounced that I am willing to say on the phone: *Darling, it is I*. If I did, I would get laughed at. Sticklers insist that this construction is grammatically correct, as the pronoun *I*, rather than its object case *me*, is the complement of the verb *is*. But you can't dismiss as grammatically incorrect a construction that is in general use, such as *it's me*. (If you work in an open-plan office, you'll have confirmation every day that this is what people say by eavesdropping on their phone conversations.) The pedants insist that the construction *it's I* is a logical relationship: the linking verb is like an *equals* sign in an equation, so what goes after it must be equivalent to what goes before it. In reality, this construction is just a carry-over from Latin syntax. Other languages don't have it. The sticklers' insistence that their recommendations follow logic is at best a huge overstatement. Their case isn't a serious option in the debate over what is good English.

Johnson's handling of the issue is far more sensible. There are admittedly limits to defining good English by citing the best writers. In Johnson's hands, and with his knowledge of the corpus of literature, it was a very expansive criterion – a good representation, if not quite a proxy, of the customs of English usage. The reason that authorities on language cite literary evidence is that it provides verifiable examples of usage over centuries. To answer Simon's gibe: a single writer may commit a solecism or several. So may a newspaper, even one as venerable as *The Times* of London or the *New York Times*. But a consistent pattern of usage, exemplified by but not restricted to the great body of English literature, is powerful evidence that constructions decried by the sticklers are an integral part of the language. That's why Part 2 of this book, setting out recommendations on usage, contains many examples of noted writers, including the greatest writers, in English. If you get castigated for a SPLIT INFINITIVE, a STRANDED PREPOSITION, a FUSED PARTICIPLE, a DANGLING MODIFIER or any of the other shibboleths held to by sticklers, you can be assured that you're in good company, with Shakespeare, Byron, Jane Austen, Dickens and many others.

Evidence from noted writers is far from the only evidence that modern lexicographers and linguists go on. The content of the language is the body of customs observed by native speakers – *norma loquendi*, the custom of speaking. That isn't limited to the famous, the notable, the eloquent and the published. It includes you, me and everyone else who forms part of the unending, unstoppable and ever-flowing discourse of English.

This is tough for sticklers to accept. The difficulty explains much of the hostile reaction to the publication of *Webster's Third New International Dictionary* in 1961, when American users discovered that a cherished name in lexicography had included non-Standard usages in its quest to describe the state of the language. (See AMERICAN ENGLISH.) An editorial in the *New York Times* lamented:

Webster's has, it is apparent, surrendered to the permissive school that has been busily extending its beachhead on English instruction in the schools. This development is disastrous because, intentionally or unintentionally, it serves to reinforce the notion that good English is whatever is popular.[27]

No, good English is not whatever is popular. But English is whatever the custom of English speakers happens to be. It's defined not by 'cultured' usage but by general usage. It's the task of a dictionary to record that usage, not to arbitrate on usages that it likes or dislikes. The language doesn't belong to the *New York Times*, the dictionaries or *The Times* of London. I'm the language columnist of *The Times* of London and English certainly doesn't belong to me. It resides in custom. The absence of an external guardian of English doesn't mean that people will lose the capacity to communicate. If enough users abandon a convention, another will take its place. There is no objective standard designating one convention better than another, but there is always a requirement that usage be understood. If it weren't, there would be no point in using it.

Custom: the raw material of communication

I'm encouraged by a comment posted online by a *Times* reader underneath one of my columns (which explained the bogus nature of the prohibition on SPLIT INFINITIVES). The reader said:

> I should like to commend this reassuring piece by Oliver Kamm and confess to being one of those people who studiously avoid split infinitives and constructions such as 'different to' and 'under the circumstances' for fear of being thought illiterate, even though I know them to be mere superstitions.
>
> On reflection, they are probably more insidious than that: snobbery maybe, or shibboleths; the linguistic equivalent of wearing the 'wrong' label suit, drinking the 'wrong' wine or shopping at the 'wrong' supermarket. (Coming from an older

generation, I am still uneasy wearing brown shoes with a blue suit!)

At present, these conventions can be safely flouted only by the supremely talented and the reckless; but the more we dare do it, the sooner we shall be less inhibited about expressing ourselves.

This is exactly right, if excessively modest. It states what's wrong with the notion that good English is what happens if you follow certain rules. Good English doesn't happen like that. You can accept all of the sticklers' prescriptions and it won't have an effect on your lucidity and expressiveness. It will merely allow you entry into the circle that cares about shibboleths. You shouldn't care about being in that circle. Instead, be aware of the way language is used by custom, rather than by the superstitions that were taught to this *Times* reader.

It's in the customs of English speakers that you'll find not the answer to what is good English, but the raw material for writing and speaking it. It isn't only the talented and the reckless who should look to custom, however. Everyone should. And as my correspondent rightly intimates, the more that the sticklers are confounded, the less inhibited will people be about ignoring their shibboleths. That's a good thing. Sticklers have influence only because they're loud and have an outlet in the media, and are popularly believed to know what they're talking about.

The history of language instruction in Britain and possibly the rest of what became the English-speaking world might have been different. The next chapter will introduce the eighteenth-century grammarians who devised many of the shibboleths that are still current today. These found a ready audience among the newly affluent classes who aspired to gentility. One of those grammarians was Joseph Priestley, the famed scientist, who was unusual and perhaps unique for his time in stressing the importance of general usage. His insight didn't gain widespread acknowledgement, however, till the scientific linguists of the late nineteenth century. And it was not till the twentieth century that it was given a full exposition in a volume called *English Usage*, published in 1917, by J. Lesslie Hall.

Hall concentrated on written sources in explaining English usage. He used literary examples to demonstrate that usage did not accord with the rules (or rather, the shibboleths) invented by the eighteenth-century grammarians. It was a radical and thorough exposition of an insight that is crucial to modern studies of language (though to more recent linguists it is the spoken word that is primary). If studies of language had followed usage, much pointless argument might have been avoided over the centuries. Generations of schoolchildren might have been spared rote learning of rules that have no relevance to clarity of communication. They would have been taught to read and write well instead.

What is good writing?

What does it mean to write well? The most convincing answer I have found among the language authorities of the early scientific approach is that of Charles C. Fries, who made a valuable study of the way common school grammar had been taught historically. He noted of these grammars that came to dominate English teaching in the late eighteenth and nineteenth centuries and their modes of reasoning: 'The standard of correctness and propriety furnished by these grammars was not based upon usage, for the grammarians insisted that "even our most approved authors offended against every part of grammar"; but it was a standard based upon Latin syntax and "reason" and expressed in arbitrary rules.'[28]

This carried through Fries' day and into the 1960s, when it fell into abeyance. Children are fortunately taught differently now. Whether deliberately or not, they are following a doctrine that Fries argued for, which is to write with appropriateness. By that, I mean to judge the register of their writing. There is no definitive answer to how far you should use colloquialisms in English: it depends on who (or, if you prefer, *whom*) you're talking to. Writing formally for an essay, whether in an exam or for publication, requires knowing Standard English. But that isn't an absolute standard: it's a way of conforming to certain conventions that are expected by the reader.

David Crystal, who has had much influence (though still not enough) in devising new ways to teach language, puts it well: 'Different usages are appropriate to different settings, and once we are aware of this we can begin to exploit the stylistic contrast involved… Competent writers know they have the ability to switch into and out of Standard English, when there is an effect to be achieved. And this is one of the linguistic skills that children have to be taught.'[29]

Appropriateness means distinguishing Standard English from 'good' English. It's a form of English that every child must know, among other varieties of language. If they are aware of the stylistic range of English, this will fit them much better in life than knowing pedantic rules. Good writing is what enables you to express yourself in a way that communicates most vividly and persuasively to the audience you're addressing. If you do that effectively, you're using good English.

Register is not all there is to effective communication; but it hasn't till recently been stressed enough in linguistic education and usage guidance, and you can't sensibly talk about style without judging first what register to adopt. It's a dispiriting feature of much academic writing and speaking that it's dull. It perambulates. Its authors know their subject but not how to express it with directness. They don't try the thought experiment that I recommend in Part 2, under STYLE: imagine you are addressing the people you grew up with, studied with, worked with or have met socially, who are no less intelligent than you but happen to know different things. That will lead you to a combination of register (knowing your audience) and language (ease of expression). This approach is far from the narrow set of rules taught by sticklers.

Jespersen argued in a book called *Efficiency in Linguistic Change*, published towards the end of his life, in 1941, that language is constantly changing in the direction of greater expressiveness. Language is what we create as well as what we inherit. And change in language has to balance two things. First, it needs to stem from the conventions of usage; a neologism, for example, must still accord with the rules of how nouns are inflected for case. Second, it needs to meet the speaker's wish for communication. The interplay of these two needs creates an efficient language: one that allows communication and conserves the energy of the speaker or writer. If you're sceptical, consider this list of words, all in current use: *ace, awesome, blast* (in the sense of fun), *crush* (in the sense of infatuation, usually unrequited), *dork, dweeb, gnarly, gross, jerk, lame, like* (in the sense of a filler word), *mega, nerd, totally, wicked* (as a term of approbation), *zit*. Perhaps you don't use these slang terms yourself. But they are not only intelligible: they are expressive and precise. They follow grammatical rules and can be assigned to standard parts of speech.[30]

Expressiveness will often lead you to ignore the sticklers' pet causes because, if followed, they create bad prose, such as this example from *The Economist*: 'The main umbrella organisation, the Syrian National Coalition, was supposed to do three things: expand its membership, elect a new leader and decide whether unconditionally to attend the Geneva talks.'[31]

You can see immediately what's happening here. The writer is following the magazine's style advice to avoid a SPLIT INFINITIVE. The adverb *unconditionally* is supposed to modify the verb *attend*. If it were inserted into the phrase *to attend*, it would read naturally. But because of a stupid rule, the modifier has been placed in a way that guarantees a stilted sentence.

Where to put a modifier isn't an invariable rule of grammar (even supposing that the prohibition on split infinitives had anything to do with grammar anyway), let alone logic. The question is answered best by asking where the modifier is most rhetorically effective. The indictment I charge the sticklers with is being heedless of good and effective prose. Their rules are not just an irrelevance but a liability, expressed with misplaced militancy and ignorance.

3
The Usage Debate

*But since good authors have adopted different forms of
speech, and in a case which admits of no standard but
that of custom, one authority may be of as much weight as
another; the analogy of language is the only thing to which
we can have recourse, to adjust these differences.*

Joseph Priestley, *The Rudiments of English Grammar*, 1761, p. xviii

Disputes over English usage are longstanding and often vehement
but their origins are not mysterious. It's possible to date them
in their current form to the years between 1650 and 1800. The
sticklers' litany of complaints has harmed language instruction and
debased public discussion of the subject, and it does so still. But
theirs isn't some pure and traditional English grammar that has
its roots in the nation's history and is being threatened by the
insidious forces of cultural relativism. Instead, it's a manufactured
product dating from a particular period when English society
was changing and the beneficiaries of that social ferment wanted
instruction. What they got was the prescriptive grammarians of
the eighteenth century, whose influence has been felt ever since,
overwhelmingly for ill.

Let's start in the sixteenth century. The language of Shakespeare
is recognisable to modern readers and is known as Early Modern
English. When Shakespeare studied at the Stratford Grammar

School (there are no attendance records of the time but it is highly likely that he was educated there), he would not have been taught English grammar. The notion of being taught your own language would have seemed quixotic at the time. The central subjects were Latin and Greek.

The early works on English grammar were contemporary with Shakespeare but it's an anachronism to regard them as fundamental parts of a grammar school or university education of the time. They had two main functions: to educate foreigners in English and to provide an economical introduction to the principles of Latin. The latter type of grammar book was specifically intended to introduce the reader to Latin grammar. It's hardly surprising that the study of English grammar should have been forced for centuries afterwards into a model that conformed to Latin syntax, but it was unfortunate even so.

These early grammar books from the sixteenth and seventeenth centuries were therefore often written in Latin or French. Ben Jonson, Shakespeare's great contemporary and rival playwright (whose knowledge of Classics was extensive), wrote an *English Grammar* that was subtitled 'For the benefit of all Strangers, / out of his observation of the English Language, now spoken / and in Use'. Note that it was for strangers.[1]

John Milton, also a Classical scholar, wrote a book, *Accedence Commenced Grammar*, published in 1669, which declared: 'Accedence Commenced Grammar supplied with sufficient Rules for the use of such as, younger or elder, are desirous, without more trouble than need, to attain the Latin tongue...' Milton's aim, in common with that of other grammarians of the time, was to use a reader's knowledge of English in order to inculcate the accidence of Latin.

It was the eighteenth-century grammars that sought to instruct

English speakers in their own tongue. Why would people want to be taught a language that they already knew? Because they wanted to speak it 'correctly'; and it was in this desire that the usage debates as we know them were forged. The growing power and influence of the middle classes entered in a vacuum where absolute royal and aristocratic power had once been. The expansion of the colonies brought new wealth and opportunities for social betterment. Gentility mattered and manuals of etiquette became phenomenally popular. (As a boy, George Washington was required by his tutor to copy out '110 Rules of Civility and Decent Behaviour in Company and Conversation'. These included: 'In Company of those of Higher Quality than yourself Speak not till you are asked a Question then Stand upright put of your Hat and Answer in few words.') Among these signs of gentility was a desire to speak correctly. The market provided the manual.[2]

The authors of these grammars were evangelists for the cause of making English usage correct, by imposing on it a standard of reason. Thomas Sheridan, in the preface to his *Dictionary* of 1780, was typical of this movement in considering 'Whether many important advantages would not accrue both to the present age, and to posterity, if the English language were ascertained, and reduced to a fixed and permanent standard?... To compass these points... has been the chief object of the author's pursuits in life, and the main end of the present publication.'[3]

The grammatical instruction of these times was, with the important exception of Joseph Priestley, unconcerned with Horace's principle of *norma loquendi*, the custom of speaking. No custom, even the usage of the best writers, could establish what correct English was. What mattered was conformity to reason, which meant conformity to Latin. As one influential study of the history of grammar teaching puts it: 'Latin grammar was not just one grammar out of many; it *was* grammar. There could be no question of "applying" Latin grammar to English. If Latin "had" a grammar it was not for English to have anything different. It could only have the same and less of it.'[4]

Today's purported rules are the direct descendants, and sometimes the very same creations, of these eighteenth-century grammarians. These rules are not the test of correct English: they are simply a remnant of a partial and misguided approach characteristic of a particular epoch and that was itself a radical departure from earlier understandings of English grammar.

There had been proposals before to regularise English usage, but English letters remained till about 1650 highly diverse in its language. Paradoxically, the decline of Latin as the language of scholarship and diplomacy coincided with an emphasis on Latin as a standard against which to judge English. It was a fateful development. English letters were increasingly judged against the rhetorical standards of Latin.

John Dryden, whose acid pen produced some of the great poetic works in English, laboured under the notion that Latin was a superior form of language. He exemplified the spirit of his time. Hence the grammatical instruction that generations of schoolchildren received was modelled on Latin. This point will sound trite but is crucial: Latin and English are not the same language. Even Latin terms when used in English become English terms. Different languages have different rules. They need not have the same ones.

Concern to fix the language in a certain state, with reference particularly to Latin grammar, prompted a proposal by the Royal Society in 1664 to establish a committee for English usage. The Society instead concentrated on science and mathematics and the proposal never came to fruition, but the idea of an official body to arbitrate on language has never gone away. The absence of an academy was regretted by Dryden with these words in 1693:

> We have yet no English prosodia, not so much as a tolerable dictionary, or a grammar; so that our language is in a manner barbarous; and what government will encourage any one, or more, who are capable of refining it, I know not: but nothing under a public expense can go through with it. And I rather fear a declination of the language, than hope an advancement of it in the present age.[5]

A proposal for such a body was included by Daniel Defoe in *An Essay Upon Projects* (1697), a collection of various rationalist schemes for social improvement. A committee of noted writers would, under Defoe's proposal, issue edicts on linguistic usage and be the sole authority capable of licensing new words: it would, in fact, 'be as Criminal then to Coin Words, as Money'.

The scheme came to nothing, but the proposal didn't die. It was taken up again by Jonathan Swift in 1712 in his *Proposal for Correcting, Improving and Ascertaining the English Tongue*. Swift was driven by a sense of outrage, much as today's sticklers are. He considered that the usage of his time 'offends against every Part of Grammar'. Among his principal complaints was the way that writers abbreviated. He took issue with the word *mob*, for example, which is an abbreviation of *mobile vulgus*. He also strongly objected to new words, much as sticklers through the ages have done. Where he saw change, he termed it barbarism. In any event, his proposal went nowhere too. It was Samuel Johnson who astutely noted the flaw in this notion, wherever it came from: 'The edicts of an English academy would probably be read by many, only that they might be sure to disobey them.'[6]

This is not quite the fate of the Académie Française or the Accademia della Crusca in Italy. These bodies still exist but their edicts are not widely read and their role is ceremonial rather than effective. While the idea of an academy never took hold in England, however, the worries that Defoe and Swift expressed did. Writers were concerned that English appeared to have no recorded systematic grammar. Johnson stated: 'That our language is in perpetual danger of corruption cannot be denied; but what prevention can be found? The present manners of the nation would deride authority, and therefore nothing is left but that every writer should criticise himself.'

Self-criticism wasn't going to satisfy the demands of the self-appointed guardians of the language, though. Education was necessary. It was this need that an English dictionary and an English grammar were intended to meet. Hence came Johnson's *Dictionary of the English Language*, published in 1755, and Robert Lowth's *Short Introduction to English Grammar*, published in 1762. These works were seen at the time as working to the same end – yet they in fact took different approaches. Johnson listened and read whereas Lowth prescribed.

Johnson didn't just provide definitions of words. He gave examples of the way that these words were used, not least by great writers through the ages: Shakespeare, Milton, Bacon and many others. He also read widely in the sciences and cited such sources as Newton and Boyle to substantiate his definitions. It took him nine years to complete his Dictionary, with a little clerical assistance. David Garrick, the actor, composed an epigram celebrating Johnson's industry compared with the French academicians: 'And Johnson, well arm'd like a hero of yore, / Has beat forty French, and will beat forty more.'[7]

Johnson's *Dictionary* exemplifies the principle that words mean what the users of a language, rather than official academies, take them to mean. To this day, sticklers fail to realise this. A pressure group called the Queen's English Society (which I have addressed) seriously proposes the establishment of a language academy on the French model and as advocated by Defoe and Swift, apparently unaware of the reasons Johnson cited for why such a venture cannot succeed:

> Swift, in his petty treatise on the English language, allows that new words must sometimes be introduced, but proposes that none should be suffered to become obsolete. But what makes a word obsolete, more than general agreement to forbear it? and how shall it be continued, when it conveys an offensive idea, or recalled again into the mouths of mankind, when it has once by disuse become unfamiliar, and by unfamiliarity unpleasing?[8]

The earliest grammar book on 'correct' usage by the eighteenth-century grammarians appears to have been Robert Baker's *Reflections on the English Language*, published in 1770. Baker was perversely proud of being unlettered and of having only a minimal knowledge of Classics. He wrote:

> It will undoubtedly be thought strange, when I declare that I have never yet seen the folio edition of Mr Johnson's dictionary: but, knowing nobody that has it, I have never been able to borrow it; and I have myself no books; at least, not many more than what a church-going old woman may be supposed to have of devotional ones upon her mantle-piece: for, having always had a narrow income, it has not been in my power to make a collection without straitening myself. Nor did I ever see even

the Abridgement of this Dictionary till a few Days ago, when, observing it inserted in the Catalogue of a Circulating Library where I subscribe, I sent for it.[9]

There is an echo of the modern pedants in Baker's bluff self-confidence. The sticklers haven't read much, at least not in the field of language. They have their preferences, which no amount of countervailing evidence of usage can shake. Baker is where this cause found its apotheosis. And in common with other grammarians of this persuasion, Baker had sport by finding supposed faults in the writings of notable authors. He made of this a democratic virtue, writing that he had 'paid no regard to Authority. I have censured even our best Penmen, where they have departed from what I conceive to be the Idiom of the Tongue, or where I have thought they violate Grammar without Necessity. To judge by the Rule of *Ipse dixit* [He himself said it] is the Way to perpetuate Error.'[10]

Baker's book is a collection of 127 purported rules about meaning and syntax. Its edicts were followed closely by other writers on grammar in the following few years, and thence progressed into the canons of sticklerdom, which reproduces hoary arguments endlessly rather than examine them against the evidence of usage. One volume that was distinctive in this flowering of grammatical caprice was Joseph Priestley's *The Rudiments of English Grammar*, published in 1761.[11] Priestley was (and remains) famed as a scientist. His most famous work was on the nature of 'airs', in which he is credited as one of the discoverers of oxygen. His interest in language was also evidence of a prolific output and an inquiring mind. Many of his works in other fields (notably aesthetics, politics and religion, for he was a Unitarian minister) deserve to be better known. He was also one of the three leading eighteenth-century grammarians.

Priestley's grammar book opens unpromisingly with his definition of the discipline as 'the art of using words properly'. Yet he recognises usage as an authority for correctness by arguing for the importance of 'all governing custom [which] shall declare in favour of the one or the other'.

It was on the principle of custom (compare it to Horace's *norma loquendi*, the custom of speaking) that Priestley granted the legitimacy of some disputed usages that modern sticklers still take issue with. Among them is the case of the relative pronoun *who* when used as an object. He urged generally and wisely a 'relaxation of the severer laws of grammar'.

Yet Priestley's recommendations were rapidly superseded in popularity by Robert Lowth's *Short Introduction to English Grammar*, published in 1762. Lowth was a Hebrew scholar and Bishop of London. His grammar book was a huge success, running through twenty-two editions by the end of the century. His philosophy has been defended by some linguists as more subtle than his reputation suggests but his approach was uncompromising. He maintained that 'the principal design of a Grammar of any Language is to teach us to express ourselves with propriety in that Language, and to be able to judge of every phrase and form of construction, whether it be right or not. The plain way of doing this, is to lay down rules, and to illustrate them by examples. But besides shewing what is right, the matter may be further explained by pointing out what is wrong.'

Lowth's was thus a declaratory, even exhortatory, approach. He set out to 'correct' general usage. Whereas Johnson and Priestley examined literature for the evidence of usage, Lowth used the works of great writers such as Shakespeare as evidence of the ubiquity of errors. The salvation for the common people resided, of course, in Lowth's account of the rules.

Priestley was not entirely alone in his diagnoses. George Campbell, a Scottish clergyman, published a *Philosophy of Rhetoric* in 1776 that sought to place rhetoric on a scientific (we would say psychological) basis. To that end, he also advanced the evidence of usage by the great writers: 'Whatever modes of speech are authorised as good by the writings of a great number, if not the majority, of celebrated authors.'

That criterion would be appreciated by modern scholars of language (though they would point to general usage, primarily in the spoken word, rather than just the great writers for evidence of the content of language). The eighteenth-century autodidacts such as Lowth by contrast looked at the evidence of usage to detect mistakes even by the mightiest and most revered writers. Nor did they agree among themselves about what constituted a mistake. Disagreement, or more accurately confusion, among sticklers about correct usage has been a feature of their protests ever since. And they failed to allow for legitimate variant uses. Their approach was consistent with the spirit of the times, in attempting to subject language to rules and in believing that chaos could be brought to order by an expression of the rationalist temper. But these weren't rules derived from the evidence of usage: they were edicts driven by preference and faulty analogy.

The temper of the times is an important reason why the prescriptive approach to English grammar became so popular and remains with us. It's far from a foolish impulse to seek to inject rationalism into public discourse, and this was very much tied up among eighteenth-century political theorists with the notion of manners. In Joseph Addison's influential *Spectator* essays, for example, there is an extended treatment of the civilising social (and not merely personal) virtues of politeness. That impulse is discernible in Priestley's work on grammar too. He uses the term 'elegant' to describe usages that are economical in their expression, such as *rather* 'to express a small degree, or excess of a quality'. Yet the rationalist temper was taken to extremes by other grammarians of the time, in their zeal for rules. The rules that the eighteenth-century grammarians devised, and that their twenty-first-century equivalents repeat, reflect little more than the accretions of linguistic mythology that have built up over 250 years. Many other usages condemned by the grammarians have become Standard, accepted parts of the language. There is no consistency in the way some rules survived in the sticklers' taxonomy of faults (though ignored in general usage) while others perished; the constant was that their advice lacked a conception of how language worked. A gulf opened between spoken English and the written word, hemmed about by shibboleths taught through the school system.

That destructive legacy persisted till well into the twentieth century. Only now, in an age of instant communication, does there appear to be a countervailing tendency, where the written word is conforming more accurately to the way people speak. As you would expect, sticklers hate it. John Humphrys, the broadcaster, bemoans this tendency and identifies the culprits: 'It is the relentless onward march of the texters, the SMS (Short Message Service) vandals who are doing to our language what Genghis Khan did to his neighbours eight hundred years ago. They are destroying it: pillaging our punctuation; savaging our sentences; raping our vocabulary. And they must be stopped.'[12]

Genghis Khan; rape; pillage; savaging: it's characteristic of the sticklers' overheated imagination and it's untrue. Humphrys vented that litany of complaints in the *Daily Mail* but he has also written similarly in the *Daily Telegraph*, one of the leading broadsheet newspapers in the UK. I wonder if he stopped to consider what contemporary critics made of the invention of the telegraph and its effect on language. In fact, texting conforms to grammatical rules: if it didn't, it wouldn't be comprehensible to its readers. Crystal cites one US study showing that less than 20 per cent of text messages it examined contained even an abbreviation. Yet abbreviations are what people such as Humphrys denounce. English has always had abbreviations in its orthography; Swift condemned the word *mob*, which not even the most hidebound stickler today would object to, and many would find indispensable.

Texters also use variant spellings, which is like using dialect (in fact, some of the words used are dialect, such as *coz* and *wot*). To be able to send a text message requires literacy, and not only the ability to use technology. Crystal writes:

> Before you can write and play with abbreviated forms, you need to have a sense of how the sounds of your language relate to the letters. You need to know there are such things as alternative spellings. If you are aware that your texting behaviour is different, you must already have intuited that there is such a thing as a standard. If you are using such abbreviations as *lol* and *brb* ('be right back'), you must have developed a sensitivity to the communicative needs of your textees.[13]

It is vastly preferable that speech and the written word converge than that they be driven apart by bogus rules. And the bogus rules are ones that, in the main, Lowth and his contemporaries and imitators devised. Here are just a few.

Lowth was hostile to FLAT ADVERBS (adverbs that take the same form as their associated adjectives, such as *bright* or *direct*) and his judgment was widely supported. Some grammarians proposed adding the *-ly* suffix to all adverbs, including such forms as *soonly*. Lowth also applied a misconceived logic against such double comparative forms as *lesser* and *worser*; the first still exists in a restricted sense (usually *the lesser of two evils*), and you sometimes see non-Standard examples of other forms. (See DOUBLE COMPARISON.)

The most notorious judgment advanced by the grammarians was the objection to the STRANDED PREPOSITION – the notion that you mustn't end a sentence with a preposition. The rule is devoid of merit or reputability but it gets repeated constantly. The prohibition on stranded prepositions comes from Dryden; no one had thought of it before. Engaging in the popular recreation of criticising writers of the past for linguistic transgressions that they would never have thought of, Dryden targeted Ben Jonson for his usage here: 'The waves and dens of beasts could not receive / The bodies that those souls were frighted from.'

Not only does Dryden criticise Jonson, he also criticises *himself* for having used stranded prepositions in *An Essay of Dramatic Poesy*. The problem, says Dryden, is 'the preposition in the end of the sentence; a common fault with him, *and which I have but lately observed in my own writings*' (emphasis added).[14]

Also down to Lowth is the insistence on a predicate nominative after a copular verb. (See IT'S I/ME.) No rule has caused more, and more pointless, suffering than the case of pronouns. The rule asserted by Lowth about pronouns after a linking verb doesn't sound right to native speakers, who almost all ignore it in speech.

Also ruled out at this time was the DOUBLE NEGATIVE construction. To this day, you'll find amateur grammarians insisting that *I can't get no satisfaction* means *I can get satisfaction*, because one negative cancels out the other, thereby yielding a positive. They're wrong. A double negative in that context is an intensifier. It has a long history in English letters (Chaucer used the multiple negative) and nobody, but nobody, misunderstands the construction when it's considered in its context.

Of the triumvirate of great eighteenth-century grammarians, however, the most prolific and influential was Lindley Murray.[15] Murray was an American-born Quaker who settled near York. He took up grammatical pedagogy after a successful career in law and business. This was due not to his originality, for his principal role was as a synthesiser and populariser of grammatical instructions, but to his being the author of the standard text on the subject. Its full title was *English Grammar, adapted to the different classes of learners. With an Appendix, containing Rules and Observations for Promoting Perspicuity in Speaking and Writing*. The book was published in 1795 and was phenomenally popular during the following century and into the twentieth too, going through at least sixty-five editions in Britain, and was also widely used in the United States. It was a huge influence on English teaching in the British Empire. Historians estimate that nearly two million copies of the *Grammar* were sold in the fifty years after its publication, and that Murray's works in total would have sold perhaps fourteen million copies. In the age of imperialism and long afterwards, English became a world language. Murray was a crucial figure in the way that it was taught and adopted.

In George Eliot's *Middlemarch*, the genteel Mrs Vincy looks down on Mrs Garth, who has won respectability:

Mrs Vincy had never been at her ease with Mrs Garth, and frequently spoke of her as a woman who had had to work for her bread – meaning that Mrs Garth had been a teacher before her marriage; in which case an intimacy with Lindley Murray and Mangnall's 'Questions' was something like a draper's discrimination of calico trademarks, or a courier's acquaintance with foreign countries: no woman who was better off needed that sort of thing.

(Richmal Mangnall was to the study of history what Murray was to grammar, in the schoolrooms of the time. Mangnall's *Historical and Miscellaneous Questions for the Use of Young People*, published in 1798, was almost literally a catechism for the schoolchildren of the first half of the nineteenth century.)

Also in *Middlemarch*, Mrs Garth attempts to educate her son in the principles of grammar, in this case with reference to Murray's account of 'Rules of Syntax'. The references to Murray had no need of annotation or explanation to readers in the late nineteenth century.

Murray's *Grammar* was highly derivative of the work of Lowth and other conservative grammarians. Indeed this was one of the sources of his success, as he was not prone to making radical distinctive judgments of his own. The ostensible reasonableness of his approach would have commended it to educators. Yet his aim was to regulate and fix the language and he held to a highly moralistic outlook. He established norms for good English drawn from appeals to logic and arguments about the essential nature of the English language. He also included orthography and pronunciation in his subject matter.

English grammar, according to Murray, 'is the art of speaking and writing with propriety'. Language to him was an acquired skill; having gained it, a user was more fit for society. And the upper classes hoped meanwhile that some objective standard could be found that would distinguish between the genuine aristocracy and the merely newly wealthy. Both these established interests and the aspiring middle classes looked to some written authority to ascertain standards of proper speech and writing.[16]

The entire second volume of the book was devoted to exercises in applying rules of grammatical analysis. Users of Lindley's *Grammar* would memorise prescriptive rules of accidence, to provide the basis for writing well. It was an approach wholly recognisable from the stickler guides that persist into the twenty-first century.

Not all of Murray's prescriptions are pointless. He sensibly defends *whose* as the possessive of *which*, on grounds of concision. He hints at the need for different registers in the use of English. Yet Murray didn't extend this last point to the notion of what was appropriate in usage. It's the same omission that characterises modern sticklers, who insist on 'correct' usage independent of all other considerations. Underlying everything, however, is Murray's insistence on memorising rules of grammar. His book provided a set of definitions and rules, which were to be learnt by heart and recited in unison, and a set of exercises where these could be applied.

America meanwhile had its own usage guru, whose name has become a synonym for lexicographical authority. This was Noah Webster. His answers to the question of correct usage may have been driven by a wish for American exceptionalism, but they were notably enlightened. He was, in effect, a reformed pedant. 'After all my reading and observation for the course of ten years,' he wrote in his *Dissertations on the English Language*, 'I have been unable to unlearn a considerable part of what I learnt in early life; and at thirty years of age can, with confidence, affirm that our modern grammars have done much more hurt than good.'

The grammars he was alluding to are those of Lowth and his followers, who tried to force English to conform with Latin syntax and label anything as incorrect usage that couldn't be defined this way. Webster continued:

> The authors [of the grammar books] have labored to prove what is obviously absurd, viz. that our language is not made right; and in pursuance of this idea, have tried to make it over again, and persuade the English to speak by Latin rules, or by arbitrary rules of their own. Hence they have rejected many phrases of pure English, and substituted those which are neither English nor sense.

Exactly. And how prescient too. It's impossible to understand Webster's views on language without grasping too his instincts as a political reformer. He was highly critical of the deference paid by the early colonists to England, specifically in the field of language. Samuel Johnson was a fierce critic of the insurrectionary movement in America and a defender of monarchy. His *Dictionary* was hugely admired by the colonists even so, and it had a powerful influence on the framers of the Constitution and the Bill of Rights. Webster was by contrast a supporter of American independence. In 1785 he published *Sketches of American Policy*, in which he argued for a new constitution that would establish the principles of American independence. His nationalist zeal inspired him to compile a dictionary that would rival Johnson's.

Webster sought to create a language for America, by adapting the English language. It was a plausible aim, given that Webster knew the unlikelihood of fashioning a complete new tongue. He foresaw that eventually linguistic change might produce 'a language in North America, as different from the future language of England, as the modern Dutch, Danish and Swedish are from the

German'. It was an overstatement but not a radical one. Webster was right about the mechanism of linguistic development.

Webster's single greatest achievement was *An American Dictionary of the English Language*, published in 1828. The name of Webster's dictionaries has been integral to American letters ever since. The book was modelled on, and intended to rival, Johnson's *Dictionary*. It used the same technique of citing authors to substantiate definitions of a word – indeed, Webster often used the same definitions and the same quotations, though he also made an ostentatious gesture of citing American authors to provide a manual of specifically American usage.

The historical significance of Webster's *American Dictionary* was twofold. It recorded American usages that would have been unrecognisable in England (notably political ones, such as *assembly* and *senate*) and it introduced American spellings. Indeed, Webster has a claim to being the most successful spelling reformer in the language. Ambitious planners for a rational alphabet have always been thwarted owing to the difficulty of persuading one generation to give up its hard-won recognition of difficult spelling conventions. Webster, on the other hand, merely rationalised a few spellings and created enduring and economical variants. Silent letters in such words as *programme*, *axe* and *catalogue* could be axed, so to speak. The endings of *theatre* and *centre* could be reversed, in accord with their pronunciation. The silent *u* in *labour* and *honour* could be dropped. The doubled consonant in the middle of *travelled* was rationalised away, to create *traveled*. It was a remarkably successful venture in creating a distinctive national orthography and it owed that success to its limited ambition.[17]

Webster expounded two crucial principles: the spoken language provides the regularities that can be formulated as grammatical rules; and to arrive at those rules means studying the way language is used. Imposing Latin categories as if they could self-evidently be taken as English forms too was pointless. So was inventing arbitrary rules. Webster maintained instead:

> In every instance grammar is built solely on the structure of language. That which is not found in the practice of speaking a language can have no place in the grammar of a language; it must be the arbitrary dictum of the compiler and of no authority. I have thought it necessary to say this much on a mistake which appears to be material. Grammars are made to show the student what a language is, not how it ought to be.

Priestley and Webster were thus unusual in grammarians of their time. Their judgments were fallible but they explicitly looked to the way native speakers used the language in order to derive grammatical rules. That's how linguists work. It's contrary to how sticklers reason.

You see this division among grammarians to this day. Lest I be accused of selecting the less thoughtful pedants for censure, consider the saner and more temperate representatives of the sticklocracy too. These are epitomised by H. W. Fowler. With his brother Francis, he wrote *The King's English* (1906). But far his most celebrated book is *A Dictionary of Modern English Usage*, published in 1926, with a second edition (edited by Sir Ernest Gowers, as *Fowler's Modern English Usage*) in 1965 and a third (edited by R. W. Burchfield) in 1996. It had a mixed reception on publication and has had minimal impact on scholarly studies of language yet it has a revered reputation. Fowler is an outlier in usage debates. His book is in many respects a pleasure and his judgments on usage are often commendably broadminded. Yet he is still a lexicographer and grammarian who advances principles first and considers usage second.

In his introduction, Burchfield notes 'the isolation of Fowler from the mainstream of linguistic scholarship of his day' and terms the book a fossil. Why, he continues, 'has this schoolmasterly, quixotic, idiosyncratic, and somewhat vulnerable book... retained its hold on the imagination of all but professional linguistic scholars for just on seventy years?'

It's an excellent question. Fowler's *Dictionary of Modern English Usage* is huge and it goes in alphabetical order. (One of its oddities is that, even so, it has an index.) Even as a book to skim, it lacks obvious attractions. Consider Fowler's entry on *dour*, which states simply: 'Pronounce to rhyme with *moor*, not *hour*.' Well, thank you, but most people from my experience pronounce it the wrong way (it was an adjective typically applied to Gordon Brown when he was prime minister, and was cited often in newspaper rooms). And if a word's variant pronunciation is widespread, it's a variant pronunciation and not an error.

Yet the book has sold extraordinarily well. Some 60,000 copies were sold in the year the book was published. It is still often cited by public figures, especially when cornered on their own usage. Many people depend on it. Winston Churchill, who was oddly insecure about his own command of grammar, was a devotee of Fowler. 'Why must you write "intensive" here?' asked Churchill of his director of military intelligence during planning for the invasion of Normandy. ' "Intense" is the right word. You should read *Fowler's Modern English Usage* on the use of the two words.'[18]

I am a reader and fan of Fowler – not for his judgments, which are founded on a misconceived moralism, but for his linguistic tolerance and wit. As a usage columnist, I find it valuable to have Fowler to refer to when readers object to an appearance of *different to* in the newspaper. (See DIFFERENT FROM, THAN, TO.) On shibboleths such as that, he maintains a sense of proportion. On SPLIT INFINITIVES too, he did much to quell an unreasoning prohibition among English readers. He aptly referred to 'literary rules and conventions misapplied or unduly revered' as 'fetishes'. His entry for Superstitions refers to 'the havoc that is wrought by unintelligent applications of an unintelligent dogma'. He adds that 'to let oneself be so far possessed by blindly accepted conventions as to take a hand in enforcing them on other people is to lose the independence of judgement that would enable one to solve the numerous problems for which there are no rules of thumb'.

These 'unduly revered' rules include, according to Fowler, the prohibition on SPLIT INFINITIVES, the notion that ALTERNATIVES cannot exceed more than two choices, the insistence that NONE must take a singular verb, the belief that *averse to* and *different to* are usages of the uneducated, the avoidance of starting a sentence with AND, and the objection to a preposition at the end of a sentence. All of these shibboleths are held today; Fowler is useful ammunition in seeing off their advocates. On split infinitives, he sensibly commented that English speakers who neither know nor care about them 'are to be envied' by those few who do.

Yet the tolerance extends only so far. You'll find the school-masterly tone when it comes to Fowler's strictures on *aggravate*, *transpire*, *eke out*, *ilk* and *discomfit*. On the loose (though in fact entirely acceptable and Standard) use of *meticulous*, Fowler refers to it as a 'wicked word' for it means not *careful* but *frightened*. This is a blatant example of the etymological fallacy, as the adjective comes from the Latin *metus*, meaning *fear*. Fowler also employed the technique of Lowth in finding fault with great authors, regardless of what would have been idiomatic at the time. Of these, he finds fault with Chaucer, Shakespeare, the Bible, Spenser, Johnson,

Burton, Pepys, Congreve, Swift, Defoe, Burke, De Quincey, Landor, Hazlitt, Peacock, Arnold and others.

Fowler is an urbane and thoughtful stickler but a stickler nonetheless, which is why linguists have tended to ignore his work. Burchfield is right in terming his famous volume a fossil, yet in injecting some academic rigour into Fowler's discussions he has tended to diminish the humour as well – which is the principal reason for reading *Fowler's Modern English Usage*.

Many later writers have tried to combine the approaches of prescription, levity and lightness of learning in writing about grammar. Unfortunately, the lightness of learning isn't deceptive. It's true of the eminent and eloquent as well as the scolding ignoramus that style guides are typically uninformed of the scholarly evidence of what language is and how it is used.

The nearest American equivalent to Fowler, in revered status if not in style, is *The Elements of Style* by William Strunk Jr and E. B. White, published in 1918. Strunk was an academic in English and White was a fine popular writer, yet their advice on style is platitudinous at best, as here: 'Make definite assertions. Avoid tame, colorless, hesitating, non-committal language. Use the word *not* as a means of denial or in antithesis, never as a means of evasion.'

Sometimes it's worse. There are good stylistic reasons, for example, not to use a COMMA *splice*, in which clauses that could function as complete sentences are separated by a comma. It's too light a punctuation mark to be effective. But it's overstating it to invoke the notion of what is proper, as Strunk and White do: 'If two or more clauses, grammatically complete and not joined by a conjunction, are to form a single compound sentence, the proper mark of punctuation is a semicolon.'

Geoffrey Pullum, a linguist who has co-authored the remarkable *Cambridge Grammar of the English Language*, is scathing about the authors' grammatical incompetence, as shown in their treatment of the passive voice and advice against it: 'What concerns me is that the bias against the passive is being retailed by a pair of authors so grammatically clueless that they don't know what is a passive construction and what isn't.'[19] (See STYLE.)

Whatever merits Strunk and White possess, their volume shows that stylish writers don't necessarily have a notion of how to convey the elements of style. The same is true of other authors who have tried their hands at style guides. Kingsley Amis was a superlative author, whose first book, *Lucky Jim*, is one of the great comic novels in English. His style guide, *The King's English* (1997), has a characteristic combativeness. He begins his entry on *kilometre* with the observation that 'perhaps sadly, perhaps not, this is hardly the place to launch an attack on the metric system...'. But the book has scant use as a manual of style and usage. It's a collection of authorial prejudices, which the reader may take or leave, and which the discriminating reader will leave. Amis has an entry on *womanese*, in which he writes: 'The word reasonable, to take a familiar case, changes meaning with the sex of its user.' It's hard to recall a time when this sort of thing was considered witty but I believe that Amis lived through it.

In this dismal genre, one outstanding intellect to contribute a volume was Michael Dummett, the philosopher. His *Grammar and Style for Examination Candidates and Others* (1993) is a fine example of a brilliant mind, who contributed notably to the philosophy of language, making assertions that are hard to credit for their dogmatism. He writes:

An effect of rapid change is that what was written only a short time ago becomes difficult to understand; such a change is of itself destructive. It cannot be helped that Chaucer presents some obstacles to present-day readers; but I have been told that philosophy students nowadays have trouble understanding the English of Hume and Berkeley, and even, sometimes, of nineteenth-century writers. That is pure loss, and a sure sign that some people's use of English is changing much too fast.

No, it isn't pure loss that language changes. It may be a net loss (though I don't believe it is) when words acquire new meanings or shift from old ones, but it's the way that language is. Nor is it up to philosophy students to arrest the pace of linguistic change. Nor do I believe that the language of the nineteenth century is becoming impenetrable to new generations. George Eliot and Charles Dickens, for example, have features that are not in fashion now, such as long and discursive sentences, yet that's just a stylistic shift; there's no need to have a cow about it.

Dummett's understated volume gains laudatory mention in *Gwynne's Grammar*, an unlikely bestseller of 2013. The philosophy of the book is highly eccentric. Among Gwynne's flights of fancy is a 'step-by-step proof (yes, a proof that really is valid!) that happiness depends partly on grammar'. This remarkable construct starts from the unexamined and gargantuan fallacy that 'thinking cannot be done without words'. I hope never to visit an art gallery with him, lest he explain how the artist first thought about the picture or sculpture in words and then converted it into an image.

Gwynne continues with a question whose portentous introduction still doesn't adequately prepare you for the coming hubris: 'I find myself provoked into raising a question of some moment. Can it be argued, dear reader, that this book is, in a way that really does matter, the single most important book in print in the English language today?'

It is, believes Gwynne, or at least he is 'only partly joking'. It's reassuring to note that he appears not to know anything about anything. Expressing his 'unconditional admiration' for Dummett's highly prescriptive book, he explains: 'Professor Dummett was neither a professional teacher of English nor even, with only one other book to his name, a remotely prolific writer.' Dummett made immense contributions to the history of analytic philosophy, and to the philosophy of logic, language and metaphysics. As well as his voluminous bibliography on philosophy, he wrote books on voting procedures, immigration and race relations, and tarot cards. Gwynne might at least have checked Dummett's entry in Wikipedia before summarising his life's work.

Unfortunately (or perhaps otherwise) for Dummett, he has to compete for Gwynne's plaudits with Simon Heffer, the journalist, whose own style guide is called *Strictly English: The Correct Way to Write and Why it Matters* (2010). Yet Heffer, whose strident stickler assertions are hard to outdo, finds himself outdone. Gwynne says regretfully that he 'can find no reference in the book to the grossly illiterate but almost universal "per capita" in place of the correct "per caput"'.

Heffer's book is stylistically of a piece with this sort of fanaticism, however. He insists, for example, that DOUBLE NEGATIVES are an offence against logic, which they aren't, and when recommending an obscure or superseded usage typically makes an appeal to logic and consistency, which doesn't get the usage debate very far. The evidence of usage is *entirely* immaterial to him. He says: 'As a professional writer, I happen to believe that the "evidence" of how I see English written by others, including some other professional writers, is not something by which I wish to be influenced.' This isn't merely an affectation: it's an error, involving a misunderstanding of language. A disputed usage is precisely that:

one that involves argument and that can't be resolved by assertion. Heffer, by design, is not interested in evidence.

It is not, in my speculation, coincidental that Heffer cites a number of 'saints' of his writing style, who include a pretty rum character. 'My final saint,' says Heffer, 'is Enoch Powell. Whatever the occasional controversy of Powell's politics, he was a superb stylist.'

Powell has been dead for some years and you have to admire Heffer's deft euphemism of 'occasional controversy'. He was not a superb stylist but a sophist, whose contributions to scholarship – eccentric dating of St Matthew's Gospel and attributing the authorship of Shakespeare to a pseudonymous nobleman – were scorned by specialists.

And with that, we come full circle in observing the sticklers' heresy. Shibboleths are not rules of grammar, let alone marks of civilisation: they are a means of keeping divisions sharp. They make no concession to usage, which is the only evidence there is of the content of the English language. The sticklers' cause is not about culture but about class. After the huge success of her book prescribing 'zero tolerance' on matters of punctuation, Lynne Truss turned her attention in her next book to modern manners. I don't believe this is coincidental.

That is indeed how the prescriptive urge started in the field of linguistic advice. In his early venture into arbitrary, made-up pedantic rules, Robert Baker vigorously criticised 'low people', especially servants and actors, for their linguistic failings. Fowler, a more civilised prescriptive grammarian, turned to newspaper coverage for his examples of linguistic infelicity because, as Burchfield puts it, these sources 'reflected and revealed the solecistic waywardness of "the half-educated" general public in a much more dramatic fashion than did works of English literature'. There is an echo of Fowler's fastidiousness in the complaint of Humphrys today that text-speak is depriving a younger generation of the skills for literacy.

I disagree with the pedants. There is nothing that they can do to arrest linguistic change. Flux is part of what a living language is, for new usages are being coined all the time by users. But the sticklers can skew the debate by repeating a series of myths, of which the most prominent is that they stand for tradition and respect for the conventions of language. They are, in fact, the heirs of an eighteenth-century heresy of dubious intellectual and moral character.

Part Two

Usage Conundrums
from A to Z

Because I say so...

The sticklers' concerns about modern usage are a narrow field. Their complaints about slovenly English are ferocious but the issues that exercise them are few. This is the paradox of the usage debate.

As Humphrys puts it: 'There are so many threats to the survival of good, plain English that it is not easy to be optimistic.' Yet the sticklers invariably focus not on 'many threats' but on the same few things. These concern the APOSTROPHE, when to use WHO or WHOM, the meanings of DISINTERESTED and UNINTERESTED, the cases of the few personal pronouns that have different forms for subject and object (*I* and *me*, *they* and *them* and so on), saying DIFFERENT TO instead of DIFFERENT FROM...

The list does go on and style manuals can be voluminous. But however dense the details and shrill the denunciations, the pedants' complaints still comprise a roster of disputed usages that is slim compared with the vast number of words and combinations of them that are possible in English. Note the crucial word 'disputed'. Pedants stand their ground so militantly on these issues precisely because there is disagreement about them. Their method of resolving the disagreement is to deny it exists. Alternative or non-Standard usages are, they say, illegitimate and born of ignorance, and that's all there is to it.

Hence the arguments about English usage go on, revolving

around a narrow subset of constructions, words and phrases. I've already referred to some of their main complaints. These include such issues as the use of DECIMATE and ENORMITY, and of HOPE-FULLY as an adverb modifying a whole sentence rather than just a verb. Yet a writer who uses ENORMITY only in the sense of *monstrous wickedness* rather than *great size* is following a tacit convention rather than an inviolable rule.

This section sets out, in alphabetical order, some of the most prominent of these disputed usages as well as other issues that writers have to make decisions on. I have used a number of style guides to illustrate the sticklers' contentions. Some of them are very bad indeed; others are more moderate and thoughtful. I explained in Part 1 that the ground on which the sticklers stand is broad, but it is a continuum. All treat the language as being subject to an external body of rules that it's their responsibility to assert. Most do it loudly; Fowler does it with wit and grace, but he still does it. The books I cite critically (or, in Fowler's case, also favourably) in this section are these:

- *Write it Right: A Little Blacklist of Literary Faults* by Ambrose Bierce (1909): Bierce was unusual though not unique among pedants in genuinely being a fine stylist. It goes with a lot of saying that this didn't qualify him for identifying bad English.
- *Grammar and Style for Examination Candidates and Others* by Michael Dummett (1993): a slim and on occasion oddly intemperate volume of highly prescriptive advice, in which landmarks of Oxford and the concerns of dons figure large.
- *Fowler's Modern English Usage* by H. W. Fowler (1926, 1965, 1996): a style guide more revered than read these days, and an outlier in prescriptive arguments, as it's often reasonable and acute.

- *The King's English: A Guide to Modern Usage* by Kingsley Amis (1997): a manual of prejudice and social comment more than linguistic advice. The advice is almost entirely unrelated to the book's subtitle. This is a tirade against modern usage rather than a guide to it.

- *Between You and I: A Little Book of Bad English* by James Cochrane (2003): a mercifully succinct volume of vituperation and bile directed against those who the author thinks are guilty of solecism. The foreword, which I also cite, is by John Humphrys.

- *Lost for Words: The Mangling and Manipulating of the English Language* by John Humphrys (2004): a populist work explained by its subtitle. Humphrys is not wrong to object to the evasive language that he sometimes encounters as an interviewer of the powerful. His observations on grammar and semantics are another matter. He can be relied on to decry the supposed loss of shades of meaning that are in fact alive and well.

- *Strictly English: The Correct Way to Write and Why it Matters* by Simon Heffer (2010): usefully summarised by Pullum as 'a cavalcade of rules that standard English does not comply with and never did, and representing them as instruction in how to write today, [which] is dishonest'. Heffer has published an expanded version of the book as *Simply English: An A to Z of Avoidable Errors* (2014).

- *The Economist Style Guide: The Bestselling Guide to English Usage* (10th edition, 2010): a well-intentioned but salutary demonstration of how a self-conscious wish to adhere to rules can result in terrible syntax.

- *Gwynne's Grammar: The Ultimate Introduction to Grammar and the Writing of Good English* by N. M. Gwynne (2013): a work of titanic silliness.

- *Garner's Modern American Usage* by Bryan Garner (3rd edition,

2009): a prescriptive exposition of modern American usage, but moderate and useful.

- *Plain Words: A Guide to the Use of English* by Sir Ernest Gowers, revised by Rebecca Gowers (2014): a classic usage guide by the reviser of Fowler, now revised by the author's great-granddaughter.
- *Bryson's Dictionary for Writers and Editors* by Bill Bryson (2009): an opinionated survey of usage by the popular writer and former *Times* sub-editor.

I add some works that are excellent in exposing the fallacies even in the best examples of this type of approach.

- *Merriam-Webster's Guide to English Usage* (1994): an outstanding and even delightful resource that examines usage debates in the light of evidence. It is an American volume of universal importance to the English-speaking world.
- *American Usage and Style: The Consensus* by Roy H. Copperud (1982): a valuable summary of the consensus of American usage guides. Outliers are easier to spot as a result.
- *The Fight for English: How Language Pundits Ate, Shot and Left* by David Crystal (2006): an argument about the usage debates rather than disputed usages, with much good sense and scholarship.
- *The Language Instinct* by Steven Pinker (1994): I refer continually to this seminal book but especially relevant for this section is the chapter on 'The Language Mavens', which leaves the sticklers' assertions looking very threadbare.
- *The Sense of Style* by Steven Pinker (2014): a guide to usage incorporating the findings of cognitive science, it is a model of good style itself.

- *The Cambridge Grammar of the English Language* by Rodney Huddleston and Geoffrey Pullum (2002): an immense work of scholarship. A much briefer undergraduate textbook based on this volume has been published as *A Student's Introduction to English Grammar* (2004).
- *The Oxford English Dictionary* is huge and definitive and I refer to it continually in what follows. I also recommend the two-volume *Shorter Oxford English Dictionary* as a desk reference.

Here, then, is where I'm prescriptive on usage. My main prescription is to be guided by the evidence of how English speakers, including great writers, use the language. And while I have stylistic preferences, and state them, I don't mean to imply that these are the only legitimate forms in Standard English.

That's where I differ from the pedantic approach. Instead of listening to the language and asking why people adopt certain usages, the pedants seek out error. There is, however, no criterion available for judging usage other than the way people speak and write. Any advice given by a language pundit needs to be consistent with that evidence.

-a, nouns ending in

The noun *data* is a Latin plural. The singular is *datum*. Not all Latin words ending in -*a* are plural but this one is. So are *media* and *strata* (the singulars are *medium* and *stratum*). They are neuter plurals. Hence in traditional English usage *data* is treated as a plural count noun. Since the middle of the last century, though, it's been increasingly used (especially in the context of computing) as a mass noun with a singular verb. It is *Times* style to treat *data* this way, as in the headline **Patients' data is sold to firms.**

The *OED* notes, of using *data* as a mass noun, that 'in general and scientific contexts it is still sometimes regarded as objectionable', and quotes this judgment from the journal *Psychologist* in 1990: 'A staggeringly large number of psychologists fail to appreciate that data should be followed by the plural form of the verb.'

That would be logical, given the word's Latin root, but so what? No one is consistent when it comes to subject–verb agreement. Apparently without realising the irony, the writer in *Psychologist* insisted that *data* had to be plural yet didn't treat *number of psychologists* as singular. That was a justified decision but it was a choice to avoid the strict syntactical logic of the sentence and go with meaning instead. (This is the principle of *notional* rather than *formal concord*; see NUMBER.)

Agenda is a singular noun in English, though it too is a Latin plural. In Latin, it means *things that require to be done* (the singular is *agendum*, which only the most doctrinaire pedants would use). *News* was originally plural and it remains so in some contexts (*some bad news*). Yet you'd be surprised to hear at the start of a broadcast bulletin: *Here are the news.*

The most prudent course with subject–verb agreement is to accept that some nouns, especially but not only those adopted direct from other languages, can be either singular or plural. I have a slight preference for treating *media* as plural because I can see a use for the singular noun *medium* (in the sense of a vehicle for communication). I would naturally refer to the print *medium* and the broadcasting *medium*, and collectively the communications *media*. But I won't criticise anyone for saying *the media is* and there is a strong case for treating *data* as singular. Statisticians and economists do refer to the singular *datum* but usually talk of a data point or observation. Few people, from my observation, instinctively refer to *two data*.

Some sticklers insist that *referenda* be used as the plural of *referendum* in English. Alan Clark, the flamboyant Conservative politician, urged the then Speaker of the House of Commons to 'strike a blow for classical revivalism' by ruling that the word should be *referenda*, but she sensibly demurred. *Referendum* is in fact a gerundive form meaning *question to be referred*. Fowler maintains that *referenda* is confusing, because it suggests this original sense of *referendum*. For that sense, we now use *terms of reference*. The firmly established English plural is *referendums*.

Latin plurals ending in *-a* can legitimately be singular in English. I go for *data* as a mass noun though I see a case for treating *media* as a count noun.

about, around, round

About and *around* are interchangeable as prepositions in the positional sense of being surrounded. In his poem 'How it Strikes a Contemporary', Browning uses *about* in this sense: 'And seen who lined the clean gay garret-sides / And stood about the neat low truckle-bed...' He might have said *around* equally well.

There is a peculiar pedantic objection, however, to using *around* in the positional sense of *next to* or *out there*. It appears to have started with Bierce, who insists: 'Around carries the concept of circularity.'

You could have fooled me. It's a purely artificial objection that would have caught out many writers. In *The Rime of the Ancient Mariner*, Coleridge writes: 'The ice was here, the ice was there / The ice was all around...'

Maybe you have the mental image of the ice arranged in a circle but I don't. I think of something less regular. It's a bizarre piece of reasoning by Bierce.

Around and *about* are also interchangeable in the sense of *approximately*, though *about* is less formal, to my ear at least. Finally, *around* and *round* in a positional sense are also interchangeable in both British and American usage.

acronym

Many usage pundits distinguish between an *acronym* and an *initialism*. An acronym is technically an abbreviation, comprising the initial letters or sounds of a name or phrase, that can be spoken as a separate word. An initialism is an abbreviation pronounced as a succession of letter sounds. Thus Nato is an acronym, whereas EU is an initialism. Opec is an acronym; BBC is an initialism.

The distinction between an acronym and an abbreviation is illustrated by the progress into the language of acronyms that become such common words that few people realise they are acronyms. Radar is an acronym coined by the US Navy in 1940 for Radio Detection And Ranging. Conversely, no one would fail to realise that the initials CIA and FBI stand for something rather than being words in themselves.

The sticklers would thus find fault with this sentence from a rugby report: **So we have to accept that ERC is in its death throes and that, for all the talk of a desire to negotiate, the body which has run the Heineken Cup for the past 18 years is set to become another one of the game's forgotten acronyms.**

It hardly needs saying, but I will say anyway, that the sticklers don't trouble to check their suspicions against a dictionary. The *OED* includes both definitions that I've just given, of which the first is this: 'A group of initial letters used as an abbreviation for a name or expression, each letter or part being pronounced separately; an initialism (such as *ATM, TLS*).'

Reserving the term *acronym* for one type of abbreviation is unnecessary. The only relevant point is to note the conventions of spelling. *Times* practice is to write acronyms (using the narrow definition of the term) with only an initial capital letter and abbreviations with capitals throughout (so Smersh but KGB). This seems to me convenient but optional.

adjectives, absolute

Absolute adjectives are a category invented by usage pundits to denote adjectives that, in their opinion, admit of no point of comparison. Gwynne insists that *unique, peerless, matchless, infinite* and *eternal* can't have comparatives (*more infinite*), superlatives (*most infinite*) or intensifiers (*very infinite*). He allows that the 'rule' that certain adjectives cannot have superlatives can be broken if used jocularly.

The rule is arbitrary and can be ignored. First, the supposedly select group of adjectives that are absolute is in fact far bigger than pedants conceive of. *Merriam-Webster* points out that most adjectives in English, perhaps an overwhelming majority of them, don't admit of a point of comparison either because they are technical or because their meaning doesn't allow it. I open *The Shorter Oxford English Dictionary* at random and come up with *rearmost*. No usage pundit I'm aware of has ever issued an edict about this adjective. Perhaps now I've mentioned it, someone will; I doubt it, though, because it doesn't fit into the customary catechism of the sticklers who complain about the decline of standards of literacy and so forth.

Second, notable as well as capable writers do use comparatives and superlatives with absolute adjectives – even the adjectives that the sticklers care about so much.

The Preamble to the US Constitution uses the eloquent phrase 'to form a more perfect union'.

Walter Scott writes in his epic poem *Marmion*, about the Battle of Flodden: 'But chief 'twere sweet to think such life / (Though but escape from fortune's strife), / Something most matchless good and wise, / A great and grateful sacrifice...'

In Shakespeare's *The Winter's Tale*, Leontes declares: 'Gentleman / Ay, the most peerless piece of earth, I think, / That e'er the sun shone bright on.'

Robert Louis Stevenson writes, in his early travelogue *An Inland Voyage*: 'The more you look into it, the more infinite are the class distinctions among men...'

These sentiments are not grammatically wrong or semantically chaotic. Their authors don't lack a sense of language, nor are they cracking a joke. On the contrary, everyone can see what they mean. In modifying an absolute adjective with adverbs of degree, they are using idiomatic language, usually as a sort of intensifier. The pedants, on the other hand, look at a construction and wonder about its logic more than its effectiveness and lucidity (let alone its poetry). The fault lies with them. You can go right ahead and use comparatives, superlatives and intensifiers with absolute adjectives; the best writers do.

When I was at school I had an English teacher who insisted that *wrong* was an absolute adjective and should not be modified with an adverb. Having carried this rule with me for much of my adult life, I'm still wary of writing *completely wrong* or *more wrong*. It's pure superstition on my part, of course, and you should pay no attention to this rule. Here's Jane Austen, from *Pride and Prejudice*, describing Elizabeth Bennet's reasoning on noting the stare of Mr Darcy: 'She could only imagine however, at last, that she drew his notice because there was a something about her more wrong and reprehensible, according to his ideas of right, than in any other person present.'

See also COMPARATIVES, SUPERLATIVES and UNIQUE.

adjectives, position

An adjective is a type of word expressing an attribute of a noun. Most adjectives can be placed either before or after a noun. Those that precede a noun are known as attributive adjectives. Those that follow (or rather, follow a verb that follows a noun) are called predicative adjectives.

Sticklers advance a bit of mumbo-jumbo about the order of attributive adjectives. Gwynne insists that the order should almost always be *opinion–size–age–shape–colour–origin–material–purpose*, and gives the self-referential example (for diffidence does not come naturally to him) 'a nice little just-published oblong-shaped attractively-coloured much-needed paperback grammar textbook'.

This sounds an impressively detailed rule until you realise that you know it anyway. The fanciful character of the example obscures this, but in fact native speakers already say *little black book* instead of *black little book*, without thinking about it. It's an example of a rule of grammar that is instinctive: attributive adjectives of size precede those of colour.

That rule is not absolutely always followed. If I wanted to stress that it was one little book rather than another that I was referring to, I'd say *the black little book* as opposed to the red one. But the rule generally holds. Note that there's nothing so elevated as a logical relationship, let alone a moral imperative, about it. The rule just *is*: it exists and makes sense in its own terms. And as you know it already, there's no point in saying any more about it in a usage guide.

adverbs, flat

An adverb is often defined as a word that describes or qualifies a verb in the same way that an adjective qualifies a noun. Adverbs in fact have many more uses than that. They can modify verbs, adjectives, phrases, clauses, sentences or indeed other adverbs.

Confusion occasionally arises from the tendency of adverbs to end with -*ly*. Some people infer from this regularity that adverbs must therefore end -*ly*, and that a word lacking that suffix isn't an adverb. Not so. Among the many exceptions is the class of adverbs known as flat adverbs.

A flat adverb is an adverb that has the same form as its related adjective. An example is *first*, which is an adjective ('the greedy columnist ate his first blueberry muffin of the morning') and an adverb ('the indolent columnist first ate a blueberry muffin').

There used to be many more flat adverbs in English usage, both as ordinary adverbs and as intensifiers, than there are now. In his semi-autobiographical travelogue *Roughing It*, Mark Twain deliciously describes the author of the *Book of Mormon*; 'Whenever he found his speech growing too modern – which was about every sentence or two – he ladled in a few such scriptural phrases as "exceeding sore"…'

That sort of phrase hasn't survived in modern usage, which is Twain's point. Yet we do have flat adverbs – a point that is apparently lost even on some English teachers. Crystal has written of his dismay on learning of the marking of a grammar test for schools.[1] One question asked children to complete this sentence with an appropriate adverb: 'The sun shone – in the sky.' One child had given the answer *bright*; extraordinarily, this had been marked as incorrect. As Crystal observes, that was the response of an examiner who was insecure about grammar.

The adverbial use of *bright* is long established in English. Crystal cites *Beowulf* and Shakespeare. I can think of many other examples. Here is Emily Brontë's *Wuthering Heights*: 'The moon shone bright; a sprinkling of snow covered the ground, and I reflected that she might, possibly, have taken it into her head to walk about the garden, for refreshment.'

As noted in Part 1, the mistaken notion that flat adverbs are poor English originated in the writings of eighteenth-century grammarians. Notable among these was Robert Lowth and his *Short Introduction to English Grammar*, published in 1762. Lowth arrived at some arbitrary principles drawn from Latin and then faulted writers who transgressed them. Thus he wrote: 'Adjectives are sometimes employed as adverbs: improperly, and not agreeably to the genius of the English language.'

Lowth thus criticised Shakespeare ('indifferent honest') and Dryden ('extreme elaborate') for this practice, which tells you something about the value of his purported rule. I believe he was the pioneer sceptic about whether flat adverbs could really be adverbs, and advocate of the notion that adverbs should have the suffix -*ly*.

Hence we have fewer flat adverbs now. They exist, though, and where they sound natural it's legitimate to use them. The expressions *buy direct*, *sell cheap*, *shine bright*, *run away quick* and *spell it wrong*, for example, are not slang: they're Standard English. It's common to hear that a footballer or cricketer *played amazing* or *good*. That's non-Standard but grammatical.

The purported rule about *-ly* adverbs can create needless problems, as with this sentence from a legal article in *The Times*: **Part of the problem is expense – the technology, premises and high standard of the bench do not come cheaply.**

The word *come* in this sentence is a copular, or linking, verb. Mistakenly believing an adverb was needed to follow it and that adverbs end *-ly*, the author wrote something stilted that no one would say in real life.

That section of *The Times* apparently has a problem in recognising adverbs, as this sentence demonstrates: **The alleged actions of a single rogue employee could end up costing one of the country's supermarkets and its shareholders dearly in the months to come.**

It's idiomatic to say *cost dear*, as *dear* is an adverb as well as an adjective. Writing artificially in order to satisfy an eighteenth-century rule that was erroneous even when it was devised ought to cost a writer dear in credibility.

See also DATES, DAYS; DIRECT, DIRECTLY; ONLY and WRONG, WRONGLY.

adviser, advisor

'I see no reason for orthography to be varied,' writes Heffer. Hmm. Standard English has many variant spellings. This is one. Both *adviser* and *advisor* are correct, and they are interchangeable.

Because the adjective *advisory* is spelt thus, you might imagine that *advisor* would be the more common spelling of the noun. There's no linguistic reason that it should be, however, and that speculation isn't supported by a search of *The Times*'s database.

affect, effect

Both *affect* and *effect* are verbs, and both have a long history in usage. Most style guides warn about confusing them. The meanings are distinct, which is to say that general usage differentiates them. *Affect* as a noun does exist but it has a technical meaning (in psychology and psychiatry) in the sense of an emotion or a mood rather than an everyday one. Its principal use is as a verb, where it means both *to put on a pretence of* and *to have an effect on*. *Effect* as a noun means principally *the state or fact of being operative* and as a verb means *to bring about, to accomplish*.

Where the words are used in place of each other in edited prose, it's usually, from my informal observation, a typographical error, as here: **While the Champions League has been a really nice distraction, it has had an affect on our domestic form.**

aggravation

There is a common view that the verb *aggravate* can't be used in the sense of *irritate*. Rather, it means *make worse*. Bierce added an unpleasant prejudice to this judgment: 'To aggravate is to augment the disagreeableness of something already disagreeable, or the badness of something bad. But a person cannot be aggravated, even if disagreeable or bad. Women are singularly prone to misuse of this word.'

The objection is often extended to using the noun *aggravation* in the sense of *irritation* or *exasperation*, as here: **While the West has stood idly by, electronic key cards have spread from hotel to hotel, bringing in their wake aggravation and annoyance.**

Is the objection right? No, it isn't. Both senses of *aggravate* and of *aggravation* have been around for a long time and have been used by notable writers, and the sense of *make worse* is only loosely related to the word's etymology anyway (*aggravate* has a Latin root from the verb meaning *make heavier*).

In Walter Scott's *Redgauntlet*, we find exactly the usage that Bierce complains about: 'It was not my business to aggravate, but, if possible, rather to soothe him in whose power I was so singularly placed.'

Here is Jane Austen, from *Persuasion*: 'Lady Russell was extremely sorry that such a measure should have been resorted to at all, wondered, grieved, and feared; and the affront it contained to Anne, in Mrs Clay's being of so much use, while Anne could be of none, was a very sore aggravation.'

This is Charles Dickens in *Bleak House*: 'All the unowned dogs who stray into the Inns of Court, and pant about staircases and other dry places, seeking water, give short howls of aggravation.'

The usage has been in the language for centuries, is widespread and has been adopted by some of the greatest exponents of English prose. *Aggravate* in the sense of *irritate* and *aggravation* in the sense of *exasperation* or *annoyance* are Standard English.

ain't

Children are routinely scolded for using this word. Its condemnation is a perfect illustration, and perhaps the perfect one, of the vagaries of usage. The *OED* records its use in writing as *an't* by the eighteenth century and as *ain't* by 1778. It is a contraction of the same form as *aren't*, *isn't* and *hasn't*, and it makes grammatical sense. Yet at some point it became a taboo word and has remained so.

You can easily imagine an alternative universe in which *ain't* became Standard and usage pundits condemned native speakers for sloppily failing to use it. Fowler comments sensibly: '*A(i)n't* is merely colloquial, and as used for *isn't* is an uneducated blunder and serves no useful purpose. But it is a pity that *a(i)n't* for *am not*, being a natural contraction and supplying a real want, should shock us as though tarred with the same brush. Though *I'm not* serves well enough in statements, there is no abbreviation but *a(i)n't I?* for *am I not?...*'

A pity indeed. Language doesn't follow logic, except its own. *Aren't* would be an alternative, as in *aren't I clever?*, yet *I aren't clever* isn't Standard English.

all right

There is a variant spelling, as here: **The Non-Proliferation Treaty still acts as a constraint on behaviour. Alright, it hasn't stopped the spread of nuclear weapons entirely**.

English usage traditionally spells **all right** as two words. This is far the more common spelling and pedants frown on the elision. As one wag put it, 'alright is alwrong'.

But it isn't. There is no logic to this rule. The sticklers presumably refrain from adding that *alright* is *always* and *altogether* wrong, *already*, even when they're *alone*. Such examples of inconsistency confirm that there is variation in English spellings and that permissible elisions are many and varied. The *OED* notes: 'Although these analogues exist, the form [*alright*] is strongly criticized in the vast majority of usage guides, but without cogent reasons.'

The spelling *alright* is often found in dialogue and monologue in literature, but not only there. Here is Gertrude Stein in *The Autobiography of Alice B. Toklas*: 'The first two years of the medical school were alright.' Waldo Frank uses the spelling colloquially in *Not Heaven*: 'It's goin' to be *alright*.'

In the absence of any cogent reasons for avoiding *alright*, it's fine to go ahead and use it as an accepted variant spelling in Standard English.

alternative

It is a fairly extreme position that *alternatives* must involve a choice of only two but there are some sticklers who hold it. Thus Heffer says: 'There can only ever be two *alternatives*. If there are – or you think there are – three or more, then they are *options*.'

The word is well established in Standard English to mean more widely a choice among several options and has been explicitly used in this sense for centuries. The *OED* cites Gladstone from 1879: 'When in doubt among several alternatives of conduct, we are bound to choose that which has the greatest likelihood of being right.'

When George Orwell writes, in his essay 'Shooting an Elephant', of only one alternative, he implies that there might have been others: 'There was only one alternative. I shoved the cartridges into the magazine and lay down on the road to get a better aim.'

although, though

These words are normally used as conjunctions. There is no difference between them. Some writers maintain that there is a difference in tone. Garner says: 'The only distinction is that "although" is more formal and dignified, "though" more usual in speech and familiar writing.'

That's a matter of aesthetic judgment and nothing else. *Though* is not an illegitimate contraction and is entirely appropriate in any form of writing. It's my preference because it's shorter.

There is only one difference, which is that *though* is sometimes used as an adverb: **It is not often, though, that you will see Ayckbourn in the West End as a punter.**

See also *TILL*.

amend, emend

Emend is far the less common word. It means principally to remove errors from the text of a book or a document. For some reason, usage pundits think it worth carefully distinguishing this verb from *amend*. The more profitable course is just to accept that most people can go through a lifetime without once having cause to use *emend* or *emendation*. I had till just now.

There is, incidentally, one slightly odd but plainly jocular use of *emend* in P. G. Wodehouse, from the novel *Psmith in the City*. Psmith, the languid protagonist, explains: 'If Comrade Bickersdyke wishes to emend any little traits in my character of which he may disapprove, he shall never say that I did not give him the opportunity.'

Either Psmith is, in character, riling his enemy with pedantry or it's a typographical error.

American English

Much misunderstanding among language pundits has arisen from the evolution of a distinctive dialect in North America. Like the US Constitution itself, it is an unusual example of a deliberately engineered and consciously planned outcome that has worked.

Much of the credit lies with Noah Webster, whose *American Dictionary of the English Language* of 1828 is historic. As discussed in Part 1, Webster was the reformer who created American spellings such as *honor*, *theater* and *traveled*. The dictionaries that still bear his name are part of America's social and cultural history.

It was the power of the Webster name that in the twentieth century caused a vitriolic debate on American usage. The third edition of *Webster's*, published in 1961, deliberately set out to record usage rather than pronounce on correctness. Critics have long since believed that the dictionary thereby blessed such non-Standard usages as AIN'T and IRREGARDLESS. It didn't, but the arguments anticipated the wider cultural controversies of the 1960s. Many people expected a dictionary to set down standards. They accused the editors of *Webster's Third* of abandoning that duty (Dwight Macdonald, the literary critic, said they had 'untuned the string, made a sop of the solid structure of English...').[2]

The notion of 'two nations divided by a common language' is a cliché but it has some truth so long as you stress the similarities. Yes, there are differences in terms (*pavement*, *sidewalk*), differences in meaning for the same term (*pants*), differences in the uses of prepositions (*meet*, *meet up with*), and the greater ease with which nouns can be verbified (and vice versa) in American than in British usage. Yet it's the same language, in differing dialects – or as I put it in Part 1, there are Englishes rather than English and certain deviant forms.

Many commentators, or at least the ones based in Britain, object to what they consider to be the incursions of American speech into popular culture. It is, however, just one more superstition to regard the dialect spoken in North America as a bastard form of English. The forms of speech and writing known as British English and American English are dialects deriving from a common ancestor, which have diverged. Neither is more authentic than the other; the idioms of both are equally legitimate. It is particularly odd when pedants complain about the assimilation of Americanisms into the language, as Standard English has borrowed extensively from other languages and dialects over centuries. The widespread belief among sticklers in Britain that 'Americanisms' are a threat to English usage has nothing to commend it. It's merely ethnocentrism and ignorance dolled up as cultural purism.

among, amongst, between

There is an enduring myth that *between* can apply to only two people or things and that *among* is required for more than two. I have in front of me an academic paper entitled *Relationship Among Economic Growth, Internet Usage and Publication Productivity: Comparison Among ASEAN and World's Best Countries*, whose authors must have been swayed by this notion in their choice of preposition. It sounds awkward in both parts of the title.

Between is my preference in each case because *among* is too vague when you're talking about a relationship rather than simply some association. The *OED* states the distinction this way: '[*between*] is still the only word available to express the relation of a thing to many surrounding things severally and individually, *among* expressing a relation to them collectively and vaguely'.

Among and *amongst* are synonymous and interchangeable. Some commentators (apparently originating with Fowler) caution that *amongst* sounds quaint, and most British publishers' house styles prefer *among*. Yet there is still plenty of evidence of current usage for *amongst*. The same holds good of *amid* and *amidst*, and *while* and *whilst*.

and

And is a conjunction. A longstanding superstition holds that it can't be used at the start of the sentence. Yes, it can. And that's an end to it.

The pedants' aversion is so unreasonable that few will state it openly but many people do observe this purported rule. Almost all, from my observation, learnt it in childhood and have never resiled from it. The reason that children are taught this rule is probably to dissuade them from writing in fragments, yet to extrapolate from this laudable aim a rule that a conjunction can't begin a sentence is absurd. A sentence doesn't necessarily exhaust a thought. It's fine to begin a sentence with *and*, just as it's permissible to use a conjunction after a semi-colon.

See also BECAUSE.

anent

Anent is an unusual preposition, meaning *concerning* or *about*. Fowler says that, excepting its use in Scottish law courts, it's 'chiefly met with in letters to the press; that is, it is a favourite with unpractised writers who, on their holiday excursions into print, like to show that they possess gala attire'. That was in 1926. Coincidentally, the only time I've seen the word in modern prose is in a letter to the press. One correspondent to *The Times*, disagreeing with readers who adopted general usage on the case of pronouns, referred to 'those who would take issue with my comments anent the predicate nominative'.

For all his idiosyncrasies, Fowler had moments of acute insight. I refer to *anent* largely to recount his advice and that example. I can't imagine any reason to use it, even in a letter to the press, unless you are a Scottish lawyer, and probably not even then.

anticipate, expect

Usage pundits are emphatic. '*Anticipate* does not mean *expect*,' declares *The Economist Style Guide*. The old grammarian's joke, repeated by *The Economist*, says that a couple expect to marry, whereas if they anticipate marriage, only one of them will be expectant.

What a riot these grammarians are. Bierce puts it less hilariously: 'To anticipate is to act on an expectation in a way to promote or forestall the event expected.'

Well, *anticipate* does carry the meaning of *forestall*, as in *Macbeth*: 'Time, thou anticipatest my dread exploits.'

But to discount the widespread use of the verb as a synonym for *expect* is arbitrary and against the historical and literary evidence. Here is H. G. Wells, in *The War of the Worlds*: 'At present the planet Mars is in conjunction, but with every return to opposition I, for one, anticipate a renewal of their adventure.'

Here is Charlotte Brontë in the opening paragraphs of her novel *Shirley*: 'If you think, from this prelude, that anything like a romance is preparing for you, reader, you never were more mistaken. Do you anticipate sentiment, and poetry, and reverie?'

The evidence of usage is nothing to the sticklocracy, however. Daniel Hannan, the Conservative politician, posted on Twitter the following comment: 'Noam Chomsky in the Guardian uses "anticipate" to mean "expect". I thought language was his thing.'

Expect such smugness if you do as Chomsky did, and then go ahead anyway.

antisemitism

The word is an oddity. So is my preferred spelling of it. The term, which is the most common for denoting anti-Jewish prejudice, was coined only in the second half of the nineteenth century by a German polemicist, Wilhelm Marr. Marr argued that Western civilisation had been infiltrated by a pernicious Jewish influence, and he established his own Anti-Semitic League in 1871 to further his demagoguery.

There is, however, no such thing as *Semitism* against which someone can be prejudiced. We are stuck with the term *anti-Semitism*, but it is as well to note its historical lineage and the ease with which it can be manipulated to do further damage. Political extremists have been known to argue that, as the word *Semite* covers very many ancient and modern peoples, they can't be accused of anti-Semitism even though they are oddly obsessed with supposed Jewish conspiracies.

It was for that reason that the philosopher Emil Fackenheim, having escaped Nazi Germany in 1940, recommended that the word *anti-Semitism* be written, without a hyphen, as *antisemitism*. I adopt this spelling: it simply makes it marginally more difficult for those who wish to deliberately misapply the term for mischievous reasons. Conor Cruise O'Brien, the historian, proposed an alternative with a similar rationale. He suggested adopting the term *anti-Jewism*. Its merit is that no one could fail to miss what it means and its ugliness is appropriate to the phenomenon it describes.

apostrophe

The apostrophe is a useful mark in denoting possession and distinguishing the genitive singular and plural. The genitive is generally formed by adding an apostrophe and the letter *s* to the noun. For a singular noun, the apostrophe precedes the *s* (as in *the author's book*). For a plural noun that ends in *s*, the apostrophe comes after it (as in *the politicians' debate*). For a plural noun that does not end in *s*, you add an apostrophe followed by an *s* (as in *the people's demands*). Possessive pronouns can function as either adjectives or nouns. The possessive adjectives are *my, your, his, her, our* and *their*. The noun (or substantival) forms are *mine, yours, his, hers, ours* and *theirs*. The possessives *yours, hers, ours* and *theirs* do not take apostrophes.

The apostrophe is also useful in indicating an elision in a contracted word, such as *don't* or *haven't*. (Though not everyone agrees. Shaw dispensed with it in early editions of his plays, only to find that actors stumbled over the pronunciation of *we'd* when spelt as *wed*, or *can't* when spelt as *cant*.)

Those are the conventions. Every so often there's a manufactured controversy in public life when sticklers discover loose or non-existent observance of the apostrophe. There's even something called the Apostrophe Protection Society that reliably kicks up a kerfuffle about street signs that omit the apostrophe. When it belatedly discovered that the famous Princes Street in Edinburgh had, till the 1830s, been known as Prince's Street, it doltishly demanded that the street's 'lazy, ignorant and appalling' signs be altered to that previous name.

Enough. The genitive (or possessive) apostrophe is a grammatical anomaly in English and its conventions are quite a recent development. The apostrophe entered the language (the form of it that we now call Early Modern English) from French in the sixteenth century, as a printer's mark to denote an elision. Its use to denote possession was, for centuries thereafter, much debated and highly inconsistent.

For example, *A Grammar of the English Tongue* (1711), by Charles Gildon and John Brightland, states that the mark could be added 'to the End of the Name … as the King's Place'. The book is dedicated 'To the Queens most Excellent Majesty'.[3]

Crystal notes in his *Cambridge Encyclopedia of the English Language* that 'even at the beginning of the 19th century there was inconsistency over whether constructions such as "the girls' dresses" should contain an apostrophe (because no letter was being "left out")'. Only later in the century was anything approaching a set of rules established for using the apostrophe. Even then, they still showed the inconsistency of much English usage. Thus an apostrophe marks possession in nouns (*the greedy columnist's blueberry muffins*) but not pronouns (*his blueberry muffins*).

That anomaly is the source of a peculiarly fierce complaint by the sticklers: the confusion of *it's* and *its*. The first is a contraction of *it is*. The possessive adjective *its* has no apostrophe. The sticklers deploy their typical invective if the possessive includes an apostrophe but you can immediately see why children (and adults) often make this mistake. Having had impressed on them that a noun requires an apostrophe to indicate the genitive, they carry the rule over to the possessive of *it*.

There is no logic to the exception, nor is there to the sticklers' complaint that the absence of an apostrophe in Princes Street is illiterate and so is the presence of one in (possessive) *it's*. Both are accidents of orthographical history.

Horobin notes: 'The spelling of [possessive] *its* with an apostrophe was in fact used right up to the beginning of the nineteenth century, and thus our modern use of *it's* exclusively as an abbreviation for *it is* is a comparatively recent phenomenon.' And he cites as an example Shakespeare's use of possessive *it's*, in *The Tempest*: 'This Musicke crept by me vpon the waters, / Allaying both their fury, and my passion / With it's sweet ayre...'

The apostrophe exists only in written English. Spoken English does not become unintelligible in its absence. Nor were our forebears unlettered for want of rules for the regular use of the apostrophe as a genitive marker. Pedants who urge zero tolerance of breaches of conventions of apostrophe usage are being anachronistic in insisting that these are part of the heritage of the language; rather, they're a recent convenience.

appraise, apprise

This distinction is stressed by usage guides. *Appraise* means to put a value on something. Large employers call their staff reviews *appraisals*. To *apprise* means *to inform* or *give notice to* (someone).

It's less common a confusion than the sticklers suppose, largely because they're used in different types of construction. You generally *apprise* someone of something. *Merriam-Webster* comments that the confusion typically occurs in speech rather than print. I can come up with a newspaper example or two but not many more, as in this sentence from an article about the First World War: **Appraised of this situation on reaching Potsdam, the Kaiser nevertheless saw Britain as the key player in a game that was suddenly moving at desperate speed.**

as, like

Sticklers have a problem with a sentence like the second one here: **On Monday morning Kenneth Proctor, a civilian utilities foreman at the Navy Yard, went for breakfast in the cafeteria of building 197, as he did every morning. But first he called his ex-wife Evelyn, just like he did most days.**

The problem is with *like*. The reasoning goes that it can serve as a preposition but not as a conjunction. To introduce the clause *he did most days*, a conjunction is needed. It should thus be *as he did most days*. The first sentence would be accepted by pedants, because the subordinate clause *he did every morning* is introduced by a conjunction.

Here's Dummett's stipulation: 'It is therefore proper to write "like me" or "unlike me", but wrong to write "like I am" or "like I do": it should be "as I am" or "as I do".'

Is there truth to this? It depends if *like* can be treated as a conjunction. Strunk and White call the usage illiterate. *Merriam-Webster*, more responsibly, summarises the historical evidence. *Like* was used as a conjunction by Chaucer and Shakespeare. After a period of abeyance, it became far more common in the nineteenth and twentieth centuries. Otto Jespersen records examples from Keats, Emily Brontë, Thackeray, George Eliot, Dickens, Kipling, Bennett, Gissing, Wells, Shaw, Maugham and others.

Like so many stickler superstitions, the insistence that *like* cannot govern a clause is contradicted by the evidence of the way the language is used. There is no inherent reason that *like* can't serve as a conjunction. Burchfield sensibly acknowledges that '*like* as a conjunction is struggling towards acceptable standard or neutral ground' and that 'the long-standing resistance to this omnipresent little word is beginning to crumble'. But even that is to understate its ubiquity.

as to

Many usage pundits take exception to the two little words *as to* in sentences such as this: **The defeat raises questions as to why Conservative Campaign Headquarters was not better prepared for a by-election that political observers had thought possible for many months.**

Their argument is that the phrase is ugly and intrusive. It is legitimate in English to write *the question why* or *the question whether*, just as it's natural to write *he asked why* or *she asked whether*. Inserting the phrase *as to* adds nothing to the meaning but merely, owing to verbiage, blunts the impact of the sentence. Dummett is representative: 'The phrase *as to* is almost always redundant, and is best avoided altogether; on the few occasions when it cannot simply be removed, the substitution of *about* will usually suffice.'

That's overstating it. The phrase *as to* is a minor prolixity. On stylistic grounds, I would always say *question whether* rather than *question as to whether*. It would be ponderous if Dorothea, in George Eliot's *Middlemarch*, were to use the longer phrase, and entirely adequate that she doesn't: 'But what has that to do with the question whether it would not be a fine thing to establish here a more valuable hospital than any they have in the county?'

There is no definitive stylistic rule about the use of *as to*, beyond using your own ear. But Dummett's strictures go beyond what's reasonable even as a stylistic preference. You could indeed replace *as to* with *about* in this sentence, from a *Times* obituary: **At the time, little was known as to how the brain initiated the Defence Response.**

But what purpose does it serve to say *about how the brain initiated*? A preposition is needed, and a two-word preposition consisting of four letters is not obviously preferable to a one-word preposition with five letters and the same number of syllables.

auger, augur

These words are homophones: they are spelt differently and pronounced alike. And this is a small spelling mistake: **Past opinions from commissioners do not auger well for Mr Salmond.**

The word *auger* isn't a verb, but a noun. An auger is a tool, shaped like a corkscrew, that's used for boring holes in wood. Here it should be not *auger* but *augur*. To *augur well* is to portend a good outcome.

These words are unrelated. No spell-checking software will correct *auger* when you mean *augur*.

My own knowledge of tools for drilling holes is extremely slim. I know what an auger is only because Emily Dickinson describes a woodpecker this way: 'His Bill an Auger is / His Head, a Cap and Frill / He laboreth at every Tree / A Worm, His utmost Goal.'

Having read the poem, I could understand the word from the context.

See also HOMOPHONE.

auspicious

Some pundits criticise a common use of this adjective. Bryson says that 'auspicious does not mean simply memorable or special. It means propitious, promising, of good omen.'

The sense of *special* has been around for a long time and is Standard usage. Here's how *The Times* uses it: **Tens of millions of Hindus have gathered in India for the world's biggest communal bath in the sacred River Ganges on the most auspicious day of the world's largest religious festival.**

Dickens uses it likewise in *Bleak House*: 'It is the old girl's birthday; and that is the greatest holiday and reddest-letter day in Mr Bagnet's calendar. The auspicious event is always commemorated according to certain forms, settled and prescribed by Mr Bagnet some years since.'

The phrase *auspicious occasion* crops up dismayingly often in after-dinner speeches but if you don't mind the cliché there's nothing wrong with the usage.

authoress

The word isn't merely the feminine of *author*. As women's emancipation proceeded in the last century, *authoress* came to bear the sense of a writer of fripperies. The insinuation is clear in Saki's comic novel *The Unbearable Bassington*: 'The authoress of *The Woman who wished it was Wednesday* had swept like a convalescent whirlwind, subdued but potentially tempestuous, into Lady Caroline's box. "I've just trodden with all my weight on the foot of an eminent publisher as I was leaving my seat," she cried, with a peal of delighted laughter.'

The term has largely fallen out of use but is occasionally revived for comic effect, as here: **This week's 'Admirable Breeziness' award goes to authoress and wearer of over half of the world's leopardskin-print clothing items, Jackie Collins.**

However great the temptation to use the word, spurn it.

There is a terrible entry about *authoress* in *Fowler*, which sneers: 'It is a word that has always been disliked by authoresses themselves, perhaps on the grounds that sex is irrelevant to art and that the word implies disparagement of women's literary abilities.'

That's in fact from the second edition of *Fowler*, dating from the 1960s. If anything, it's even worse than the entry by Fowler himself in the first edition. There, Fowler says that the word is 'regarded with dislike in literary circles'. Remarkably, it's the later edition that interpolates the gibe about 'authoresses themselves'. The original Fowler adds that the public 'may be trusted to keep a useful word in existence' and bafflingly maintains that there is a still greater need for a feminine of *doctor*.

Authoress isn't useful and it's barely in existence. Even a jocular mention is a mention too far. Sex is indeed irrelevant to art, and *authoress* is a slighting term that can be applied only to female writers. That imbalance is an anachronism. While it's possible to distinguish, say, Barbara Cartland and Virginia Woolf by referring to the first as *authoress*, we have to refer to both Jeffrey Archer and Joseph Conrad as *authors*. It's better to judge the output of inferior writers direct, rather than insinuate a judgment through a term that can apply only to inferior writers who are women.

I once made this case in a column, whereupon a *Times* reader rebuked me on the Letters page by pointing out that Jane Austen had described herself, in a letter to the Prince Regent's librarian, as 'with all possible Vanity, the most unlearned, & uninformed Female who ever dared to be an Authoress'. My point is made. The most persistent misreading of Jane Austen is to overlook her understated and effective irony.

There is one historical instance of *authoress* that I can think of that's justifiable, but it's a literary oddity. Samuel Butler, author of the fine semi-autobiographical novel *The Way of All Flesh*, also wrote a book called *The Authoress of the Odyssey*, published in 1897. It was initially considered a hoax, in the manner of Oscar Wilde's short story 'The Portrait of Mr W.H.' (which purports to identify the mysterious dedicatee of Shakespeare's sonnets). But it is a serious study, in which Butler argues that Homer's *Odyssey* was written by a young Sicilian woman who depicted herself in the figure of Nausicaa. Hence the arresting title.

As we know nothing about the historical figure of Homer, Butler's argument relies on drawing biographical inferences about the author from the work, which is a dangerous technique. But it has its admirers. James Joyce, who owned the book, may have recalled Butler's argument when he wrote the Nausicaa episode in *Ulysses*.

Butler does not represent an important exception to this general rule. An authoress is a writer of trifles, not a female writer. Bierce describes it and the related *poetess* as foolish words. So they are, for they denote foolishness and in a way that is out of kilter with modern mores and hence general usage. The words *actress* and *poetess* (which I've dispensed with in this book in favour of *actor* and *poet*) are similarly likely to fall out of common use.

baleful, baneful

The adjectives have similar meanings and the distinction is subtle, which in principle makes them a potential cause for pedants. *Baleful* means *menacing*; *baneful* means *destructive*. In Book 1 of *Paradise Lost*, John Milton describes Satan thus: 'Round he throws his baleful eyes, / That witnessed huge affliction and dismay, / Mixed with obdurate pride and steadfast hate.'

That's a precise use of *baleful*. Both words have the connotation of evil, but something is *baleful* if it threatens harm and *baneful* if it causes it. Both adjectives are quite often used to modify the noun *influence* and the distinction is so slight that it matters little which you choose.

basis, on a regular

Fowler cites *on a provisional basis* as an example of periphrasis, or saying things in a roundabout way. *On a regular basis* (or *on a daily basis*, or *on a weekly basis*) is susceptible to the same criticism. Cochrane says: 'It can hardly ever be necessary to use this formula ... unless it is to make a mock of a particular kind of pompous or bureaucratic discourse.'

It's often an awkward adverbial phrase but not always. My Pedant column appears in *The Times* on Saturdays but occasionally I miss a week through indolence. It would be legitimate, though not mandatory, to say that the column appears on a weekly basis (for that's when it's scheduled) rather than that it appears weekly (which is not literally true).

because

Can you begin a sentence with *because*? Of course. Many people who write to me have a recollection of being told in childhood that it was bad English. As with starting a sentence with AND, a pedagogical instruction not to write in fragments seems to have congealed into the belief that coordinators are ungrammatical when starting a sentence.

Because isn't even a coordinating conjunction like *and* or *but*. It's usually treated as a subordinating conjunction (one that joins a subordinate clause to a main clause). With a subordinating conjunction, it's possible simply to rewrite the sentence by reversing the clauses (*because I was hungry, I ate everything on the plate* can be rewritten as *I ate everything on the plate because I was hungry*). You would have to be a very extreme pedant indeed to argue that beginning a sentence with a subordinating conjunction (such as *unless* or *although*) is ungrammatical. It isn't.

because, the reason is

See REASON IS BECAUSE, THE

beg the question

To *beg the question* means to assume in your premise the truth of your conclusion. It is widely understood now to mean simply to raise a question or make a debatable remark.

To philosophers, *begging the question* is a logical fallacy known as *petitio principii*. For an example of question-begging in this sense, consider Sarah Palin, the hapless former US Republican vice-presidential nominee. As a candidate for Governor of Alaska in 2006, she was asked whether she supported the teaching of Creationism alongside evolution in school science classes. She replied: 'Don't be afraid of information and let kids debate both sides.'

The notion that Creationism is information rather than religious dogma is what scientists dispute. Mrs Palin had presupposed her conclusion, that Creationism had a rightful place in school science, in her premise.

The alternative sense of merely raising or prompting a question is widespread, however, as here: **Germany's kneejerk decision to slow extensions to the lives of its fleet of nuclear power plants begs the question why it wants to part-own a uranium enrichment company at all.**

There is no stopping its wider usage and the technical sense can withstand a dual use.

between you and I

No phrase drives the sticklocracy to greater distraction and dismay than this. Cochrane explains that he chose the title *Between You and I: A Little Book of Bad English* because it is 'such an egregious example of Bad English'.

Well, *between you and I* is permissible. I would write and say *between you and me* instead, but that's a convention of usage, not a rule of grammar.

Almost all style manuals disagree with me on this, but I modestly submit that they're wrong. Take Cochrane's explanation. He maintains that because *between* is a preposition, it must be followed by the object and not the subject case of the pronoun (so *me* rather than *I*). He calls this a 'basic rule of grammar'. A construction such as *between you and I* is, he says, an 'oddity, which seems to have emerged only in the last 20 years or so' (this was in 2003). Dummett maintains that it is 'a false genteelism'.

In fact, the construction goes back centuries and in contexts that have nothing to do with attempts to sound refined. In *The Merchant of Venice*, Shakespeare has Antonio say to Bassanio, in a letter, 'all debts are cleared between you and I'. Byron uses the construction and there are several examples in the works of Mark Twain, such as this one, in a letter in 1856: 'Now, between you and I and the fence you must say nothing about this to Orion...'

There's no point in castigating Shakespeare's grammar (though some do). That's to betray an anachronistic grasp of language. *Between you and I* may have been in common and educated use in Shakespeare's time, for all we know. And what pedants would regard as confusion between the subject and object cases of pronouns abounds in other noted writers too. 'Yet so it was,' writes John Bunyan in *The Pilgrim's Progress*, 'that through the encouraging words of he that led in the front, and of him that brought up behind, they made a pretty good shift to wag along.'

What's the explanation? Inflection for case has largely died out in English. The exceptions are a few pronouns that have both subject and object cases. Pronouns that do inflect in this way take the object case after a preposition (*to me, between us, for them*). It's a convention of usage that the case of a pronoun is not affected if it is conjoined to another. That's why grammar sticklers insist that it must be *between you and me* instead of *between you and I*.

Yet the convention about the cases of conjoined pronouns isn't required by any rule of English grammar. The fact that articulate users of English say things such as *invited Michelle and I* (the phrase is President Obama's) suggests that chaos doesn't ensue by relaxing the convention. *Between you and I* is frowned on by pedants but it's perfectly possible to imagine that it might have been accepted as the Standard form of this construction. All it takes is a loosening of the rule governing the case of personal pronouns in coordinate phrases in object position.

See also *IT'S I/ME*.

blond, blonde

This is a good example of knowing a rule only by examining the way the word is used. There is no inherent reason why *blonde* as a noun should apply only to females but that's how usage has it: **The Grand Budapest Hotel is a child's idea of a beautiful, grand hotel, a gleaming old-fashioned pink spa cake of a hotel, run by the camp Monsieur Gustave (Ralph Fiennes), who only makes love to blondes (nothing childish about that).**

In all other respects, as an adjective applied to people or as an adjective applied to things (especially but not only hair), *blond* and *blonde* are interchangeable. There is nothing wrong with this sentence: **With her bright eyes, blond hair and winning smile, Gut still radiates a sunny warmth, even on bitter days in the mountains and after a young lifetime spent in pursuit of her talent.**

Nor is there with this (which comes from the arch-stickler Bierce's short story 'The Affair at Coulters'): 'In face he was of a type singularly unlike the men about him; thin, high-nosed, grey-eyed, with a slight blonde moustache, and long, rather straggling hair of the same colour.'

bored of

Sticklers deplore the phrase. They insist that you can be *bored by*, *bored with* but not *bored of* someone or something. There is no logic to this. It's just a choice of preposition. Writers have traditionally used *by* or *with* but it's a natural extension of the language to use *of* as well.

You can be *tired of* the sticklers' complaints, and you can be *wearied of* them; why, then, should you not also be *bored of* them? Burchfield, in the third edition of *Fowler*, comments: 'A regrettable tendency has emerged in recent years, esp. in non-standard English in Britain and abroad, to construe the verb with *of*.'

What is recent is not intrinsically wrong or regrettable. And there is in fact a consistent if rare pattern of *bored of* in English. Here is Ezra Pound, from *Redondillas: Or Something of That Sort*: 'I am bored of this talk of the tariff, / I too have heard of T. Roosevelt.' There are occasional uses in other twentieth-century works. This is from *The Dance of the Veils* by Sax Rohmer, the writer best known for the Fu Manchu novels: 'As a matter of fact, it was she who was bored of the life she led in Limehouse – in chilly, misty Limehouse...'

What seems to have happened is that an established but occasional usage has become much more common in the past twenty or thirty years, especially among a younger generation. There's no good reason for objecting to it. *Bored of* will be accepted as Standard usage before you know it, and so it ought to be.

born, borne

Usage guides deal with the distinction but it's surprising how rarely the words are confused given their closeness in meaning and spelling. Both are past participles of the verb *bear*. The spelling *born* is the passive of giving birth (*he was born*) and can be used also as an adjective (*she was a born winner*). Other senses have the spelling *borne*: **Egypt said yesterday that it has discovered its first human case of a camel-borne virus that has been sweeping through the Middle East, killing nearly 100 people.**

The spellings were once interchangeable but the distinction has hardened. Still, it may not have been clear to this *Times* writer, who plays on the idea that lion cubs were *born* to parents who were themselves *borne* through tunnels: **It gives new meaning to the phrase: 'Born in captivity.' A pair of lion cubs this week became the first to be born in the Gaza Strip to parents that were smuggled into the blockaded territory through tunnels four years ago.**

brutalise

The verb *brutalise* and adjective *brutalised* have more than one meaning. They are commonly used in the senses *to treat brutally* and *to have been treated brutally*. The *OED* cites Robert Louis Stevenson from *Travels with a Donkey in the Cévennes*, from 1879: 'God forbid ... that I should brutalise this innocent creature.'

There are two other meanings of *brutalise* cited by the *OED*, however. One is as an intransitive verb meaning *to live or become like a brute*. The second is as a transitive verb meaning *to render brutal, to imbue with brutal nature*.

The difference between treating someone brutally and rendering someone brutal is subtle. That makes it odd that it hasn't been more of a shibboleth for sticklers (though Christopher Hitchens, who was a sensitive and eloquent user of language, did worry about losing the sense of *render brutal*).

Here's a passage from a column by George Orwell in 1944:

'This deliberate brutalising of millions of human beings is part of the price of society in its present form. The Japanese, incidentally, have been experts at this kind of thing for hundreds of years.'

A *brutalised* society is one that suffers a coarsening and atrophy of its moral sensibilities. Orwell makes an important point about the nature of warfare. Even in just wars there may be a cost to the victims of aggression that goes beyond the destruction of life and extinction of liberty.

The Hitchens preference is well represented in published sources, though. Here is Oscar Wilde in *The Soul of Man Under Socialism*: 'As one reads history . . . one is absolutely sickened, not by the crimes that the wicked have committed, but by the punishments that the good have inflicted; and a community is infinitely more brutalised by the habitual employment of punishment, than it is by the occurrence of crime.'

The persistence of *brutalise* and *brutalised* defies Hitchens's worries about the loss of a word. As with so many other disputed usages, words can bear different meanings according to the context. You can use *brutalise* in either sense.

bunkum

Bunkum is one of my favourite words. It has been invoked by Sir Paul Nurse, the Nobel laureate, in his campaign against junk science. That's the best use for it: as a synonym for nonsense and especially quackery, such as homeopathy, astrology, reflexology and similar superstitions.

But it's worth being aware of the origin of the term, lest any stickler stick on it. *Bunkum* traditionally denotes sentiments that are insincere and empty, especially those that are uttered in politics. The term originates in a speech made in the nineteenth century by

Felix Walker, a US Congressman representing Buncombe County in North Carolina. He interrupted important legislative business in order to 'make a speech for Buncombe'.

In his novel *Pudd'nhead Wilson*, Mark Twain recounts a political speech whose author 'said he believed that the reward offered for the lost knife was humbug and bunkum'. That's what *bunkum* is: humbug or cant, especially of a political variety. It's often paired with the noun *balderdash*, but (like *flotsam and jetsam*) these aren't the same thing. Technically, the pseudoscientific movements that were Sir Paul's targets talk *balderdash*, and the vote-seeking politicians who affect to be open-minded about them talk *bunkum*.

Or you can use them interchangeably. No one can reasonably object.

circumstances, in/under

There is a strong stickler objection to the phrase *under the circumstances*. *The Economist Style Guide* declares briskly: 'Circumstances stand around a thing, so it is in, not under, them.'

This is a rank bad piece of reasoning. Who says circumstances stand around a thing? The pedants define it that way in order to force their own stylistic preference. The real reason they insist on *in the circumstances* is etymology and that alone: *circum* means *round* or *around* in Latin; therefore circumstances must encompass. It's an instance of the etymological fallacy. It does not follow that the present-day meaning of a word or phrase should be similar to its historical meaning. Fowler is dismissive of the reasoning for *in the circumstances*, calling it puerile – which is pushing it; rather, it's a preference deriving from a mistaken approach to language.

In any event, writers on both sides of the Atlantic ignore

the stipulation. Thomas Hardy writes, in *Far from the Madding Crowd*: 'It seemed rather ungenerous not to tell Coggan, under the circumstances, for Coggan had been true as steel all through the time of Gabriel's unhappiness about Bathsheba...'

Here's Herman Melville, in *White Jacket*: 'Under like circumstances, a merchant seaman goes to his bunk, and has the benefit of a good long sleep.'

Likewise Charles Dickens, from *A Tale of Two Cities*: 'He walked up hill in the mire by the side of the mail, as the rest of the passengers did; not because they had the least relish for walking exercise, under the circumstances, but because the hill, and the harness, and the mud, and the mail, were all so heavy...'

And so on and on. It is enough to say that *in the circumstances* is fine and so is *under the circumstances*. Both make sense to the reader. Choose whichever you prefer.

claim

In their book *The King's English* (1906), the Fowler brothers, in one of their least considered judgments, raised an objection to the verb *claim* when used in the sense of *assert, maintain* rather than, in a broad sense, *to stake a claim*. (The latter sense can be illustrated by the words read by Bassanio in *The Merchant of Venice*: 'Turn you where your lady is / And claim her with a loving kiss.')

That objection is continued by Gowers, who declares that, where new meanings arise such as 'the enlarged meanings of *anticipate* and *claim* in [the places of] those of *expect* and *assert* ... they are clearly harming the language by "blurring hard-won distinctions"'.

The word 'clearly' is doing a lot of work in that judgment. Enlarged or alternative meanings by no means blur distinctions. Nowadays, even Gwynne uses *claim* in this sense, perhaps not realising that other pedants object to it: 'I turn to an interesting feature which I claim to be a considerable merit of this book.'

His modest claim is as wrong as wrong can be, but not because of his use of *claim*. On the contrary, it illustrates a virtue of the word. Unlike *assert* or *maintain* or *contend*, it suggests an element of doubt or contention. The word is useful in this sense and there's nothing wrong with it.

classic, classical

Usage manuals are firmer on the distinction between *classic* and *classical* than is justified on the evidence of usage. 'One would have thought that these two were settled down,' complains Amis, who wants to reserve *classic* as a noun or adjective meaning *ideal* or *standard* and *classical* as an adjective applied in the first place to styles of art (and, though he does not say so, to ancient Roman and Greek civilisation).

It's far from unknown, and far from wrong, to find them (as adjectives) the other way round. The *OED* gives instances over four centuries of *classic* as applied to ancient history, including this from *The Times* in 1956: *The Roman warriors and matrons are marshalled in their classic landscape with as much ease as ingenuity.*

Likewise Richard Steele in the *Spectator* from 1712, using *classic authors* in the sense of *the Classics*, rather than great works of any period: 'All the Boys in the School, but I, have the Classick Authors in *usum Delphini*, gilt and letter'd on the Back.'

In the use of *classical* to mean *standard* or *archetypal*, there are again examples throughout the past four centuries, including the grammatical advice of Lindley Murray in 1808: 'Classical authority consists of speakers and writers, who are deservedly in high estimation.'

Amis is especially irate at the name of the (then recently established) commercial radio station Classic FM for not calling itself Classical FM, which merely underlines the point. It's usual to distinguish between the two words as adjectives but not obligatory.

comma

The comma is a punctuation mark with many uses. Among them are its functions in separating items and framing a relative clause. It's an economical way for a writer to denote whether a clause is restrictive or non-restrictive to use (or omit) a pair of commas (see THAT, WHICH).

The common practice in modern prose is to use what's known as light punctuation. This means a more sparing use of (especially) commas than you'll find in prose from a century or more ago. That modern practice is to my taste. Fashions in orthography change, to the extent that one practice of an earlier age would be wrong now: inserting a comma between subject and predicate. It was common in the eighteenth century, as here, from *A Modest Proposal* by Jonathan Swift: 'my reason is, that these children are seldom the fruits of marriage, a circumstance not much regarded by our savages, therefore one male will be sufficient to serve four females.'

Merriam-Webster even cites Lindley Murray, the seminal grammarian himself: 'The first thing to be studied here, is grammatical propriety.'

Weighing down a piece of prose with commas tempers a writer's fluency. There is a cost, though, at least as far as sticklers are concerned. A hostile *New Yorker* reviewer of Lynne Truss's polemic on punctuation faulted her for not using the comma properly in the dedication to her book. The dedication was 'to the memory of the striking Bolshevik printers in St Petersburg who, in 1905, demanded to be paid the same rate for punctuation marks as for letters, and thereby directly precipitated the first Russian Revolution'.

The reviewer, Louis Menand, wrote that Truss had made an error by not placing a comma before a non-restrictive clause. He meant that there should have been a comma after 'St Petersburg'. Truss was referring to the striking Bolshevik printers in aggregate. And in strict syntax, it would have been better for her to insert a comma. However, she probably felt that the punctuation would be too heavy if she did. If that was her reasoning, it was sound. I'd have done the same. But I'm not the one who's declaring a zero-tolerance approach to purported orthographical errors. She is.

Debate over commas tends to focus on two other issues in particular. One is the Oxford comma. This is a comma preceding a conjunction, which itself connects the last item in a list to the previous items. A comma before a conjunction isn't necessary but it's possible to construct examples where one is supposedly needed to avoid ambiguity, as when *The Times* referred to a royal banquet of **lamb and bread and butter pudding with ice cream**.

Is that ambiguous? It's stylistically clumsy but it's not disastrous. The banquet menu is one example where I would use an Oxford comma, or hyphenate the phrasal adjective (*bread-and-butter pudding*). Yet the occasional ribbing from pedants claiming to have found a solecism is a price worth paying to avoid excessively heavy use of punctuation. Use your instinct for what reads fluently.

Second is the issue of the so-called comma splice, or comma fault. This is where a comma is used to join two independent clauses. Critics object that the comma is not a strong enough mark to do this. Instead, you need a more emphatic mark. Typically, a stickler would use a semi-colon, a full stop or (where the second clause explains or illustrates the first) a colon. Alternatively, you could use a conjunction, namely a part of speech that connects words, phrases or clauses.

Is the objection to the comma splice right? I dislike comma splices and don't use them. In newspaper articles, where I need to stick to a limited word count, I typically use shorter sentences than I do in other forms of writing. To call a comma splice incorrect is going too far, though.

Here's an example of a comma splice: 'I have found your white mittens, they were folded up within my clean nightcap.' The sentence is by Jane Austen – from a letter rather than a published work, but she's an author who does use the comma splice occasionally. Tastes in punctuation aren't constant. It makes no sense to accuse Jane Austen of incorrect use of the comma, as no one would have levelled that charge against her at the time. Her conventions of usage were not ours.

It irks me when language sticklers insist on the 'correct' use of punctuation without acknowledging where these marks, which aid a reader's comprehension, are matters of convention. The conventions of prose in the eighteenth and early nineteenth centuries were closer to speech than those of the twentieth century. In spoken English, people do generally run their sentences together. I can well see a use for comma splices in direct or reported speech.

A novelist might find that this form of punctuation adds realism. *Merriam-Webster*, from which I've taken the Jane Austen quotation, also gives this example from John Updike (in *Bech is Back*): 'The Ambassador ... responded with a blast of enthusiasm. "Those weren't tough questions, those were kid-glove questions."'

Is Updike wrong in using the comma splice? He assuredly isn't. He's captured the way a character expostulates, with two clauses that naturally follow each other. With clauses that are more obviously independent than these, it does no harm to stick to the convention of using a stronger break than a comma when joining them. It's thus different from other conventions, such as the destructive prohibition on split infinitives.

comparatives, superlatives

Sticklers are insistent on when to use the comparative (*younger*) and the superlative (*youngest*). A comparative is usually an adjective with the suffix *-er* and a superlative is normally one with the suffix *-est*. Heffer complains: 'One often hears reference to "the eldest son" when there are only two sons available; or "the youngest child" when there are only two children.' He argues that for a superlative to be used requires more than two people or objects of comparison.

As so often happens, great writers fail the pedants' exacting standards. Jane Austen has scarcely begun recounting her tale of *Emma* before revealing that its heroine 'was the youngest of two daughters of a most affectionate, indulgent father'. Anthony Trollope writes in *Castle Richmond*: ' "The truth was, she did not like to leave me," said the countess, whispering prettily into the ear of the eldest of the two girls...'

Likewise, it is a commonplace of sporting commentary that *the best team won* rather than *the better team won*. It would be at best pointlessly pedantic to maintain that this is ungrammatical. And in any event, *the best team won* is an entirely legitimate construction. It's also permissible to use the superlative of two subjects that are simply not measurable on the same scale. If two people go for a job and one is clearly superior, it would be idiomatic to say that the best candidate was selected.

By all means follow the rule, which will produce grammatical sentences, that only comparatives and not superlatives should be used when referring to two subjects. But it's not required and sometimes it's misleading to choose a comparative and economical to choose a superlative. In a general election campaign, you would idiomatically use the phrase *best candidate for prime minister* even though in practice it's invariably a choice of two politicians, leaders respectively of the Conservatives and Labour. There are many other exceptions to the convention.

Sticklers also worry fruitlessly about the use of comparatives, superlatives and intensifiers (*very young*) with what they insist are absolute adjectives that have no point of comparison (see ADJEC-TIVES, ABSOLUTE and UNIQUE).

compounds

English speakers often find it funny that German has very long words. These are typically compounds of several words. Some of them, as Mark Twain said, are so long that they have a perspective. But many are either coined opportunistically or are technical terms. And one virtue of German compounds is that, in fitting together words that belong together, they are always clear. Compounds in English, on the other hand, can be ambiguous if they're not punctuated.

That's not a grammatical error but it is a question of good style. English-language newspapers are lax on this point because of the need for compression in headlines. I used to receive a publication called *Distressed Debt Investor*, whose title could be interpreted as a comment on the emotional state of the investor. Here *distressed-debt* is a phrasal adjective; joining the words with a hyphen makes it clear.

It's good practice to hyphenate phrasal adjectives that may not be clear on first reading. In fact, I recommend hyphenating all phrasal adjectives (*the six-year-old girl*, *the little-read columnist*, *the open-and-shut case of blueberry-muffin theft*), not as a grammatical point but as a courtesy to the reader, who then won't need to work out the meaning from the phrase's context.

See also COMMA.

comprise, compose

The distinction between *comprise* and *compose* is a major shibboleth. Cochrane is clear on what it is. The words are close but not identical on meaning 'when correctly used'. Like many other pundits, he defines the correct use thus: 'The parts *compose* the whole; the whole *comprises* (or *consists of* or *is composed of*) the parts.'

Not quite. There are instances of parts that comprise a whole. Here is Herman Melville in *Moby Dick*: 'Nor do heroes, saints, demigods, and prophets alone comprise the whole roll of our order.'

The sticklers in practice don't object so much to this active use of *comprise*. Their ire is reserved for the passive construction *comprise of*. It's common, as used here: **A brace of Brahms is rarely far away in a recital of German lieder, but how often has an entire evening been comprised of the composer's songs?**

Merriam-Webster observes that this disputed usage has been in existence for more than a century. The active version of the disputed usage is older still. Neither is unclear in the context; both are legitimate. Cochrane gives an indication of what's exercising him in condemning 'the typical estate agent's phrase' using *comprised of*. He doesn't like the language of trade. Commercial usage has its faults but this isn't one of them.

conventions

The conventions of English usage are not the same as the rules of grammar. They are acquired through explicit teaching rather than instinct. An example of a convention is the use of the apostrophe with the genitive case. It's wrong to say: *The dog ate it's breakfast.* The genitive forms of the definite personal pronouns don't have apostrophes: *my, your, his, her, its, our, their.* That's always true. Yet (see *APOSTROPHE*) the conventions for when to use and when not to use the apostrophe were established at quite a recent stage in the development of written English. They might have turned out differently.

You can think of the notion of convention this way. In front of me is an electrical adaptor. If I'm at home in London, I don't need it, because every electrical appliance I own has a three-point plug and my home has three-point sockets in the walls. If I travel to Europe, I take the adaptor and plug its two round points into the wall. If I travel to the United States, I take the adaptor and plug its two flat points into the wall. These national differences are neither right nor wrong. They're just differences. When I go elsewhere in the UK, I don't trouble with the adaptor because I know that my laptop and phone can be plugged into a socket wherever I can find one. There is a convention that a three-point plug will fit a socket.

Language is similar. There are differences of language and differences of dialect but there is no sense in which one language or dialect is right and proper and another is wrong and improper.

See also *AMERICAN ENGLISH.*

credence, credibility

A fine distinction between these words is, from my observation, quite a recent cause in sticklerdom. The argument goes that a sentence like this simply mixes up closely related nouns: **A document found by Human Rights Watch in Libya's external security office lends credence to the claims.**

The pedants insist that *credence* means *belief* or *trustful acceptance*. The word wanted in the quoted sentence would be *credibility* or *support*.

They would also have a problem with this: **The Office of Fair Trading's referral to the Competition Commission of the proposed acquisition of Chi-X, by Bats Global Markets, tests credulity.**

The writer means that the referral was hard to believe. Yet the noun *credulity* means *gullibility* (the adjective is *credulous*). Again, the word the sticklers would want is *credibility*, meaning *believability*.

Compounding the confusion, say the sticklers, some writers use *credulity* when they really mean *credence*, as here, in an article on the European Commission: **The demands for a 6 per cent budget rise must stretch the credulity of even the most sympathetic European taxpayer**.

Is there anything in this? The phrase at issue is *give credence to* or *lend credence to*. And there isn't really a problem. It's longstanding usage to say that a person *gives credence to* something. As Dickens writes in *Oliver Twist*: 'But, then, the thought darted across his mind that it was barely eleven o'clock; and that many people were still in the streets: of whom surely some might be found to give credence to his tale.'

The stickler complaint comes when it isn't a person who gives or lends credence, but something inanimate – such as a document or other piece of evidence. It's possible for a person to give credence to something, because belief is a human quality. But an object can't have belief; it can have believability.

Merriam-Webster sensibly comments that the lexicographer's difficulty here is in fact not with *credence* at all but with *belief* and *believability*, as *credence* is applied to people and inanimate objects in the same constructions. With objects, it appears to be a twentieth-century construction but it is well established. You can use it; *believability* is not a widely used term.

crescendo

Many sticklers object to this sort of usage: **When Jackie Tyrrell accepted the Liam MacCarthy Cup as Kilkenny captain in 2006 he launched his thank-yous in the usual sequence, beginning with the invisible faces in the back-room team, rising to a crescendo of gratitude for the manager.**

They spy a solecism in the use of *crescendo* to mean *climax* or *peak of intensity*. They insist that the term in fact means a gradual increase in intensity. In music, this is true; that doesn't make the extended sense of *crescendo* wrong. It's an established usage, not least when referring to crowds. Here is P. G. Wodehouse in his early school story *The Gold Bat*: 'Sometimes the evenness of the noise would change to an excited *crescendo* as a school three-quarter got off, or the school back pulled up the attack with a fine piece of defence.'

Even an orderly crowd is unlikely to increase the intensity of its sound gradually if it's excited.

Feel free to use *crescendo* in either sense but you'll probably find more occasions for the extended one.

danglers

Danglers (especially dangling participles) are strongly criticised by sticklers. Here's an example: **Dominic Raab, the Tory MP for Esher & Walton, said: 'Having helped bankrupt the eurozone and delivered the biggest anti-EU election results in history, the chancellor can be forgiven for treating the commission's advice as spam when it arrives in his inbox.'**

Raab has used what's known as a dangler. Sticklers would claim that this is a grammatical error. That's too strong a criticism but I would still count Raab's comment as poor style.

The pedant's objection is that the implied subject of a participle or other modifier must be the same as the subject of the main clause. For example, Humphrys cites this statement from a radio bulletin: 'Driving in from the airport, the flags were fluttering proudly.' To this, he adds with laboured irony: 'What accomplished flags they must have been.'

Raab's comment raises a similar issue. The subject of the main clause is the Chancellor. Sticklers would therefore giggle that a Conservative MP has accused a Conservative Chancellor of bankrupting the eurozone and delivering the biggest anti-EU election results in history. That's not what Raab meant. Instead he wished to level the accusation against the European Commission.

Pedants feel strongly on this point. Humphrys says that the dangler 'should be a hanging offence'. They're wrong. Danglers aren't a grammatical error. That sort of construction is often found in edited and even great prose. For example, Shakespeare gives these words to the ghost of Hamlet's father: 'Now, Hamlet, hear. / 'Tis given out that, sleeping in my orchard, / A serpent stung me.'

Something that is clear (it was Hamlet's father who was sleeping and the serpent that stung him) and common can't be counted an error. Consider the idiomatic phrase *having said that*, or certain words that have become prepositions, such as *concerning*, *regarding*, *respecting*, *following* and so on. You often find them beginning a sentence but it would be pointless to object to them on the ground that they're danglers. (Some pedants do make just that argument. Dummett insists that if you write *having said that*, you are using a participle and must provide a noun for it to qualify. You can ignore that advice.)

There is, however, a stylistic issue. Pullum states it precisely. Danglers, he says, are 'not a disastrous blunder or a major display of ignorance' but are 'a minor discourtesy to the reader'.[4]

The discourtesy happens when the subject of a modifier isn't clear or the reader is attracted to the wrong choice of subject by clumsy positioning. That isn't a problem with Shakespeare's dangler or with Humphrys' example of the flags. Perhaps, too, you fully understood Raab's comment on first reading. I had to read it twice, though.

dashes

Dashes are useful marks. They help achieve the modern preference for lighter punctuation. A single dash can take the place of a colon – like this. A pair of dashes – like this – can be used in the same way as brackets or a pair of commas. I find the dash valuable as a less formal way than other marks in indicating a pause. Great stylists have used them – they are a famous part of the poetry of Emily Dickinson, who came to prefer them to exclamation marks. Her poems became less outcries to God or the reader and more about the poet and her states of mind.

As in most matters of style, though, what's appropriate for a great writer can be wearing when used indiscriminately by others.

The dash is useful, but pairs of dashes for every parenthetical comment can look breathless – more appropriate to an informal letter than prose for a wider readership.

dates, days

Some people object to a construction like *he works Saturdays*. There's nothing wrong with it. It's an adverb of time. *Merriam-Webster* refers to it as an adverbial genitive of time. It's well established in Standard English, if more common in American than British usage.

decimate

Sticklers insist that to *decimate* something is to *reduce it by a tenth* (it derives from the punishment in Roman legions of selecting by lot and executing every tenth man). The problem is that when it is used in this sense it's often done with self-consciousness as if the writer knows that most people use it differently. A *Times* report, for example, stated: **Marks & Spencer is to decimate its supply base in an attempt to turn around its flagging clothing performance.**

The report added, lest anyone misunderstood the term: **It is removing about 10 per cent of womenswear ranges.**

Providing a definition of a term is to implicitly acknowledge that it's widely used in a different way. And this is true with *decimate*. In conventional speech, to *decimate* something is to reduce or destroy a large part of it, without the implication of its being a tenth. The word has long been used in an extended sense without confusing anyone.

Charlotte Brontë wrote in a letter in 1848 about conditions

at the Clergy Daughters' School at Casterton (it's quoted in Mrs Gaskell's *Life of Charlotte Brontë*): 'Typhus fever decimated the school periodically; and consumption and scrofula, in every variety of form bad air and water, bad and insufficient diet can generate, preyed on the ill-fated pupils.'

It's unlikely that she means the disease killed every tenth girl. Why would its effects be so predictably regular? Similarly, in H. G. Wells's short story 'The Stolen Bacillus', a scientist describes the effect of cholera to a visitor who he doesn't realise is an anarchist terrorist: 'Once start [the bacillus] at the water supply, and before we could ring him in, and catch him again, he would have decimated the metropolis.'

At the very least, the word *decimate* isn't useful enough to insist on a meaning derived from etymology. Those who insist that it must, by its construction, mean a tenth are invariably inconsistent about it anyway. They do not insist that December must be counted the tenth month owing to its Latin root.

decline fallacy

This is my term for an assumption made by many language pundits. Underlying the discrepancy between linguists' accounts and newspaper columnists' views is that many of the pundits instinctively confuse *change* in language with *decline*. That's an error. I don't yield to these critics in valuing language and caring about the way it's used. But where they see a new solecism, barbarism or instance of illiteracy, I marvel at the inventiveness of the human imagination in finding new ways of expressing complex ideas. We do need conventions of usage. They provide a shared stock of references and mode of communication, and they encourage clarity. The life of the mind is a more hospitable place when they've been absorbed. But what makes up English conventions is not the arbitrary preferences of authorities: it's how native speakers actually use the language. When conventions fall into disuse, they're replaced with *something*, not nothing. It makes no sense to castigate this new *something* as wrong. It's what the language is.

delusion, illusion

Usage guides caution that these nouns are closely related but they are not interchangeable. Fowler has an extensive discussion and a sensible one. An *illusion* exists purely in the imagination. A *delusion* is an idea that misleads and deceives; it carries the connotation of a misapprehension that is destructive. *Merriam-Webster* says that sometimes the senses are interchangeable but in most they are not – and that 'when you have a context in which either word fits comfortably, you will probably choose *illusion*'.

Here's an example of the alternative choice. In Charlotte Brontë's *Jane Eyre*, the clergyman St John Rivers urges Jane to marry him and accompany him on missionary work. Jane imagines that she hears a 'known, loved, well-remembered voice' calling her name. It's the voice of Edward Fairfax Rochester. She reflects the next morning: 'I asked was it a mere nervous impression – a delusion? I could not conceive or believe: it was more like an inspiration.'

The noun *delusion* is right. It conveys the starkness of Jane's choice. She worries not merely that the voice is an illusion but that it may lead her astray; and then she dismisses the possibility. Among the reasons for *Jane Eyre*'s greatness is that the reader is absorbed in the conflict between Jane's longing for passion and her sense of spiritual struggle. Jane subverts conventional expectations of a woman's role and obligations. Within that narrative, even the single word *delusion* enriches the reader's understanding.

different from, than, to

Is it wrong to say *different to*? Many people maintain that it is and that the correct expression is *different from*. The oddity of this judgment is that it's widely held but not well represented even in traditional usage guides.

One exception is, as you would expect, the vituperative Gwynne. In a section on *special prepositions*, he comments: 'Sometimes they are important simply because to give the wrong preposition is illiterate, as "different to something" is wrong and "different from something" is correct.' The judgment is apparently supposed to stand as an absolute truth, as no argument for it is provided. Meanwhile, Heffer declares his own anathema: 'different than', he says, is 'an abomination'.

In fact, *different from*, *different to* and *different than* are all correct though not equally common. *Different from* is the most usual form. *Different to* is more often used in Britain than in America. *Different than* is predominantly an American usage but that doesn't make it an illegitimate variant elsewhere. Indeed it's useful for concision because it can be followed by a full clause. It would be cumbersome to rewrite this (from the *New Republic* magazine) using either of the other variants: 'But as Sharon famously observed, the world looks different through the eyes of a minister or opposition leader than it does through the window of the prime minister's office.'

None of these constructions is an abomination. You can use any of them. And if you maintain, as Gwynne does, that *different to* is illiterate, you have the problem familiar to the ill-informed stickler of having to explain why so many notable writers have ignored the stipulation.

'Mr Rochester, as he sat in his damask-covered chair, looked different to what I had seen him look before,' recounts Jane Eyre in Charlotte Brontë's novel.

'Unquestionably it is a very common phrase of modern intellectualism to say that the morality of one age can be entirely different to the morality of another,' writes G. K. Chesterton in *Heretics*.

'But this, under the circumstances, was quite different to Mary's plan,' says Mrs Gaskell in *Mary Barton*, thereby violating two edicts of the sticklers (who insist on *in the circumstances*) in a single sentence.

'There had been another "affair" in the house that morning, though of a nature very different to the "rumpus" which had occurred between Lord Fawn and Lady Eustace,' writes Anthony Trollope in *The Eustace Diamonds* (thereby also breaching the sticklers' arbitrary edict against using *which* as a relative pronoun in a defining relative clause).

The most common justification for insisting on *different from* is that it follows the pattern of *differ from*. To which my response is: so what? One of the reasons I'm sympathetic to Fowler is that he's often brisk with this sort of spurious reasoning, which in this case he terms 'a hasty and ill-defined generalization'. Derivatives, Fowler argues, need not conform to the construction of their parent verbs, and he's right. *Different to* is no less legitimate a construction than *averse to*.

dilemma

Sticklers are precious about preserving *dilemma* against this sort of usage: **The banker's dilemma 2008: too much lending. The banker's dilemma 2014: too little lending.**

'The word should not be used by SLIPSHOD EXTENSION for *plight* or *predicament*,' insists Garner.

Garner is following Fowler's stipulation: 'The use of dilemma as a mere finer word for difficulty when the question of alternatives does not definitely arise is a SLIPSHOD EXTENSION; it should be used only when there is a pair, or at least a definite number, of lines that might be taken in argument or action, & each is unsatisfactory.'

The earliest citation for *dilemma* in the *OED* is from the sixteenth century and it refers to the discipline of rhetoric. A dilemma is a form of argument in which an adversary is confronted with alternatives that are equally unfavourable (hence the phrase *horns of a dilemma*). The term has a technical meaning in formal logic too but not even the most obdurate stickler insists that it's illegitimate to use it in other contexts. They just insist that there must be an element of unpalatable choice.

It's not hard to show that this imagined restriction is yet another made-up rule. Fowler's entry itself acknowledges an extended use. The *OED* records as early as 1590 a popular use of *dilemma* as a choice between two or ('loosely') several equally unfavourable alternatives, from which it is a short step to a condition of doubt. Its second citation in this extended sense is from Shakespeare, *The Merry Wives of Windsor*: 'In perplexity, and doubtful dilemma.'

Merriam-Webster cites the judgment of the pioneering Columbia linguist George Krapp from 1927 that the use of *dilemma* without the implication of alternatives was 'now in general colloquial use as a synonym for *predicament, uncomfortable position, a fix*'. What was then colloquial use should in the twenty-first century be counted established. It is not a slipshod extension but a natural one. You should have no qualms about using it in this sense.

Gowers rehearses a common and misguided complaint that '*dilemma* originally had a precise meaning that it would be a pity not to preserve'. The word has long had more than one meaning.

These are in any case overlapping. Using *dilemma* in the extended sense doesn't stop Gowers or anyone else from using it in a restricted one if that's what they insist on.

direct, directly

Direct is an adjective (as in *the direct route to Outer Mongolia*), and also an adverb. As an adverb it is thus a FLAT ADVERB, as its adverbial and adjectival forms are the same. You often see advertisements urging you to *buy direct*. That is not a colloquialism: it is Standard English.

Directly is also an adverb. In most contexts it's interchangeable with *direct* apart from one. *Directly* is the form that's used to mean immediately. If the Editor of *The Times* tells me to go to Outer Mongolia directly and never come back, then he means that I should do it without delay.

discomfit

There is, says Fowler, 'a tendency to use this in too weak or indefinite a sense'. There is an established sense of the verb *discomfit* meaning to *rout* or *defeat utterly* (especially in battle). As Orcanes says in Marlowe's *Tamburlaine the Great*: 'Be now reveng'd upon this traitor's soul, / And make the power I have left behind / (Too little to defend our guiltless lives) / Sufficient to discomfit and confound / The trustless force of those false Christians!'

That's what Fowler is referring to. The weaker sense, he maintains, is an erroneous extension of *discomfort*, with which it has no connection. Bryson agrees: 'Discomfit has nothing in common with discomfort besides sound; it means to rout, overwhelm or completely disconcert.'

In fact an intermediate sense of *discomfit* has been around for a long time. The *OED* cites an example from 1425 for 'frustrate the plans or hopes of, thwart, foil; to throw into perplexity, dejection, or confusion'. It notes that *this* definition is now chiefly used in a weaker sense of causing discomfort. Here's a typical example: **I was rather moved, and also discomfited, to read that a 42-year-old man, Peter Farrell, from East London, has donated a kidney (to a woman he had never met) in an attempt to atone for the wrongdoings he committed as a younger man.**

If the weakest sense of *discomfit* is indeed a slipshod extension from *discomfort*, that doesn't obviate the fact that gradations in being discomfited (the noun is *discomfiture*) exist. The equivalence of *discomfit* with *causing discomfort* is well established in usage by now.

discreet, discrete

Most style guides caution against confusing this pair of phonetic-ally near-identical words. Their explanation is that *discreet* means *prudent* or *tactful*, whereas *discrete* means *separate*. The second is not often used (at least, I don't often see it) but it can be found in newspaper editorials: **But while the critics have justice on their side on discrete issues, they lack a sense of the wider significance of the Pope's mission.**

That distinction is Standard usage but it hasn't always been so. According to the *OED*: 'The emergence of *discrete* as the accepted spelling of the present word (more closely reflecting the form of its classical Latin etymon) is shown in dictionaries from the 18th cent. onwards, and probably reflects an attempt to differentiate the two words in writing.'

If, as in an earlier era, the spellings were treated as interchange-able, nothing would be lost. The distinction itself is so forced that Fowler made his own stipulation. Whereas *Merriam-Webster* says (accurately) that the words are homophones, Fowler urges that *discrete* be stressed on the first syllable (like *concrete*) as 'both natural in English accentuation ... & useful as distinguishing the word from the familiar *discreet*'. I've never heard anyone follow this practice.

In the meantime, you're liable to be interpreted as making a mistake if you use *discrete* for *discreet*. If you can live with that, you can justifiably treat them as variant spellings for each other.

See also HOMOPHONE.

disinterested, uninterested

Mixing up *disinterested* and *uninterested* is a cause of huge concern to pedants. *Disinterested*, they'll tell you, means *impartial*, whereas *uninterested* means *unconcerned about* or *uninvolved with*. Almost all usage guides deplore the use of *disinterested* to mean *uninterested*.

'"Disinterested" is an excellent word with a precise meaning,' says Humphrys. 'Now that it is used interchangeably with "uninterested" by those who should know better, its meaning has been destroyed. It is sad to lose a good word.'

This is overwrought. The word has not been lost at all; it merely has an additional shade of meaning that Humphrys dislikes. Yes, the word means *unbiased*. That is not its only meaning, however. The first citation for *disinterested* in the *OED* is in the sense of *not interested*. It's from John Donne in 1631: 'If there be cases, wherein the party is dis-interested, and only or primarily the glory of God is respected and advanced, it [suicide] may be lawfull.'

The *OED*'s first citation for *disinterested* in the sense of *impartial* is from 1659. Burchfield notes that this sense has been in continuous use since the seventeenth century, whereas the sense of *bored* was in use till the eighteenth century and then revived in the twentieth century.

This appears to be true, though I have found an earlier twentieth-century example of the supposedly wrong use of the noun form than the *OED* gives. It's from Jack London's novel *The Mutiny of the Elsinore*, published in 1914: ' "Well, he's buried," I observed. "Oh," she said, with all the tonelessness of disinterest, and went on with her stitching.'

A meaning that is recorded from the seventeenth century, was revived at least 100 years ago and is in general use now is not wrong. Cochrane grudgingly allows, on the strength of Burchfield's evidence, that the issue is 'not quite as cut and dried as it appears, but it is surely a matter of practical common sense to preserve two separate words for two distinct meanings'.

When usage pundits resort to appealing to common sense, you know they're on linguistically weak ground. Many English words have dual or multiple meanings, yet native speakers are never in doubt about which sense is intended. They can always tell what's meant from the context. The adjective *interested* means different things in different contexts (such as an interested party in a business transaction, or an interested reader of a book), yet no one ever mistakes what's intended by it. Why, then, should *disinterested* be reserved for only the sense that the pedants prefer?

Cochrane unintentionally demonstrates the emptiness of the complaint in his own insistence on the purity of the word's meaning. He calls the disputed usage 'such an old favourite' that the BBC received more complaints in the 1980s on this word than any other, apart possibly from *hopefully*.

Well, yes; lots of people insist on it. Doesn't that suggest that the word is hardly likely to lose this shade of meaning? What is the point of decrying the use of it as a synonym for *uninterested*? It's not enough for the sticklers to be smug about their own command of language. They apparently have some temperamental need to denounce those who don't conform to their own usage. If you wish to use *disinterested* in the sense of *bored*, you can.

double comparison

This dismal story appeared in *The Times*: **A teenage grammar purist has shamed a supermarket chain into changing the wording on its cartons of fruit juice. Albert Gifford, 15, says that he nearly poured juice on his Weetabix when he noticed that Tesco claimed its oranges were squeezed at their 'most tastiest'.**

Albert was so indignant that he resolved to march to his local Tesco but then settled on writing a letter of complaint. The newspaper quoted him thus: 'Of course, this [wording] could be either "most tasty" or simply "tastiest" but to say "most tastiest" is just wrong.' Tesco accepted the complaint and promised to change the wording. I don't think it should have done.

The phrase *most tastiest* isn't 'just wrong'. It's an example of double comparison. This is the use of *more* or *most* with an adjective that is already inflected for the comparative or superlative. Double comparison isn't part of modern Standard English but that's merely a convention of usage. It was common in Early Modern English. Shakespeare used double comparison freely. I'd hate to see Albert's reaction when he comes to read *Julius Caesar*: 'This was the most unkindest cut of all.' How about *Othello*? 'She comes more nearer earth than she was wont.' (Compare *A Midsummer Night's Dream*: 'What worser place can I beg in your love … ?')

The double comparison has largely fallen out of use since but there's no grammatical reason for avoiding it. Standard English readily uses *most*, like VERY, as an intensifier in ways that would also offend a pedantic standard of logic. Are you really *most grateful* for something as trivial as a dinner invitation? And, while we're at it, how can you send *very best wishes* to someone? Surely it should be enough to say *best wishes*.

Yet these are idiomatic phrases that even obdurate pedants would have a hard time objecting to. It's but a short step from that type of construction to intensifiers with adjectives inflected for the comparative and the superlative.

double genitive

A double genitive is a construction such as *the pen of my aunt's*. The aunt's possession of the pen is indicated first by the preposition *of* and then by the genitive form of the noun *aunt*. Some people find this odd, reasoning that it would be enough to say *the pen of my aunt* and that the double genitive is redundant.

In fact the double genitive has been Standard in English for a long time. Here (with my italics) is Anne Brontë, from *The Tenant of Wildfell Hall*: 'Shortly after, they both came up, and she introduced him as Mr Huntingdon, the son of a late friend of *my uncle's*.'

In Jane Austen's *Pride and Prejudice*, Mr Bennet says of the foolish Mr Collins: 'Nay, when I read a letter *of his*, I cannot help giving him the preference even over Wickham, much as I value the impudence and hypocrisy of my son-in-law.'

Non-native English speakers find the double genitive peculiar but it's an idiom that native English speakers adopt naturally. Stare too long at a double genitive and you may think it offends logic. That shouldn't be a cause for concern, as language has its own rules. Anyone who would insist on saying *a friend of me* rather than *a friend of mine* is elevating dogma over fluency and idiom.

But if you do worry about it, consider that the genitive in English has more functions than to indicate possession. A possessive genitive (*a portrait of the Queen's*) is different from an objective genitive (*a portrait of the Queen*).

The objection that the double genitive involves a redundancy is really quite odd. There is also a redundancy in *I am*, where both words are first-person singular, and in *these books*, where both words are plural. I have yet to come across a pedant who would object to these redundancies, though, or advocate *we was* instead of *we were* to avoid redundancy.

double negative

A double negative is the use of two negative words in the same clause to express a single negative. Phrases such as *I can't get no satisfaction* or *it don't mean nothing* get castigated by sticklers for supposedly having two negatives that cancel each other out.

They're wrong. Double negatives are not Standard English but they do make grammatical sense and are unambiguous. They are intensifiers. Some languages use double negatives in just this way, without confusing anyone. French has double negatives (*je ne sais pas* or *je ne sais rien*) and no one claims they violate logic. There is also double negation in Standard English in such constructions as *neither the columnist nor the Editor knew the answer*.

When they make pronouncements on the logic of English constructions, the sticklers ignore context. It's a huge omission. In context, no one misunderstands DOUBLE GENITIVES (which are Standard English) or double negatives used as intensifiers (which once were, but aren't now).

due to

Sticklers object to the use of *due to* in this sort of construction: **First-time homeowners expect to spend 14 years 'stuck' in their existing property due to difficulties raising a deposit and a lack of affordable homes.**

Style guides typically describe *due* as an adjective. They maintain that it remains an adjective in the phrase *due to*. It must therefore have a noun or noun-phrase to qualify or complement. In the sentence above, it has none. Instead, *due to* has been used as a prepositional phrase.

The simplest way of rewriting that sentence to satisfy the stickler's objection would be to replace *due to* with *owing to*, which is a prepositional phrase. Alternatively, we could say: 'First-time homeowners expect to spend 14 years "stuck" in their existing property. Their plight is due to difficulties raising a deposit and a lack of affordable homes.'

In the second rewritten example, the phrase *due to difficulties raising a deposit and a lack of affordable homes* is the complement of the noun *plight*. To what purpose? *Due to* is used widely as a prepositional phrase. Pick up any newspaper and you'll generally find it. Moreover, the development of *due to* as a prepositional phrase has precedents in English usage. *Owing to* is one of them. Like *regarding* or *concerning*, *owing* is a participle that has come to be used as a preposition. There's nothing wrong in that. It's one of the most obvious features of English that words come to change their functions, even if we dislike particular instances. If *due to* as a prepositional phrase offends you, don't use it. But it's Standard English.

effete

This is a notably elastic term. It's used in the sense of weakness, as applied to people: **It is safe to say the Labour leader has not burst into the public imagination as a rugged action hero. But it would be wrong to think that the effete caricature expresses real weakness.**

But note also this usage: **Isn't there a very fine line between calling all gay men great listeners and talkers and labelling them as effete gossips?**

These are not the same meanings of *effete* and you have to work out from the context what each writer means (and you can do it, as sticklers often fail to credit). In the first example it clearly denotes weakness. In the second it means something more like effeminacy (the writer's implication being, of course, that this is a false and pejorative stereotype of gay men).

These aren't what earlier writers typically meant by the term. In his portentous mystical poem 'The World-Soul', Ralph Waldo Emerson writes: 'When the old world is sterile, / And the ages are effete, / He will from wrecks and sediment / The fairer world complete.'

By *effete*, he means worn out or exhausted. By the time Spiro Agnew, as US Vice-President, denounced his critics in 1969 as 'an effete corps of impudent snobs who characterise themselves as intellectuals', the term had acquired a highly derogatory sense. (Agnew, by the way, had imaginative speechwriters, whereas his extemporised insults were crude abuse.)

Effete is a good example of how meanings shift. The word issues etymologically from Latin (*ex* and *foetus*) and was an adjective primarily, meaning simply *recently having borne offspring*, applied to female animals or women. It went from there to mean *exhausted by bearing*, and was applied in this sense to moribund hens by the scientific encyclopaedist Pliny; by extension it was applied by the agricultural writer Columella to soil made barren by over-farming, and similarly (by Lucretius) to the earth in general. A further metaphorical broadening of its range appeared when Virgil used it of a person's exhausted physical strength, and of old age (indeed Cicero did so too). Emerson will have been aware of at least the poetic Latin sense of the word, and this is probably what he thought he was saying.

In summary, the first definition given in the *OED*, from 1660, is (applied to animals) *ceasing to produce offspring*. It has evolved through the sense of exhaustion to weakness. Even if (as I suspect, but can't prove) use of the term to denote effeminacy was in the first place someone's misunderstanding, born of a common first four letters, it's still become part of the language. It's a definition that's recognised and used, however it came into general circulation.

elder, older

The usual practice is that *elder* is a comparative of people (as in *Pieter Breughel the Elder*) and *older* is a comparative of both people and things (*his older brother* is equivalent to *his elder brother*). It's not invariable and not mandatory, but it's conventional. *Elder* is also a noun, meaning someone of advanced years (whether literally or metaphorically), as in Emily Brontë's poem 'The Elder's Rebuke': 'Thus spake the ice-blooded elder gray: / The young man scoffed as he turned away...'

enormity

The word is one of the big pedantic shibboleths. The pedants would deplore a usage such as this, from the President of the European Central Bank, talking about Ireland's guarantee to the banks: 'It was extremely difficult in Ireland because of the enormity of the exposure. I never stated that the Irish government made a mistake extending this guarantee to Irish banks...'

Heffer speaks representatively for the sticklers on this (he is specifically criticising President Obama for referring to the enormity of the task ahead): 'an enormity is something bad, a transgression: it is not simply something big. One should speak not of the *enormity* of the task, but of its *enormousness*: even if one is President of the United States.'

Well, how many people do speak of enormousness, apart from the sticklers? You can see its logic and sense but it is simply not widely used. Herman Melville uses it in, naturally, *Moby Dick*: 'Some idea may hence be had of the enormousness of that animated mass, a mere part of whose mere integument yields such a lake of liquid as that.' That is exceptional. It is not a noun that finds favour with other writers, or even with him.

The earliest citation in the *OED* of *enormousness* in the sense of enormous size is in 1802. Earlier usage of the word, again cited in the *OED*, carries a different sense – that of moral transgression or wickedness. John Donne, in a sermon of 1631, reflected: 'Such is the infinitenesse, and enormousnesse of our rebellious sin.'

The irony is exquisite. Sticklers insist on *enormousness* when referring to something of enormous size. Yet early usage of this unpopular word has the sense of what the sticklers want to refer to as *enormity*.

Heffer insists that the *OED* has not accorded *enormity* the definition of *enormous size*, which is strictly true. That's because the entry hasn't been updated. That usage has plenty of historical and literary warrant yet was labelled 'now regarded as incorrect' by the *OED* in 1891 without explanation. That arbitrary judgment has been reversed in the *Concise Oxford Dictionary* and it is just a matter of time before the *OED*'s entry is brought into the twenty-first century, reflecting usage that is long established.

Enormity is properly used to refer to wickedness, as Sir Leicester Dedlock does in Charles Dickens's *Bleak House*: 'I wish my people to be impressed with the enormity of the crime, the determination to punish it, and the hopelessness of escape.'

It is also properly used in the sense of great size, as in H. G. Wells's *The First Men in the Moon*: 'At first as I peered into the radiating glow this quintessential brain looked very much like an opaque, featureless bladder with dim, undulating ghosts of convolutions writhing visibly within. Then beneath its enormity and just above the edge of the throne one saw with a start minute elfin eyes peering out of the glow.'

And it is also properly used for many shades of meaning in between. This passage, also from Wells (it's from *Tono-Bungay*), evokes both the sense of monstrousness and the sense of great size: 'Each day one feels that the pressure of commerce and traffic grew, grew insensibly monstrous, and first this man made a wharf and that erected a crane, and then this company set to work and then that, and so they jostled together to make this unassimilable enormity of traffic.'

With *enormity*, the sticklocracy is once more insisting on a single meaning by the technique of arbitrarily asserting it. It is a useful and concise word that can do duty in several ways, expressing subtle distinctions, which are conveyed by the context.

exceptionable, exceptional

Exceptional means *out of the ordinary*; *exceptionable* means *objectionable*. Usage guides caution against mixing them up though there is scant evidence that this is a problem. *Exceptionable* and *unexceptionable* aren't often used. Here is Charles Lamb in a letter from 1800: 'I am still on the tremble, for I do not know where we could go into lodgings that would not be, in many respects, highly exceptionable.'

One of few examples in modern usage that I can come up with is from a *Times* leader: **Mr Phillips should be applauded for his simple, unexceptionable and acute observation that for civic purposes what matters is a common citizenship under the rule of law.**

This shouldn't be taken as indicating that *exceptionable* is in everyday use, for embarrassingly that sentence was written by me and I probably picked up the word from a usage guide. But as the issue is raised by the sticklers, yes, *exceptionable* and *exceptional* are different adjectives. The only serious example I can cite where they're confused is by G. K. Chesterton in *Tremendous Trifles*: 'Now Mr Balfour is a perfectly sincere patriot, a man who, from his own point of view, thinks long and seriously about the public needs, and he is, moreover, a man of entirely exceptionable intellectual power.'

factoid

Factoid means an assertion that is widely accepted as true and is often made, but is false. It is a recent coinage but a useful one. Garner gives the derivation. It was invented by Norman Mailer in his 1973 biography *Marilyn* to denote 'a fact that has no existence before appearing in a magazine, newspaper, or other mass-media outlet'.

Garner records, however, that *factoid* was adopted by *USA Today*, a mass-market newspaper, in the 1980s to describe the easily digested chunks of news that are typical of its style. That usage spread to other news organisations, on both sides of the Atlantic. A reviewer who praises an author for assembling a list of factoids is almost invariably praising an accumulation of small but interesting details.

That's life and it is an interesting example of how no one has ownership of the language. *Factoid* is a word that was carefully crafted. The suffix *-oid* means *resembling but not the same as*. So an anthropoid is a simian that resembles a human. A *factoid* in its original sense means something that looks like a point of information but is not.

See also INVENTED WORDS.

farther, further

Farther and *further* are both comparatives of *far*. They are also adjectives, adverbs and verbs (as a verb, *farther* is rare but it does exist). There are some pundits who still insist on distinguishing the comparatives. 'In the best usage,' says Garner, '*farther* refers to physical distances, *further* to figurative distances.'

It's a distinction you can safely ignore. I use *further* in all comparative senses.

fewer, less

Almost all style guides insist that *less* applies to mass nouns and *fewer* to count nouns. Here is the edict of Strunk and White: '"Less" should not be misused for "fewer". Therefore "He had less men than in the previous campaign," should be "He had fewer men than in the previous campaign." '

Dummett is still firmer: 'An important elementary distinction in the foundations of mathematics is thus reflected in English grammar. This is one case in which a victory, over supermarket chains, has recently been scored by those resisting linguistic pollution.'

He alludes to the campaign some years ago to get supermarkets to change their signs from things like *ten items or less* to *ten items or fewer*. The stores give way too easily on linguistic matters. The rule stated by Dummett, and Strunk and White, is a piece of folklore. Like so many items of pedantry, it was dreamt up by an eighteenth-century grammarian without any warrant in usage.

According to *Merriam-Webster*, it was Robert Baker who, in *Reflections on the English Language* (1770), invented the *less/fewer* rule. He did so, moreover, with caveats ('I should think'; 'it appears to me') that you won't find in modern style manuals.

Yes, *ten items or fewer* is fine. So is *ten items or less*. Dummett's argument that the English language incorporates an important mathematical distinction is exceptionally odd when you consider that *more* applies both to count nouns and to mass nouns.

In choosing *less* or *fewer*, what should guide your choice is what's pleasing to the ear. Sometimes that may cause you to choose *less* with count nouns. In Bernard Shaw's play *The Doctor's Dilemma*, Sir Patrick Cullen declares to Sir Colenso Ridgeon: 'And for all you know, Bloomfield Bonington kills less people than you do.' That sounds less fussy, to my ear, than 'kills fewer people'. It's permissible on grounds of usage.

first, second, third...

When you advance an argument, you may want to make it clearer by enumerating the points you are making. *Times* leader writers do this quite often, distinguishing between their first, second and third points, and so on. There are different practices in this.

The obvious way to start is *firstly*, but this term has many critics. It's an adverb, but so is *first*. It appears that some nineteenth-century pundits who favoured *firstly* did so on the misunderstanding that *first* was not an adverb.

Some sticklers, however, insist that, because *first* can serve as an adverb, there is no need to write *firstly*, and thus, in an enumeration of points, the first one should be labelled *first*.

The argument goes on, however, that *second*, *third* and so on are not adverbs. They can serve only as adjectives. You can say *I first drank a large whisky*, but you cannot say *I second drank a large whisky*. This is the stickler objection to enumerating points as *first*, *second*, *third*... If you write them this way, say the purists, you are in effect using adjectives without nouns. The stickler solution is thus to write *first*, *secondly*, *thirdly*... Alternatively, the stickler provides a noun for the adjectives to qualify, in this form: *I have three disagreements: first, that...; second, that...; and, third, that...* Here the adjectives *first*, *second*, *third* qualify the noun *disagreements*.

Fowler sensibly comments that the preference for *first* over *firstly* in formal enumerations is 'one of the harmless pedantries in which those who like oddities because they are odd are free to indulge'. In doing so, he earns the ire of the most excitable pedant of all. Gwynne is incensed that 'Fowler patronisingly and contemptuously dismisses two centuries of English literature... It is surely not unfair to call the manner in which he treats the subject outrageous.'

This is a fine example of Fowler's wisdom and his imitators' (or at least this imitator's) haplessness. Fowler is frequently questionable but generally reasonable. What Gwynne says is unreasonable. *Second* is in fact used adverbially (or as a quasi-adverb, as the *OED* says) all the time. In a parliamentary debate, *the Leader of the Opposition speaks second.* If you enumerate points as *first*, *second* and *third* (and so on) rather than *first*, *secondly* and *thirdly*, your meaning is clear, your grammar is fine and you are using short words. That's an end to the matter.

As for the solution of enumerating points as *first, that* . . . ; *second, that* . . . , it is a convoluted contrivance for resolving a non-existent problem. Instead of saying that you have three points and then listing them, why not just state them? The simplest way of enumerating them is to accept that using the adjectives *second* and *third* adverbially is unambiguous, comprehensible and unobjectionable.

See alse ADVERBS, FLAT.

flaunt, flout

Almost all usage guides refer to the distinction between these similar-sounding verbs. To *flaunt* is to display ostentatiously. To *flout* is to express contempt for, in word or action. The injunction against confusing them seems to me excessively loud, given that not many people do it, but it's as well to be clear on the distinction.

Humphrys laments: 'When words with wholly distinct meanings become synonymous with each other – flaunt and flout, for instance – we begin to lose the capacity for discriminated expression.'

This would be nonsense even if he were talking about a weightier issue of language than a simple confusion between two words on the ground of similar appearance. If *flout* really did acquire the meaning of *ostentatious display*, this wouldn't destroy its current meaning. And if it lost the sense of *registering contempt*, another verb would take its place. The capacity for discriminate expression is part of what it is to be human; it isn't bestowed on us by a set of words.

former, latter

There's no real justification for the view that *former* and *latter* must be reserved for pairs rather than be applied to more numerous items. *First* and *last* are also possible for pairs. A better objection to *former* and *latter* is that they may be confusing to the reader. Use your judgment. Don't assume that it will be as clear to the reader what you're referring to as it is to you.

fortuitous

The adjective *fortuitous* means *occurring by chance*, as in this formidable sentence:

> It appears hardly fortuitous that the Government announced yesterday that it would publish a strategy for supporting Service personnel, their families and veterans on the very day when a new defence lobby group, headed by three former chiefs of the Defence Staff, called for an immediate increase in spending to make up for critical shortages of equipment and support for troops in Iraq and Afghanistan.

The word is often now used to mean *fortunate, lucky*. It's likely that, in an interview from *The Times* with Arnold Wesker, the playwright used the word in the first sense and the interviewer interpreted it in the second:

When the Royal Court rejected the play, it was suggested to Wesker that he rewrite it so that Ronnie does eventually turn up. He refused. It set the pattern for a career that, he insists, has been 'fortuitous', but also fractious. 'It put me on guard against directors for the rest of my career.'

There is no obvious reason why fractiousness should be seen as tempering a fortuitous career unless a fortuitous career is seen as something good. That is why I think the interviewer has taken the second interpretation, which I doubt is what Wesker meant. That doesn't mean the second sense is wrong and the first right. Both senses are right and the context might have been made clearer by the writer.

In the traditional usage of *fortuitous*, there is an implicit contrast between chance and deliberateness. Knowing this does help in appreciating the term in many literary contexts. In Chapter 11 of *Emma*, Jane Austen recounts the meddling schemes of her heroine to bring together Mr Elton, the clergyman, and the sweet but dim Harriet Smith:

> The coming of her sister's family was so very near at hand, that first in anticipation, and then in reality, it became henceforth her prime object of interest; and during the ten days of their stay at Hartfield it was not to be expected – she did not herself expect – that anything beyond occasional, fortuitous assistance could be afforded by her to the lovers.

Emma doesn't mean that her assistance will be of good fortune (those who know and love the book will find an irony in that very possibility). She means that she will offer it by chance, as the occasion presents itself.

The secondary meaning of *fortuitous* is noted by Fowler, who calls it a mistake. He considers that it is 'sometimes confused with *fortunate*, perhaps through mere sound'. Perhaps it is, but a meaning that becomes established isn't rendered illegitimate because of an initial confusion over sounds. And *fortuitous* in the sense of *fortunate* is so widely used some eighty years after Fowler that many are unaware of its traditional meaning. *Merriam-Webster* usefully notes, however, a shade of meaning between *by chance* and *fortunate*. It is used of chance occurrences that have a fortunate outcome. One of the examples cited by *Merriam-Webster* comes from Doris Lessing's *The Good Terrorist*: 'She panted into the underground, snatched a ticket from the machine, belted down the stairs, and there was a fortuitous train.'

I note with shame that on first reading this outstanding novel on the obsessions of political extremism, I underlined Lessing's use of *fortuitously* in (genuine) pedantic irritation. The Nobel laureate had every justification for using the word in this extended sense that has its roots firmly in the traditional meaning and is in fact a useful addition to the language. If you use the word to denote good fortune, I'd recommend keeping this sense of chance – not to assuage the pedants but to avoid any possible confusion such as the one I believe happened in the Wesker interview. In any event, you can discount such grumpy complaints as this typical one from Cochrane: '*Fortuitous* does not mean "fortunate" and *fortuitously* does not mean "by happy chance", but an increasing number of speakers and writers seem to be unaware of this.'

There is a useful word that is almost identical in sense to *fortuitous* in its traditional definition. It is *aleatory*. It comes from the Latin word for *die* (the singular of *dice*, which is also legitimately used as a singular in English). The phrase *alea jacta est* (*the die is cast*) is attributed to Caesar, as he crossed the Rubicon. It appears frequently in the Asterix books, notably from a laconic pirate as the ship goes down after an encounter with the Gauls.

fraught

Fraught means *laden* or *equipped*. The associated noun is *freight*. It is a past participle of a now obsolete verb and is widely used with the preposition *with*. Charles Dickens writes in *Little Dorrit*: 'The habit, too, of seeking some sort of recompense in the discontented boast of being disappointed, is a habit fraught with degeneracy.'

That much is Standard and agreed. The sticklers object to an extended sense of *fraught*, used adjectivally, as here: **The euro crisis, America's fraught debt talks and Britain's own sputtering recovery are making for extremely hazardous seas.**

Cochrane inadvertently undermines his own objection to this usage by beginning: 'People who describe a situation as *fraught* seem to know what they mean to say, and people who hear them seem to understand what they are saying…'

Exactly. People who use it adjectivally mean *vexed*, *tricky*, *stressful*, *tense*, and people who hear it understand the same thing. It's a word in general usage. Cochrane's complaint, echoing the etymological fallacy, is that that isn't how the word started, and that something might in principle be *fraught* with delightful possibilities.

So it might, but this hypothesis doesn't lend weight to his ill-founded objection.

free gift

This phrase, much used in magazine copy, has oddly become a cause for the sticklers, who object that it's a tautology. 'Next time you are offered a *free gift*,' writes Cochrane, 'ask yourself – or better still, the party offering – whether there is any other kind, a *gift* being something that is given, not sold.'

How droll. Well, actually there is another kind of gift: a compelled one, such as forced tribute paid by a conquered people. The opposite of a compelled gift is a free one, and the distinction is far from trivial. In an Easter Sermon, Charles Kingsley declared that 'not to us is the praise of any national greatness or glory, but to God, from whom it comes as surely a free gift as the gift of liberty to the Jews of old'.

The sticklers haven't stopped to consider this one before pronouncing anathema on a legitimate usage that is at worst an idiom.

fulsome

This sort of usage is disputed: **She appeared on the verge of tears as she spoke about a fulsome apology the sisters emailed Ms Lawson and Mr Saatchi, in which the Grillos addressed the couple as 'mother and father'.**

A *fulsome* apology, maintain the sticklers, is not a *copious* one but a *cloying* and *insincere* one. They regret that the meaning of this adjective is slipping away. It's true that *fulsome* has long carried a disparaging connotation, though the sticklers slightly exaggerate this.

Charlotte Brontë puts in the mouth of her narrator, Lucy Snowe, this sentiment in *Villette*: 'That worthy directress had never from the first treated me otherwise than with respect... Not that she was fulsome about it: Madame, in all things worldly, was in nothing weak.'

Fulsomeness in this scene would be inappropriate rather than offensive to the senses. Indeed, by implying something that is *excessive*, the traditionalist interpretation of *fulsome* shades into the newer one of *copious*.

Except it isn't a newer definition: it's an older one! As often happens, the pedants consult usage guides in issuing their advice rather than the evidence. The earliest use of *fulsome* given by the *OED* is from 1325, and it means *abundant, plentiful, full*.

Meanings shift. In this case, a meaning from Middle English has become part of general usage again. There's nothing wrong in this, nor are the sticklers at fault in using another definition. Where they are culpable is in insisting that only their own preferred definition is the true one. Context can tell you the way the word is intended – which does place the onus on the writer to ensure that it is indeed clear from the surrounding material.

fused participle

Should it be *the Editor objected to the columnist using split infinitives* or *the Editor objected to the columnist's using split infinitives*?

This is a question about fused participles. A fused participle is the name given by Fowler to a construction such as the first example. The sticklers' argument would go like this:

In both versions of the sentence, the participle (the *-ing* word) is being used in effect as a noun, and is thus known as a gerund. In the second version, the subject of the gerund is the columnist, and that subject is marked with the genitive (or possessive) case. In the first version, the noun *columnist* is not in the possessive case. Fowler objected to this type of construction and modern sticklers follow him on this. They argue that the subject of the gerund, being unmarked for case, doesn't bear a proper grammatical relationship to the noun. The Editor's objection is not to the columnist, they argue, but to the action of the columnist in using split infinitives, and the columnist should thus be in the possessive case.

It's a piece of pedantry that, like so many others, doesn't accord

with the way English has been used for centuries. There is a long
tradition of using gerunds with subjects that are not possessive;
indeed it's longer than the tradition of using the possessive with
gerunds. Jespersen demonstrated numerous historical examples of
the use of fused participles. It's characteristic of the sticklers that
they issue their stipulations without first consulting this evidence.

Dummett is disarmingly frank about this. He writes: 'Almost
all of this entry [in his style guide] was written before I became
aware that this point, like the split infinitive, has become a focus of
active resistance to objectors: the authority of Jespersen is invoked
to license locutions like "Despite Morocco accepting".'

Dummett was a philosopher of brilliance; yet here, outside
his subject, he is flying by the seat of his pants. His riposte on
discovering that there is scholarly objection to his argument about
fused participles is that 'such phrases grate on my ear'.

That's not quite as feeble a rejoinder as it may appear; it merely
undermines his case. What sounds natural and pleasing to the
ear is exactly the criterion you should use when considering this
type of construction. The possessive form (*the columnist's using split
infinitives*) is more formal, but the unmarked form (*the columnist
using the split infinitive*) isn't wrong. On the contrary, the unmarked
form (or fused participle) sounds natural, and more like speech. It's
emphatically better if what you're stressing is the columnist rather
than the use of split infinitives.

So, on the reasoning of Fowler and his followers, a fused
participle is one that is treated as being joined to a preceding
noun or pronoun, instead of as a gerund requiring a subject that is
marked for the possessive case. They are hostile to fused participles
and will do their utmost to 'defuse' them, just as some people are
hostile to split infinitives. This is a controversy where the pedants

once again confuse their own preference with grammatical rules. You should do what sounds more euphonious.

I've so far accepted, for the sake of argument, the grammatical terms advanced by the pedants in their objection to fused participles. Yet a great deal hinges on their view that the participle in the fused participle construction is being used as a noun, and in fact it isn't. It's really a fairly ordinary verb form. It is modified by an adverb (*I heard them singing raucously*) and it takes an ordinary object (*I heard them singing madrigals*). On the other hand, you genuinely have a participle being used as a noun in something like *this raucous singing of madrigals*, with an adjective and an object preceded by *of*.[5]

Bear in mind too that, contrary to the pedants' complaints, there are some constructions where you cannot do anything except use a fused participle, such as this one: *The idle columnist was responsible for nothing being done about the Editor's instructions.* Also this one: *The Editor objected to there being so many mistakes in the column.* You can rephrase these if they offend your ear but you don't need to. They are grammatical Standard English.

-gate

Any new scandal, or even mere mistake, in public life risks having the suffix *-gate* added to its real or manufactured name by un-enterprising journalists. The word thus invented is both a neologism and a cliché. A neologism is a newly coined word. It ought not therefore to be a cliché, which by definition is an outworn word or phrase. What makes it a cliché is the suffix. The Watergate scandal that forced the resignation of President Richard Nixon happened in the 1970s. Yet few political scandals since have escaped the suffix.

It's applied by journalists without discrimination and with dispiriting inevitability. It doesn't mean anything and is hardly likely to be an aid to understanding for readers below the age of fifty. But the cliché is self-perpetuating. It's an odd practice. The use of *-gate* was encouraged by William Safire, a columnist for the *New York Times* on both politics and language. Safire had served as a speechwriter in the Nixon White House. He retained an admiration for the disgraced President, and partly owing to that loyalty habitually used *-gate* to refer to malfeasance, or even just mild embarrassment on the part of other politicians. Some of his coinages were admittedly very funny. In his book *Safire's Political Dictionary* he noted that 'charges leveled at Congressman Daniel Flood in 1978 were called "Floodgate," and charges that some contractors were double-billing the government reminded those acquainted with British English of the possibilities of *double-billingsgate*'.

I've long thought that this peerless polemicist's wit was wasted on the White House but it was effective. When Bill Clinton's affair with Monica Lewinsky became public, newspapers called it *Monicagate*, of course. The *New Republic* magazine asked its readers for an alternative name; one came up with *Bimbroglio*. But the term, which was a caustic comment on Clinton rather than Lewinsky, did not catch on.

My complaints about the ubiquity of the *-gate* label are beside the point. Every time I see it, I reflect that Safire achieved what he set out to do and normalised the crimes of a president. My strictures will have no effect on this journalistic practice, but it is long past time to close the *-gate*.

See also INVENTED WORDS.

gerunds

See *FUSED PARTICIPLE*.

good, well

If you ask an acquaintance *how are you?*, and get the reply *I'm good*, you are unlikely to retort indignantly that you had asked about their wellbeing and not their moral character. Nor should you. Though often deplored in English, *I'm good* instead of *I'm well* is a Standard construction.

An adjective is in any case often used after the linking verb *to be*. If the Editor of *The Times*, seeing me with my feet up, head back and eyes closed, asks *how are you?*, my best answer among the few available is *I'm busy*. This sentence is identical in form to *I'm good*, comprising a subject pronoun, a linking verb and an adjectival predicate.

hanged, hung

It's a common view that *hanged* is the correct past and past participle of *hang* when referring to a person whereas *hung* applies to an object. The distinction provides the opening to one episode ('The Great Game') of the BBC series *Sherlock*. A convict says: 'Mr Holmes, everyone says you're the best. Without you, I'll get hung for this.' Holmes replies: 'No, no, no, Mr Bewick. Not at all. "Hanged", yes.'

The pedants are wrong. The distinction between *hanged* and *hung* is not a rule of grammar but an accident of history. The *OED* sets out a complex history in which *hang* developed from two Old English verbs. *Hanged* was superseded by *hung* in the sixteenth century, except in the sense of execution – possibly because of the tendency of archaic forms to be retained in legal language.

Even so, notable writers over centuries have used the *hung* form in the way that sticklers maintain is ungrammatical. Samuel Pepys records in his diary, for 4 July 1667: 'The judge seems to be a worthy man, and able: and do intend, for these rogues that burned this house to be hung in some conspicuous place in the town, for an example.'

In *An Address to the People on the Death of the Princess Charlotte*, Shelley writes: 'The execution of Brandreth, Ludlam, and Turner, is an event of quite a different character from the death of the Princess Charlotte. These men were shut up in a horrible dungeon, for many months, with the fear of a hideous death and of everlasting hell thrust before their eyes; and at last were brought to the scaffold and hung.'

Many years after he had won a *not proven* verdict in the *cause célèbre* of Madeleine Smith in Glasgow in 1857, her advocate, Lord Glencorse, remarked: 'The jade should hae hung.'

These sources are not making a mistake in saying *hung* instead of *hanged*. They are using a legitimate variant form. By all means maintain a scrupulous distinction between *hanged* and *hung* if you wish. It has no obvious value, however, and is hardly worth troubling with. The reason people insist on this purported rule is probably just that it's easy to spot when someone breaks it. Many cherished shibboleths of language are like that.

historic present

'Shakespeare buys a house.' For some reason, this sort of sentence causes dismay among a certain type of commentator. Calling it an example of the *historic present*, John Humphrys launched a campaign against it in the summer of 2014. By this, he meant the use of the present tense to describe a past event. It is, if Humphrys is to be credited, an irritating and pretentious affectation of broadcasters and writers that gives a 'bogus, an entirely bogus, sense of immediacy'. Perhaps aware that (as I've argued throughout this book) expressing a personal dislike of a construction isn't the same as identifying in it an error of usage, Humphrys buttressed his argument by saying that the historic present is illogical, for the events it describes happened a long time ago.

That isn't a strong objection. Use of the present tense to describe a past event can be an effective narrative technique so long as your audience understands that it's wielded for deliberate effect. There is nothing 'illogical' about it: the English tense system, like grammar itself, conforms to its own logic and set of rules. We naturally use constructions that are in the present tense yet referring to future events, as in 'I am meeting the Editor tomorrow'. There's no reason, other than personal taste, to object to its use when referring to events in the distant past, and personal taste isn't an argument about grammar at all.

See also TENSES, SEQUENCE OF.

Hobson's choice

Hobson's choice, as any pedant will tell you, technically does not mean a choice between bad options. It means no choice at all. The phrase is popularly associated with Thomas Hobson, who drove the coach between Cambridge and London from 1564 to 1630. Hobson owned the local stables and would hire out his horses, but his customers had to take whichever horse was closest to the door. The horse was thus literally Hobson's choice and not the customer's. John Milton wrote a poem about him: 'Here lies old Hobson; Death hath broke his girt, / And here, alas, hath laid him in the dirt...'

It's rare to find this use of the term outside (literally) the Magic Circle. Magicians use the phrase to describe the illusion that you have a free choice when, for example, selecting a playing card from a pack. In practice, the magician will ensure that you pick the one they want.

Unless you are writing about magic or Milton, it's probably best to avoid the term, as it's become a cliché. But there is a variant of Hobson's choice that appears in newspaper headlines. My term for this usage is 'Great Historical Questions to Which the Answer is No'. One genuine example from the *Daily Mail* is: 'Will opening this tomb prove Shakespeare didn't write his plays?' Another from the same source is: 'Was Jesus taught by the Druids of Glastonbury?'

When a writer has an absurd hypothesis and no evidence, the rational course is to cast it as a question and force an answer to it while giving the reader the illusion of choice. Spotting examples of this Hobson's choice for the credulous is a continually rewarding recreation.

homophone

Homophones are a pair (or larger number) of words that are pronounced the same but spelt differently and that have different meanings. Here are some common confusions between homophones. All come from *The Times*.

> **1. Unusually, Sir John has written a forward to the SRA's financial statements explaining the relationship between Network Rail and the SRA.**

Sir John has written a foreword.

2. A bad experience at the Paris Opera four years ago, when a vocal chord haemorrhaged during a run of *Cesare*, is another example.

The usual spelling is *vocal cord*, and many people consider *vocal chord* or *spinal chord* to be erroneous. It's possible that, because vocal cords are usually referred to in the context of singing, writers tend to reach for a musical term. Cords and chords don't have the same root, as the musical *chord* is unrelated to the string *cord*. I don't object to *vocal chord* (it's not a convincing criticism to treat it on grounds of logic) but I don't spell it that way.

3. The principle behind retribution is thus the payment of a debt (part of a 'just desserts theory', in other words).

The idiom is *just deserts*, not *just desserts*.

4. Monotonous rows of grey box files, stationary bought by mail order, plastic pen-holders, staplers and blank notebooks are hardly an exciting alternative to actually being at the office.

Stationary is an adjective meaning *motionless*. The collective noun for paper, notebooks and so on is *stationery*.

5. The principle reason for giving up pay television is that subscribers believe that they do not watch it enough.

The writer meant *principal reason*. This may be the most common of all confusions of homophones.

See also AUGER, AUGUR and DISCREET, DISCRETE.

hopefully

Hopefully is an adverb. It's derived from the adjective *hopeful*. There are many instances of adverbs in English that modify clauses or sentences, but this one causes controversy due to the sticklers' objections.

To understand their criticism, consider this sentence: *Disgracefully, the idle columnist is late again*. The sentence is modified by the adverb *disgracefully*. The adverb is derived from the adjective *disgraceful*.

Now consider this one: *Hopefully, the idle columnist will not be late this week*.

The sticklers maintain that a sentence or clause modified by an adverb ought to be capable of being rewritten in the form *it is disgraceful that...* But this can't be done with the adverb *hopefully*: it makes no sense to say *it is hopeful that...*

That's the objection to *hopefully* used as a sentence adverb. Pedants accept that the usage is ubiquitous but frown on it as casual speech, not acceptable in writing. Their objection to it, as with so much else, is immoderate. Heffer writes: 'This tiresome usage is now so ubiquitous that those who object to it are sometimes dismissed as pedants. It remains wrong, and only a barbarous writer with a low estimation of his readers would try to pass it off as respectable prose.'

This judgment is quite arbitrary. English has many coinages that are far less logical than *hopefully*. For example, the adjective *balding* is a participle that has no verb. And the adverb *thankfully* provokes far less hostility than *hopefully* when used to modify a clause or sentence (*thankfully, the idle columnist has at last submitted his article*).

Hopefully is one of those questions of usage that provoke strong feelings for no obvious reason. Amis says that the political use of *hopefully* signifies 'a dimwit at best'. Yet there is no serious danger of ambiguity between the different senses of *hopefully*, any more than there is with *surely* or *naturally*, which are also used as sentence adverbs.

See also IRONICALLY.

hove

You occasionally find a verb *to hove*, as here: **The [Scottish independence] referendum is hoving into view.**

This is a complaint of one or two pedants. They maintain that it should be *heaving* rather than *hoving*, as *hove* is an archaic past-tense form of the intransitive verb *to heave*. That form (as opposed to *heaved*) is used now only in nautical contexts. Here is Tennyson's *Morte d'Arthur*: 'Then saw they how there hove a dusky barge, / Dark as a funeral scarf from stem to stern, / Beneath them…'

In fact there is a verb *to hove* but it's marked as obsolete by the *OED*. It means to be posed, or to hover. Here it is in Spenser's *Faerie Queene*: 'A little bote lay hoving her before.'

It makes complete sense to refer to a political issue as *hoving*, even where it isn't quite what the writer meant to say.

however

The placement of *however* in a sentence generates strong opinions. Strunk and White are representative in insisting that, when the word is used in the sense of *nevertheless*, it must not be placed at the start of the sentence. This is the type of construction they're objecting to: **However, the retired printer who was indeed given a Treasury bill for £1 million in 2003, will be happy**

to receive perhaps £10,000 when it is offered at specialist auctioneer Dix Noonan Webb on April 24.

The pedants will allow *however* at the start of a sentence only if it's used in the sense of *no matter how*, as here: **However remote, however unpromising, a city on the up is generally worth a visit.**

What's the reason for the rule? There isn't one; nor is it a genuine rule of grammar. It's a shibboleth. Place *however* at that point in the sentence where it emphasises the contrast most effectively.

hyphens

See *COMPOUNDS*.

icon, iconic

The words are 'grotesquely overused', says Heffer. Maybe. The sense of *iconic* as being *important* or *representative* (especially in the context of popular culture) is quite recent. It is as yet only a draft addition to the *OED* and the first citation is from the 1970s. There is no reason why the noun and adjective shouldn't be used in figurative contexts, though. In the *Guardian*'s slogan that *comment is free but facts are sacred*, no one has difficulty in understanding that the *sacred* bit is not a literal description of religious veneration. Heffer's use of *grotesquely* is itself figurative.

imply, infer

This ranks high among the sticklers' causes. Their complaint is that the words have different meanings yet are continually confused. Specifically, they believe *infer* is frequently used where it should be *imply*.

To *imply* is to *express indirectly*, *insinuate* or *hint at*. To *infer* is to *draw a conclusion*, or *reason from one thing to another*. A sentence such as this, which uses *infer* to mean *imply*, brings down imprecations from the pedants: **However, the link identified by a team from Duke University, North Carolina, is not as novel as the headlines infer and, for my money, the most exciting advance in this field stems from much closer to home.**

The story of *imply* and *infer* is more complex than is acknowledged by those who are loudly concerned with the state of the language. Burchfield comments: 'The clarity of the distinction between *imply* and *infer* is often questioned, and with a certain justification.'

That is right. *Merriam-Webster* gives a detailed account of the development of *infer*. In fact the word has been used to mean *imply* since at least the sixteenth century, when it's found in a statement of Sir Thomas More: 'The fyrste parte is not the proofe of the second, but rather contrary wyse, the seconde inferreth well ye fyrst.'

The sticklers' objection particularly concerns the personal *infer* in the disputed sense – that is, the word *infer* or *inference* used in the sense of *imply*, where the subject is a person. This is different from More's usage. The non-personal *infer* used by More is, says *Merriam-Webster*, not really a matter of controversy, having appeared in dictionaries ever since.

From my experience, the non-personal sense is in fact vigorously disputed by usage pundits, though not by informed lexicographers, which is what *Merriam-Webster* means. It does have impeccable literary precedent over centuries.

Here is Milton, in *Paradise Lost*: 'Consider first, that Great Or Bright inferrs not Excellence.'

Here is Walter Scott, from *Peveril of the Peak*: 'Neither did the violent language of the minister, supposing that to be proved, absolutely infer meditated violence.'

And here is Scott again, from *Ivanhoe*: 'The evidence of Malvoisin was skilfully guarded. But while he apparently studied to spare the feelings of Bois-Guilbert, he threw in, from time to time, such hints, as seemed to infer that he laboured under some temporary alienation of mind...'

But let's stick to the personal *infer*. *Merriam-Webster* considers this use relatively recent. Its earliest example is this, from a letter by Ellen Terry in 1896: 'I should think you did miss my letters. I know it! but... you missed them in another way than you infer, you little minx!'

But you can see the logic of the personal *infer*. The original sense of *infer* recorded in the *OED* is *bring on*, or *induce*. This is followed by many obsolete senses, and you can't of course establish a word's meaning from its origins. Note, though, that the sense of personal *infer-as-imply* does have a link to the original meaning of the word.

It's primarily since the Second World War that usage pundits have mounted a campaign against personal *infer*, and I can quote many vitriolic comments about its supposed barbarism, illiteracy and disrepute. The usage is none of those things. It has a discernible link to the history of the word and is merely an extension of the non-personal sense recorded as early as the 1530s.

Don't let anyone bamboozle you into supposing that the disputed usage is a solecism. The evidence of its use is so widespread that personal *infer* is highly likely to become Standard even in the newspapers of the usage pundits (my newspaper does not yet accept it, and I don't regard it as an essential cause to change it). And then, the word will develop according to usage, as all words do, with – perhaps – future pedants objecting when people use it in a different sense from personal *infer-as-imply*.

inherent, innate

The usual distinction that's drawn between these adjectives is that something that is *innate* is *inborn*, and thus should refer to living things. In *Jane Eyre*, the protagonist remarks of her charges in the village school: 'Many showed themselves obliging, and amiable too; and I discovered amongst them not a few examples of natural politeness, and innate self-respect, as well as of excellent capacity, that won both my goodwill and my admiration.'

A stickler would take issue with this usage: **Monaco life might be perfectly palatable for some, but I could never reconcile myself to its innate hedonism.**

The sticklers' preferred adjective here would be *inherent*. I don't buy it. There is a continuum of the use of *innate* that stretches from people to organisms and even abstract nouns that are nonetheless made up of people or organisms. In his story 'A Daughter of the Aurora', Jack London writes: 'The man whose sled he led down the last stretch was bound to win. There could be no doubt of it. But the community had an innate sense of the fitness of things, and not once was Joy vexed by overtures for his use.'

A community may have an innate quality. President Kennedy similarly declaimed on *the innate powers of resistance* of democracy. And the *OED* records a highly extended use of *innate* from *Nature* in 1890, in a reference to diamonds within rock.

Innate should have some connection to the idea of something that is native and natural, but otherwise don't worry about it.

intellectual

In most European languages, the noun or adjective *intellectual* is a neutral description. But in English it has often carried an implication of being somehow too clever. That meaning was encapsulated in George Orwell's dismissive comment, about a type of left-wing thinking, that 'one has to belong to the intelligentsia to believe things like that: no ordinary man could be such a fool'.

The media's use of *intellectual* as a catch-all term for a thinker whose words carry weight is more recent. It is a good thing that anti-intellectualism should be superseded by a public interest in ideas. But there is a disadvantage in the promiscuous use of 'intellectual'.

Richard Posner, an American judge, wrote a fine book called *Public Intellectuals: A Study in Decline*. His subject was the many academics who write outside their field for a general audience, especially on politics. This work was, Posner concluded, of generally low and declining quality. It employed standards of evidence and reasoning that would not be acceptable in scholarly studies.

The opinions of well-known people on political issues may be newsworthy because they are famous. But their views carry, at most, no more intrinsic weight than those of any other intelligent non-specialists, and probably less, because non-specialists are usually willing to admit error, whereas politically engaged intellectuals, in my experience, rarely are. The term *intellectual* is valuable; but be aware of what's going on underneath it.

interjections

Well, these are useful for rhetorical effect and should not be overlooked. Oh yes, they do not have a grammatical function but they help to establish a mood.

invented words

Invented words can be divided between *nonce words* and *neologisms*. A nonce word is invented for short-term convenience. Edward Lear's *runcible* is a celebrated nonce word. *Stagflation* was coined in economic debates in the 1970s as a shorthand way of describing the unexpected combination of weak growth and high inflation. It was a nonce word that served a need and became widely used.

If a nonce word does gain popularity then it becomes a *neologism*, literally a new word. Dictionaries record these, though there is no guarantee that they will thereby remain in currency. *Yuppie* is a neologism that you now rarely hear; my guess is that it will have died out within a decade. The development of language is not consciously planned, and there is no inherent reason why some neologisms persist and others fall out of favour. But if a new word is useful, it has a better chance of survival.

See also FACTOID and -GATE.

ironically

Ironically is thought by some commentators to be overused. If there is irony involved, so the argument goes, it should be obvious to the reader without being signposted.

There are two ways of using *ironically*, though. One is as an adverb, and it's unobjectionable. Here is D. H. Lawrence, from

The Trespasser: 'Helena smiled ironically. "And are you ready for your supper?" she asked, in the playful, affectionate manner she had assumed.'

The form that some sticklers object to, however, is the use of *ironically* as a sentence adverb. It is in that respect like the sentence-adverbial *hopefully*, which is firmly established but that they also object to. *Ironically* can be useful in that it indicates the writer's opinion of a statement or circumstance, without any necessary implication that the reader should think likewise.

See also HOPEFULLY.

irregardless

Yes, it's a real word. Don't believe the sticklers who maintain otherwise. The earliest citation for it in the *OED* is 1912, in the *American Dialect Dictionary*. It is likely to be a blend, either inadvertent or jocular, of *regardless* and *irrespective*. Should you use it? It's tempting, given the scorn in which it's held by people who are wrong on most points of usage.

Nor is it a serious objection that *irregardless* ought semantically to mean the opposite of *regardless*. The same is true of the pair *valuable* and *invaluable*, yet no one describes *invaluable* as not a real word. Similarly, if we describe a measure as *very approximate*, we don't necessarily mean that it is very close – even though a consistent stickler ought to insist that, as *very* is an intensifier, a very approximate measure ought to be more precise than an approximate one.

Even so, I recommend avoiding *irregardless*. The reason is not that it's wrong: it's just non-Standard usage, and *regardless* will do the job precisely.

-ise/-ize

The suffix *-ise* is common in British usage and so is the suffix *-ize*. The second is standard in American usage. Fowler prefers *-ize* for most verbs, on the grounds that the suffix is in its origin Greek or Latin and that it's pronounced that way. Suit yourself. It's also recreational sometimes to add the suffix to a stem in a way that sticklers will wince at. In the *Times* leader department, we have a verb to *leaderise* (adjective, *leaderisable*) for that reason.

it's I/me

Should you say *it's I* or *it's me*? Traditional grammarians are in no doubt: it should be *it's I*. Their reasoning goes like this.

The verb *to be* is a copular, or linking, verb. A copular verb connects the subject to a complement. It's like an *equals* sign in an equation. The subject isn't performing an action; the verb (for example, *be* or *become*) is connecting that subject to other information. The nominative is used for the subject of a verb and must logically also be used for the complement. (Technically, a copular verb takes a predicate nominative – that is, a predicate noun in the nominative, or subject, case.)

It's a bogus rule. It's near-universal usage among native speakers to use the object case for a pronoun after a linking verb. 'Lay on, Macduff,' cries Macbeth, 'And damn'd be *him* that first cries, "Hold, enough!"'

Almost everyone says *it's me*. It's the norm that pronouns following a verb take the object case: you get nominative case as a subject of a finite clause, genitive case as a possessive, and accusative case more or less everywhere else. *I* after a copular verb sounds more formal than *me* and you may wish to use it in formal prose; but you should never feel that it's required.

See also BETWEEN YOU AND I.

jargon, gobbledegook

Jargon is unintelligible or meaningless talk or writing, or gibberish. The *OED* adds acutely in brackets that it is 'often a term of contempt for something the speaker does not understand'.

That's right. Jargon is widely disparaged. The term is usually interpreted as meaning wilfully obscure language. In fact, there's a use and a place for jargon, and the sticklers should pipe down about it.

It's usually a good idea to write in a way that accords with normal speech patterns but there are exceptional cases. It's not only legitimate but economical to use jargon when addressing a specialist audience that knows the subject and where a jargon term can save a lengthier explanation. The Plain English Campaign, an aggressively ignorant pressure group, received deserved derision many years ago when it criticised Gordon Brown, then Shadow Chancellor, for using the term *post-neoclassical endogenous growth theory* to a group of economists. It called this gobbledegook. *Endogenous* means *having an internal cause or origin*. Endogenous growth theory suggests that changes in savings behaviour and in government policy can affect the long-run growth rate of the economy. The argument made by Brown was that government intervention could help stimulate technological progress and increase the long-term growth rate of the economy. Whatever the merits of that argument, the language is not nonsense. It is jargon.

All academic disciplines have their technical terms, and *endogenous growth theory* is an example of technical economics jargon. That doesn't mean it's impenetrable. Once you know what endogenous means, you can make an intelligent guess about what endogenous growth theory is about. The legitimate use of jargon is all about context.

The Plain English Campaign reliably behaves absurdly. It bestows an annual gobbledegook award that is not about English usage so much as a populist suspicion of ideas. Past winners include Donald Rumsfeld, the US Defense Secretary, for this brilliant analysis: 'Reports that say that something hasn't happened are always interesting to me because, as we know, there are known knowns; there are things we know we know. We also know there are known unknowns; that is to say we know there are some things we do not know. But there are also unknown unknowns – the ones we don't know we don't know.'

The campaigners described it as 'truly baffling', but the joke was on them. Gobbledegook is pretentious usage. Rumsfeld's statement was intricate but clear. The intricacy was intended to be funny, and it succeeded. As Geoffrey Pullum put it: 'The quotation is impeccable, syntactically, semantically, logically, and rhetorically. There is nothing baffling about its language at all... Hate Rummie if you want for political reasons, but don't try to get grammar or logic on your side. There is nothing unintelligible about his quoted remark, linguistically or logically.'

The Plain English Campaign also gave an award for gobbledegook for this statement by Richard Gere, the actor: 'I know who I am. No one else knows who I am. If I was a giraffe and somebody said I was a snake, I'd think "No, actually I am a giraffe."' The idea may be odd but the language is perfectly comprehensible.

See also STYLE.

Kafkaesque

Kafka is a writer to relish, but the adjective *Kafkaesque* is an overworked eponym. It is one of the few literary clichés to excite journalists as much as ORWELLIAN. It carries the sense of one who suffers harassment or victimisation but this misses out a large part of Kafka's mental world.

Some peculiarly flatfooted translations of the original German by Edwin and Willa Muir in the 1930s obscured the surreal humour in Kafka for English readers. His writings are meant to be funny. On stylistic grounds, I recommend restricted use, with an explanation, if used at all – which largely nullifies the point of using a shorthand term such as this.

lead, led

The past tense and participle of the verb *lead* is *led*. It does occasionally happen in edited prose that these are rendered as *lead*, presumably on the model of the spelling of the past tense and past participle of *read* and the pronunciation of the base metal *lead*. You can see why it happens; there's nothing to be done except learn it.

lie, lay

This is a confusing pair of verbs. The verb *to lie* means *to take a recumbent or prostrate position*. If applied to an inanimate object, it means *to be at rest*. The verb is intransitive: that is, it cannot take a direct object. The verb *to lay* means to set down. It is transitive. Consider Auden's beautiful words: 'Lay your sleeping head, my love, / Human on my faithless arm...' The direct object of the verb is 'your sleeping head'.

The past tense of *lie* is *lay*, and the past participle is *lain*. The past tense and the past participle of *lay* are both *laid*. There is a widespread but informal practice of treating them as interchangeable. Here are some examples, all from *The Times*, where the context (being more formal than casual speech) suggests that the verbs are being mixed up.

- When the Queen lay a wreath at Islandbridge to the Irish soldiers who were killed in the Great War while serving in the British Army she symbolised the joining of the two nations. When she lay a wreath in the Garden of Remembrance to commemorate the Irish men who were killed in the cause of independence, fighting against the British, she symbolised their rupture. (The Queen *laid* a wreath.)
- The stadium has laid dormant since Montreal Expos, as they were at the time, upped sticks and moved to Washington. (The stadium has *lain* dormant.)
- A year ago there was so much stock laying around Sainsbury's stores that hundreds of them needed tents erected in their backyards to accommodate it all. (The stock was *lying around*.)
- Imiela, a railway maintenance worker, prowled around London and the Home Counties in search of secluded spots to carry out attacks before laying in wait for lone women and children. (He was *lying in wait*.)
- Then ... he laid low for several months before suddenly embarking on a spree of armed robberies. (He *lay low*.)
- A New Zealand police officer is laying low after being caught making lewd remarks about a civilian colleague. (He is *lying low*.)

In Standard usage, the past tense of *lie* and the present tense of *lay* are the same word. Treating them as interchangeable is non-Standard usage but that's a matter of register rather than an error of grammar. Bob Dylan's line *Lay, lady, lay, lay across my big brass bed* is entirely appropriate to the context.

likely

This is from an American newspaper about one of my favourite modern novelists: 'In his book *John Updike's Early Years*, scholar Jack De Bellis discusses a real Updike classmate who was likely the model for some portion of Joan.'

The use of *likely* as an adverb is common in American usage but has had its American detractors even so. In British usage, sticklers would insist on replacing it with *probably*, on the grounds that *likely* is an adjective. But that objection is no more than defining a word in such a way to rule out one of its uses. It's an adverb too, which is commonly qualified by *more, less, most* or *very* and so on. It violates no rule of grammar to use it as an unqualified adverb.

literally

A minor squall among commentators happened in 2013 when someone noted that Google listed two meanings of *literally*, of which the second was: 'Used to acknowledge that something is not literally true but is used for emphasis or for strong feeling.'

It expressed exactly the fears of those who believe that standards of English are in decline. For how can the same word mean one thing and its opposite? It's the type of development anticipated by Cochrane when he warned about 'using the word in *literally* the opposite of its correct sense and committing a serious abuse of language'.

It's no such thing. The second definition is not the opposite of its 'correct' (i.e. Standard) sense at all, and the meaning of *literally* hasn't changed. The word used in its non-literal sense is an intensifier – as when Nick Clegg, then Deputy Prime Minister, referred to political critics who were 'literally on another planet'. Other words have followed the same course: *absolutely*, *totally*, *perfectly* and *really*, among others. I don't recommend using *literally* in that way, because it's a vogue word – but I'm inconsistent because I do use the others I've cited as intensifiers. There is no good linguistic reason to object to the non-literal *literally*.

lowest common denominator

The term *lowest common denominator* is often used as a metaphor for low standards, as here: **ITV's programmes exhibit a 'remarkable lack of diversity' and are targeted at audiences of the 'lowest common denominator', the broadcaster's own senior executives have said.**

If you look closely at the phrase, you find an oddity: a lowest common denominator is not a low number. In mathematics, it is the least common multiple of the denominators (the bottom numbers) of a set of fractions. For example, the lowest common denominator of [⅓] and [¼] is 12, because it is the lowest number into which both 3 and 4 can be divided exactly.

Why do writers use lowest common denominator to denote low standards or attenuated ambition? My guess is that they see the word *lowest* and think no further. However, that doesn't mean the term is illegitimate. There are many idioms that appear to violate logic when you look at them closely (such as *fall between the cracks*). They're still idioms used in speech, like this one.

malfeasance, misfeasance

You probably don't need the noun *misfeasance* but it's occasionally seen in print, as here in discussing the banks: **But since the FSA was well aware of that approach and approved it, it can hardly accuse the old HBOS board of any serious misfeasance in approving it too.**

Misfeasance means *transgression* or *trespass*. A *misfeasance* is always wrong, but it isn't as strong as *malfeasance*. A *serious misfeasance* is therefore, more concisely, a *malfeasance*.

masterful, masterly

Sticklers make much of this distinction. *Masterful* means *dominating* or *imperious*. If, however, you are *masterly* then you show a skill worthy of a master. Most style guides define them in this way, though in fact the distinction is largely the creation of Fowler, who acknowledges that 'some centuries ago both were used without distinction in either of two very different senses'.

Fowler adds hopefully that the differentiation is 'now complete'. Well, no. Here's Aldous Huxley in *Crome Yellow*, using *masterful* in a sense of admiration for skill: 'Fascinated and horrified, Denis pored over the drawing. It was masterful. A mute, inglorious Rouveyre appeared in every one of those cruelly clear lines.'

If you use the words interchangeably and allow the context to determine the meaning, you will be in good company and have every justification.

may, might

'It should be a matter of grave concern that the word *might* as the past tense of *may* seems to be in danger of disappearing from both written and spoken English,' says Cochrane. The hyperbole is absurd but this is one prescriptive question on which a clear distinction can matter. You do find in current usage the occasional use of *may* where *might* would normally go, and this substitution genuinely may cause ambiguity. *Merriam-Webster* says candidly: 'No one has a satisfactory explanation for why these substitutions occur, and we are as stumped as everyone else.'

The traditional usage is that *may* indicates an open question, whereas *might* indicates a possibility that existed in the past but does not exist now. I have for years kept an example of the careful maintenance of this distinction within a single sentence. It comes from a review in the *Observer* of the second volume of Sir Ian Kershaw's biography of Hitler. The reviewer, Peter Conrad, writes: '[Hitler] made up military strategy as he went along and may have lost the war because of muddled tactics: if the Germans had reacted more swiftly on the Normandy beaches, Kershaw reckons, they might have beaten back the Allied invasion.'

Let's interpret this. It is possible that the Nazis' defeat in the Second World War was due to muddled tactics (rather than, say, superior Allied force). So those tactics *may* have lost them the war: we don't know. The Nazis did not beat back the Allied invasion on the Normandy beaches, however. That possibility was once open (according to Kershaw's book), but it never happened. So the Nazis *might* have repelled the Allies.

Because of the use of *may* and *might*, the reader knows what is an open historical question and what is a settled one. Everybody knows that the Nazis fortunately did not beat back the Allied invasion on the Normandy beaches. But there may be discussions about history that are also of immense importance yet less well known; the difference between *may* and *might* sometimes matters and is a prescriptive recommendation worth observing.

militate, mitigate

The issue with these words is that they are occasionally confused owing to their phonetic similarity. *Militate* (usually followed by the preposition *against*) means *to be a powerful or conclusive factor* (against). *Mitigate* means *to alleviate* or *give relief from*, especially in the legal sense of *mitigating circumstances*.

They are different words with different meanings. Almost all usage guides include them though the problem is scarcely momentous. Not many people use the words. If you do, it's worth observing the difference. The issue is very similar to FLAUNT, FLOUT – two words that sound similar but have no connection.

myriad

Fowler says that 'it is well to remember' that the original sense of *myriad* is *ten thousand*. Perhaps he meant the etymological root, as *myriad* has been used in the sense of *countless numbers of things* since the sixteenth century. You're on firm ground in using it that way.

myself

Sticklers insist that *myself* serves as a reflexive pronoun (*I cut myself*) or for purposes of emphasis (*I myself have climbed Everest*). Most linguists would consider it more accurate to say that *myself* is reflexive in all its uses but there are various perfectly acceptable uses where there is no antecedent expression with the same referent.

One such use is to serve in place of the first-person singular personal pronoun in either subject or object case (i.e. *I* or *me*). Sticklers would scorn such constructions as *there are three people here apart from myself* or *the Editor and myself have parted ways*. But in compound phrases such as these, the use of *myself* solves the question of which case to use.

That will sound infuriating to the sticklers but it's not always clear in English which case the personal pronoun should take. Should it be *my brother is bigger than me* or *my brother is bigger than I*? Writers have often taken the sensible decision to pre-empt debate and objection by using 'myself' for such decisions, as in Samuel Butler's *Erewhon*: 'This was to meet the second difficulty: the first gave me less uneasiness, for when Arowhena and I next met after our interview in the garden I could see that she had suffered not less acutely than myself.'

Indeed the same writer, in the same novel, happily uses *myself* even when the decision on case is more straightforward: 'During all this time both Arowhena and myself had been dreaming, and drifting towards an avowed attachment, but had not dared to face the real difficulties of the position.'

See also YOURSELF, YOURSELVES.

nauseous, nauseated

This is one of the odder causes for purists. *Nauseous* is not an especially common word yet it occupies a prominent place in their pantheon of confidently asserted usages. Bryson makes this distinction: '*Nauseous* is an adjective describing something that causes nausea ("a nauseous substance"). To feel sick is to be *nauseated*.'

The issue is, as ever, more complex than that a word has a single meaning that is disregarded. The *OED* records three definitions of *nauseous*, of which the first is *inclined to sickness or nausea*, with citations from the seventeenth century. It marks this definition as rare or obsolete, but it has come back into fashion and will surely be recorded as such. *Merriam-Webster* says: 'Any handbook that tells you that *nauseous* cannot mean "nauseated" is out of touch with the contemporary language. In current usage it seldom means anything else.'

It's most often used, *Merriam-Webster* points out, as a predicate adjective (coming after the verb), especially in the construction *feeling nauseous*. Meanwhile, the sense of *nauseous* favoured by sticklers (though it isn't the oldest sense) is being transferred by usage to *nauseating*, as in this theatre review: **The terrible Rwandan sequence is accompanied by the frying of sliced flesh, complete with nauseating odour.**

The word *nauseated* is, on the evidence of the archive of *The Times*, becoming hard to find. Thus language changes, and the change is measured in only a few years. Why sticklers should be anguished about the process is hard to explain except that *nauseous* is a shibboleth.

no one, no-one

It's Standard practice to write this as two words. As an indefinite pronoun it can be either singular or plural. See NONE for this difference between formal concord (which holds that the verb must be singular) and notional concord (where meaning takes precedence over strict syntax).

none

Sticklers insist that *none* means *not one* and is singular. Heffer is especially emphatic on the matter. 'Therefore,' he says, 'one writes "none of us *is* free tonight", "none of us *was* there", "none of us *has* done that", and so on. The dictionary now says that the use in the plural is common. That does not mean it is correct.'

What hogwash this is. *None* can be singular or plural. This isn't some modern heresy. It's always been like this. Where do you start?

Thomas More, from *Utopia*: 'None are suffered to put away their wives against their wills, from any great calamity that may have fallen on their persons...'

Samuel Johnson, from *Rasselas*: 'The time is already come when none are wretched but by their own fault.'

John Dryden, from *A Satire Against Sedition*: 'None of your ornaments are wanting; neither the landscape of your Tower, nor the rising sun; nor the Anno Domini of your new sovereign's coronation.'

Shakespeare, from *Richard III* (it is the King speaking): 'I will converse with iron-witted fools / And unrespective boys: none are for me / That look into me with considerate eyes...'

Shakespeare, from *Love's Labours Lost* (it is the Princess speaking): 'None are so surely caught, when they are catch'd, / As wit turn'd fool...'

P. G. Wodehouse, from *The Girl on the Boat*: 'All watering-places on the south coast of England are blots on the landscape, but though I am aware that by saying it I shall offend the civic pride of some of the others – none are so peculiarly foul as Bingley-on-the-Sea.'

Tennyson, from *Sir Galahad*: 'I hear a voice but none are there...'

Robert Frost, from 'The Trial by Existence': 'And none are taken but who will, / Having first heard the life read out …'

You get the drift. *None* is not necessarily singular. Sometimes it is; sometimes it's plural. A useful (though far from rigid) test is whether the writer is considering an entire group or a specific member of it. As so often in usage, what sounds natural when you consider it this way is the answer you should go with.

nouns as verbs

Converting nouns to verbs will always be condemned by someone yet it's been part of the language for centuries. You may feel uncomfortable hearing some business guru use *transition* as a verb, but the verbs *rain*, *audition* and *button* have entered the language by the same route. Likewise, adjectives become nouns ('for ye have the poor always with you', says Jesus in St Matthew's Gospel) and nouns become adjectives ('Perchance before I see the Autumn leaves, / I may behold thy city…', wrote Oscar Wilde in his poem 'Ravenna').

number

It's a genuine rule of the grammar of Standard English that nouns and verbs must agree in number. A verb must be plural if the noun-phrase that is its subject is plural. A pronoun must agree in number with its antecedent. As with other rules of grammar, it doesn't need to be taught. Native speakers of Standard English know by instinct that if the noun or noun-phrase is singular, so must be the verb. (There are speakers of non-Standard forms who say *we/you/they was*, and who therefore need to learn that Standard English has *we/you/they were*.)

It's possible to lose sight of noun–verb agreement in a convoluted sentence. But the principle of agreement needs to be observed with an eye to sense rather than zealotry. This sentence, for example, is fine: **But now there are a growing number of complaints about sloppily drafted letters and error-strewn memos coming out of the Whitehall machine.**

The noun *number* is singular but the phrase *a number of* follows the convention known as synesis. This is where a grammatical construction conforms with meaning rather than strict syntax. Linguists also refer to it as the principle of notional (rather than formal) concord. The meaning of *a number of complaints* is *several complaints*. As *several complaints* is plural, the construction *a number of* should be paired with a plural noun and a plural verb.

The need for a plural verb is still more obvious if you turn the construction round, as in this example from Charles Dickens, in *A Tale of Two Cities*: 'In front of [the Guillotine], seated in chairs, as in a garden of public diversion, are a number of women, busily knitting.'

See also NONE and THEY.

oblivious

Obliviousness, insist the pedants, is not a state of *unawareness* but a state of *forgetfulness*. The preposition that follows the noun *obliviousness* and the adjective *oblivious* is therefore logically *of*, not *to*.

They are half right. *Forgetfulness* is one meaning. It is not the only one. The alternative sense of being heedless or unaware has been established for at least a century. It is this second meaning used by Thomas Hardy in *Far from the Madding Crowd*: 'She was a misty shape, and well she might be, considering that her original was at that moment sound asleep and oblivious of all love and letter-writing under the sky.'

You can use *oblivious* and *obliviousness* in either sense legitimately. My preference is to distinguish them by using the preposition *of* after the word when used in the sense of forgetfulness and *to* otherwise.

only

Vast amounts of printers' ink have been spilt on the question of supposed misplacement of *only*. Heffer is representative of a common piece of advice in newspaper handbooks: '*Only* should be positioned as close as possible to the word it qualifies, otherwise it will qualify a word the writer does not intend it to.'

This is too sweeping. It is common to place *only* before the word it qualifies but that doesn't exhaust the possibilities, nor is it true that a 'misplaced' *only* qualifies the wrong word. The pedants' objection appears to have its origins in (yet again) those eighteenth-century grammarians – in this case, Lowth, who insisted that an adverb is placed 'close or near to the word, which it modifies or affects'.

The demands of prosody frequently override this supposed rule, with no ambiguity resulting. The jazz song 'I Only Have Eyes for You', from the 1934 film *Dames* (and frequently revived thereafter), doesn't imply that the other organs are uncaring. *Merriam-Webster* usefully provides examples of 'misplacement' from Dryden to Doctorow, via Ruskin, Waugh and T. S. Eliot. It is rare that you will find a genuine and uncontrived example of ambiguity. Place *only* where the rhythm of the sentence suggests it should be placed.

Orwellian

Like KAFKAESQUE, the term has outstripped a close connection with the author. Orwell wrote in *Nineteen Eighty-Four* about total-itarianism and its practices. The practices – linguistic manipulation of invasive technology – are the symptoms not the subject. I much prefer the use of *Orwellian* when a writer is aware of the power of the term and simultaneously the way its overuse has dulled this sense. Christopher Hitchens used that approach admirably in a column about North Korea: 'One tries to avoid cliché, and I did my best on a visit to this terrifying country in the year 2000, but George Orwell's *1984* was published at about the time that Kim Il Sung set up his system, and it really is as if he got hold of an early copy of the novel and used it as a blueprint.'

Less gifted writers turn to *Orwellian* as a complaint against surveillance, as here, where the head of a mental health char-ity complains about an ankle bracelet equipped with satellite technology, to be worn by dangerous psychiatric patients: **There is something inhuman and Orwellian about technological systems designed to control behaviour.**

Regardless of the merits of the case, that remark must be an overstatement. As Leopold Labedz, the Sovietologist, wrote: 'For Orwell the problem was the technology of power rather than the power of technology.' Orwell's dystopia is about totalitarianism, not tracking devices.

Even so, it's pointless to rail against an extended use that is now established. Clichés are not necessarily wrong. They're more powerful, though, when flagged as clichés.

parameter, perimeter

Parameter is a technical term in various disciplines, including geometry, maths and music. It is used, to the dislike of some reasonable people who know language as well as these disciplines, in the sense of *limits*. A *perimeter* is a ring or space surrounding something. *Parameters* (plural) is common now in edited prose in the extended sense of a limit. You may not need it, and I've never used the word in that sense, but there it is: **He has just revealed that he has been living with Parkinson's disease for three years – 'ironically it is a neurological disorder,' he says – so it is fascinating to hear Bannister talk of pushing new parameters.**

parts of speech

Words are usually classified according to the function they have in a sentence. The traditional grammatical distinctions are between eight parts of speech: *nouns*, *pronouns*, *verbs*, *adverbs*, *adjectives*, *prepositions*, *conjunctions* and *interjections*. Insisting on a rigid distinction between different parts of speech is a shibboleth, though. Standard English often makes use of the same word in different ways (notably in using adjectives as adverbs).

pedantry

Pedantry is an excessive concern with petty details and a slavish adherence to literalness. It can be a mass noun or a count noun (*pedantries*). Robert Walton, the narrator in Mary Shelley's *Frankenstein*, draws a distinction between *pedagogy* (my word) and *pedantry*:

In M. Waldman I found a true friend. His gentleness was never
tinged by dogmatism, and his instructions were given with an
air of frankness and good nature that banished every idea of
pedantry. In a thousand ways he smoothed for me the path of
knowledge and made the most abstruse inquiries clear and facile
to my apprehension.

That's not how the language debate proceeds, unfortunately. Amid
all the potential expressiveness of language, pedants are concerned
instead with a narrow subset of disputed usages. Pedantry is worse
than trivial. In the language debate it's also wrong. It is wrong in its
understanding of how language works, for language never breaks
down or loses grammatical structure. And it is wrong even on the
details that it champions. If a particular construction is in general
use in Standard English, that's Standard English, whatever the
pedants say. Normally, these language sticklers not only overlook
general usage but also ignore historical usage.

A regard for general usage is the approach I adopt in my weekly
column for *The Times*. The column is called 'The Pedant'. It's a
joke (the title, I mean, not the column). There are precedents for
ironic appropriation of a label. *Methodism* was once a term of derision. *Queer* was adopted by campaigners for homosexual equality
and robbed of its derogatory connotation. *Pedant* is not a term I
naturally choose but I adopt it for my column in the same spirit
as *Slate* magazine runs a column about economics called 'dismal
science'. Readers who expect a pedantic discourse can, I hope, be
persuaded that language works differently. English reflects what its
users say and write rather than arbitrary judgments of correctness.

Whereas I use the term *pedant* with irony owing to its derogatory connotation, Pinker notes derisively an alternative label that
has been adopted with pride. William Safire, the columnist for the

New York Times, described himself as a 'language maven', from the Yiddish word meaning expert. Of this, Pinker remarks sardonically: 'Maven, shmaven! *Kibbitzers* and *nudniks* is more like it.' It is a theme of this book that language reflects how we perceive the world rather than determining it. Labels are what we make of them.

plupluperfect

The *plupluperfect* is a made-up term for a construction that you occasionally hear in speech but almost never see in print. It involves the inclusion of a redundant auxiliary in the past perfect (or pluperfect) tense. *Merriam-Webster* gives an example (from a radio interview with a politician) of *if I had've been there*, whereas the Standard construction would be *if I had been there*. The most usual extra auxiliary in the present-day variant of the plupluperfect is *have*, shortened to *'ve*. Of this, *Merriam-Webster* concludes: 'The construction would have to be judged non-standard in ordinary written discourse, but we have no evidence that it ever occurs there, at least in the edited varieties.'

Well, there is evidence of its occurrence in edited print: I found an example in *The Times*, whose rugby columnist wrote about reminiscing with his teammates. He used the plupluperfect extensively:

It was about listening to The Judge tell the same stories with the same mannerisms and inflections and still laughing, not because they were necessarily funny but because you wanted to laugh, after what you had been through together; knowing on a fundamental level that if I hadn't have pushed, he couldn't have scrummaged, and if he hadn't have lifted and cleared, I couldn't have jumped; that individually we were nothing, but together we could make a difference.

That's a non-Standard use of English that is highly unusual in appearing in print; and it's a good piece of writing. It's an example of the flexibility of English. A construction that a fastidious sub-editor might have 'corrected' (but didn't) has added to the effectiveness of the prose. It conveys the atmosphere of a drinking session where rugby players are swapping anecdotes. The long sentence replicates the speech patterns of the raconteurs.

Merriam-Webster asks why a writer might want to use the plupluperfect and advances two reasons. First, an extra auxiliary adds emphasis to the pluperfect. Second, the plupluperfect may be related to the limits of the modern use of the subjunctive mood. The article I've quoted uses it in the conditional clause of a counterfactual statement (*if I hadn't have pushed*), thereby creating a sort of pluperfect subjunctive.

There is in fact a long history to the plupluperfect. The *OED* notes that 'in the 15th and 16th centuries occur many instances of redundant *have, had,* in the compound tenses'. The latest that it records is from Laurence Sterne's *A Sentimental Journey Through France and Italy* (1768) where the narrator says of a monk he meets in Calais: 'Nature seemed to have had done with her resentments in him.'

In exceptional circumstances in present-day English, it's an effective and imaginative use of English, though not Standard.

point

The use of a point (in English orthography it's known as a full stop, in American orthography it's known as a period) signals the end of a sentence that is in statement form. Note the qualification. It isn't necessary to put a point after a question mark.

portmanteau words

A portmanteau word blends the sounds and meanings of two words. The term was coined by Lewis Carroll, who was particularly good at forming portmanteau words. In *Through the Looking-Glass*, he says of the vanquisher of the Jabberwock: 'He left it dead, and with its head / He went galumphing back.' The verb *galumph* is a portmanteau word that blends *gallop* and *triumph*, with the comic connotation of ungainly movement.

Charles Dickens was an occasional deviser of portmanteau words too. In *Bleak House*, there are two instances of *wiglomeration* (from *wig* and *conglomeration*), coined for comic effect. The difference between Dickens's portmanteau words and Carroll's is that some of Carroll's entered the language. They thereby became neologisms (see *INVENTED WORDS*), used by English speakers who may not realise that they were once specifically invented by an author.

An example of an inadvertent portmanteau word comes from Sarah Palin, the former US Republican vice-presidential candidate. In an interview in 2010 she urged President Obama to *refudiate* a particular viewpoint. *Refudiate* blends *refute* and *repudiate*. Unfortunately, it speedily became clear that this was neither a slip of the tongue nor a joke: Mrs Palin genuinely thought that the word existed. On having her error pointed out, she wrote: 'English is a living language. Shakespeare liked to coin new words too.'

preposition

A preposition is a short word indicating the role of a person or thing in a relationship or action. The choice of the 'correct' preposition is often arbitrary. The traditional insistence that *DIFFERENT to* is wrong has nothing to be said for it. Common speech patterns trump supposed logic.

preposition, stranded

The two rules that everyone 'knows' about grammar are the prohibition on SPLIT INFINITIVES and the prohibition on ending a sentence with a preposition. See the entry on the first for the pedants' case. On the issue of stranded prepositions, you might think the stickler argument so manifestly peculiar that it wouldn't need to be dealt with at all. It is an absurd case, but the effects of this belief are rife. Here is part of an email sent to me by a *Times* journalist who has evidently been taught that way: **Finally (and this is merely a request for some free grammar education) you write 'which Israeli voters had lost faith in'. I'd always want to write 'in which Israeli voters had lost faith'. Is that wrong of me? Or ugly of me? Or unnecessary? Or what?**

The prohibitions linger. Violations of these rules spark numerous letters of complaint to newspapers; yet both rules are utterly fanciful. They're superstitions that should be disregarded.

The prohibition on ending a sentence with a preposition was an invention of John Dryden. Being a Latinist, he tried to force English grammar to conform to Latin models. Fowler cites many examples of classic authors who put prepositions at the end of sentences, and gives the sensible advice to 'follow no arbitrary rule'.

Prepositions often do stand before the word they govern (*the columnist is under the table*) but this, it hardly needs to be said, isn't the only place for them. There are some constructions in which it's essential that the preposition comes at the end of the sentence. One is a restrictive relative clause introduced by *that*, such as: *It was the mythical grammatical rule that we were goggling at.*

It's also common practice to put the preposition at the end of a question, such as *who are you waiting for?* rather than *for whom are you waiting?* (No one but a prig would use the second form of that question in speech, and few others would use *whom* in the first, so I haven't either.)

Another example is where a clause is used as the object of a preposition, as in this sentence from Dickens's *David Copperfield* (cited by Jespersen): 'He never raised his eyes from what he was about.' Here the clause *what he was about* is the object of the preposition *from*. There is no obvious way of avoiding a stranded preposition here.

The prohibition on stranded prepositions is bogus and has twisted people's natural patterns of writing. The only question to consider here is whether a preposition is too weak a word to end the sentence on. If the climax of the sentence, in meaning, comes at the end, with the addition of a preposition, recast the sentence to put the preposition earlier. Otherwise don't, and ignore the objections.

One peculiarity of the stickler objection to stranded prepositions is that the same person will often also espouse the THAT, WHICH rule in relative clauses, namely that you must have *that* in a restrictive relative clause. These two made-up rules are incompatible, though. You can't say *the man to that I talked*: it has to be *the man that I talked to*.

presently

There is nothing wrong with using *presently* in the sense of *at the moment*. The *OED* cites examples from Chaucer onwards, including Ruskin ('Our presently disputed claims'). This sense, it advises, was 'apparently avoided' in literary use between the seventeenth and mid-twentieth centuries but it continued in regular use. It is entirely legitimate. How do you tell the difference between this sense and the meaning *in a short while*? By the context, namely the tense of the verb that it modifies.

primrose path

This established literary metaphor seems to be acquiring a secondary meaning (noted by Garner), as in this comment by an educational psychologist in the *Atlantic*: 'A writing assignment may guide student thinking toward substantive issues in, say, history, or it may guide students down a mental primrose path.'

The sense that I can make of this from the context is that a writing assignment may mislead a student. That isn't what's traditionally been known as a *primrose path*: it's a garden path. A primrose path is a course of pleasure ending in ruin. The phrase has a strong Shakespearean pedigree. In *Hamlet*, Ophelia warns her brother against dissipation in sensual pleasure: 'But, good my brother, / Do not, as some ungracious pastors do, / Show me the steep and thorny way to heaven; / Whiles, like a puff'd and reckless libertine, / Himself the primrose path of dalliance treads, / And recks not his own rede.'

Similarly, in *Macbeth*, the porter speaks of 'the primrose way to the everlasting bonfire'. The first published work of Bram Stoker, the author of *Dracula*, is a novella called *The Primrose Path*. It is a rather conventional Victorian morality tale of the ruin caused by alcoholism.

prior, subsequent

Sticklers insist that *prior* is an adjective. For example, it is used that way by Darcy in Jane Austen's *Pride and Prejudice*, where he writes to Elizabeth that 'thither also went Mr Wickham, undoubtedly by design; for there proved to have been a prior acquaintance between him and Mrs Younge'.

Whether the sticklers' objection to another use of *prior* is on grounds of style or of grammar is not clear to me, perhaps because it's not clear to them. In any event, many of them object to the use of *prior to* as a compound preposition. Their criticism is that the phrase is stilted and pompous, when there is an obvious alternative for a preposition meaning the same thing, namely *before*.

Their objection is extended similarly to *subsequent* as used here by Fred Goodwin, former chief executive of the Royal Bank of Scotland, complaining about his pension arrangements: 'Subsequent to this, you approached the chairman of the group remuneration committee to suggest that I should waive certain share related awards.'

Sticklers can see no case for *subsequent to* and would insist instead on *after*.

As usual in these disputes, the pedants ignore the evidence of usage. Here's George Eliot in *Romola*: 'But in this stage of the business, the friends of the accused resisted the appeal, determined chiefly by the wish to gain delay; and, in fact, strict legality required that sentence should have been passed prior to the appeal.'

This is a Standard and well-established use of *prior to* as a prepositional phrase. Note, however, the context in which Eliot is using it. Fowler, the most sensible of the prescriptivists, prefers *before* but makes an exception 'in contexts involving a connexion between the two events more essential than the simple time relation'. That's the sense of the legal circumstances that Eliot describes.

Likewise, Adam Smith in *The Wealth of Nations* uses *prior to* in the sense of a necessary connection and not simply of chronology: 'As subsistence is, in the nature of things, prior to conveniency and luxury, so the industry which procures the former, must necessarily be prior to that which ministers to the latter. The cultivation and improvement of the country, therefore, which affords subsistence, must, necessarily, be prior to the increase of the town, which furnishes only the means of conveniency and luxury.'

Even so, that principle establishes the common use of *prior to* as a prepositional phrase. Its extended sense of *one thing preceding another* is widespread and longstanding. Here is Herman Melville, in *Moby Dick*: 'I take it, that the earliest standers of mast-heads were the old Egyptians; because, in all my researches, I find none prior to them.'

This usage is now common practice in all forms of writing, and certainly in newspapers, as here: **Prior to the 1986 All-Ireland final, the Cork management sat down one evening to discuss how they were tactically going to set up against Galway.**

Chiding this usage, Bryson urges that you use *prior to* only if you are comfortable also with saying *posterior to*. His mockery is misplaced, for the simple reason that *prior to* is idiomatic whereas *posterior to* is not. The evidence of their usage is beyond argument: people use the first and not the second. There is nothing wrong with *prior to*. You can use it without qualms. The same point applies to *subsequent to* instead of *after*.

pronouns

Pronouns are words that stand for a noun or noun-phrase. There are various types of pronoun. Indeed, the same word can serve as a different type of pronoun according to the context in which it's used. (*Who*, for example, can be either an interrogative pronoun or a relative pronoun.)

Personal pronouns are: *I, me, you, he, him, she, her, it, we, us, they, them*. Inflection for case, which has otherwise died out in English, is retained for five of these personal pronouns – that is, they have a subject and an object case. These cause confusion even for native speakers but the choice of case should reflect natural speech patterns. (See IT'S I/ME.)

Reflexive pronouns are: *myself, yourself, himself, herself, itself, ourselves, yourselves, themselves*.

Possessives are: *my, mine, your, yours, his, her, hers, its, ours, their, theirs*.

Demonstratives are: *this, that, these, those*.

Interrogative pronouns are: *what, which, who, whom, whose*.

Relative pronouns are: *that, which, who, whom, whose*. The object case for the relative pronoun *who* (namely *whom*) is rarely used in speech. There is a good argument for avoiding it in writing too. See WHO, WHOM.

Reciprocal pronouns are: *each other, one another*.

Indefinite pronouns are: *everything, somebody, anyone, nothing, nobody, all, some, each, both, none, either* and so on.

publicly

There is no reason that the spelling *publically* should exercise sticklers quite as much as it does. Consistency will get you only so far. You might argue that the adjective is *public* and not *publical*, so the adverb ought to be *publicly*. By contrast, the adjective *economical* (as well as *economic*) does exist, and the adverb is properly spelt *economically*. Likewise, the adjective *magical* is in common use, and the adverb is *magically*. But this line of reasoning is easily contradicted. There is no such word as *barbarical*: the correct adjective is *barbaric*. Yet the adverb is *barbarically*.

You can use *publically* as a legitimate variant spelling.

question

A question is a sentence that asks for information or an answer. A direct question, even if intended rhetorically (*could you please come in?*), is traditionally given a question mark but it isn't mandatory. A parent who says testily *will you please stop it!* is not making a genuine inquiry. The sense of that statement would dictate an exclamation mark, even though strict syntax would require a question mark. Go with sense, not with strict syntax.

reason is because, the

Generations of grammarians, along with today's sticklers, would object to this type of construction: **Bailey, a marine biologist, argues otherwise – and the reason is because his book isn't really about the fish at all.**

Pedants maintain that *because* means *the reason that*, so that *the reason is because* is in effect saying *the reason is for the reason that*.

Yet notable writers have used *the reason is because*, including Philip Sidney in his *Apology for Poesy*: 'His reason is because Poesy dealeth with…'

Likewise John Dryden wrote in his *Discourse on Satire*: 'The most perfect work of poetry, says our master Aristotle, is tragedy. His reason is because it is the most united; being more severely confined within the rules of action, time, and place.'

A phrase that is idiomatic and grammatical, and has a literary history, is defensible. The same, by the way, is true of another phrase that sticklers object to, which is *the reason why*. They insist that it should be *the reason that*. The argument, on similar grounds, is that the phrase is a redundancy, as the *why* implies a reason. It's like saying *reason* twice.

This is all misguided. Let's accept, for sake of argument, that *the reason why* involves a mild redundancy. Why is that illegitimate? You can make an argument against *the time when* or *the man who* on the identical argument of redundancy. Yet not even the most rabid stickler, as far as I know, has ever argued that it must be *the time that* and *the man that*, on the grounds that *time* already includes the concept of chronology and *man* implies an animate being. (In fact, some of the letters I receive object to a phrase such as *the man that*, arguing that it must be *the man who*. In fact, either is permissible and both are long established.)

You can write any of *the reason that*, *the reason why* or *the reason is because*.

recollection, remembrance

Some usage guides suggest that there is a subtle stylistic distinction between these words. Recollecting something, they argue, is not quite the same as remembering it. The verb *remember* implies retrieving a memory that is easily recovered. When you recollect something, you are doing something different: you are applying conscious effort to find a thought that is stored further back in your mind.

Jane Austen observes this distinction. In *Emma*, the affable but obtuse Harriet Smith collects and transcribes riddles into a volume made up by the meddlesome Emma Woodhouse. Emma's father 'was almost as much interested in the business as the girls, and tried very often to recollect something worth their putting in. "So many clever riddles as there used to be when he was young – he wondered he could not remember them! but he hoped he should in time." '

That is a delicious portrait of a useless man, drawn without malice. The *recollect* implies that Mr Woodhouse has put much effort into this trivial exercise. His *remember* implies, however, a self-deprecating attitude no less appealing for being accurate.

That distinction between the verbs *recollect* and *remember* is sometimes replicated in that between the nouns *recollection* and *remembrance*. Recollection requires some mental exertion; remembrance is the act of remembering.

Remembrance is often used in solemn contexts (such as Remembrance Day), and it also has a biblical ring ('Rejoice in the Lord, ye righteous; and give thanks at the remembrance of his holiness,' says the psalmist in the King James Version). But there is no reason that it should be confined to such cases.

The best-known English title for Marcel Proust's *À la recherche du temps perdu* is *Remembrance of Things Past*. This is a translation by C. K. Scott Moncrieff, published in 1922. The title (itself drawn from Shakespeare's Sonnet 30, in which the poet summons up 'remembrance of things past') is intended to convey Proust's theme of spontaneous memory, though Proust himself disliked it.

You can observe the distinction carefully if you wish but, as *Merriam-Webster* points out, it isn't really that strong. It quotes Emily Dickinson, in a letter, using *recollect* as a synonym for *remember*: 'Thank you for recollecting my weakness...'

It's a matter of stylistic preference.

refute, deny, rebut

The distinction between these verbs is among the principal causes in sticklerdom. To *refute* a proposition means that you *disprove* it. For example, on the fortieth anniversary of the Moon landings, NASA issued a statement about the conspiracy theory that these landings had been faked: 'Conspiracy theories are always difficult to refute because of the impossibility of proving a negative.'

That is a very precise use of the verb. NASA rightly observes that a conspiracy theory can't be disproved. That makes it unlike a scientific theory, which advances hypotheses that can be tested. Scientists continually try to *refute* theories to arrive at better explanations. Conspiracy theorists do the opposite: they explain conflicting data by positing an even wider conspiracy than the one they had first thought of.

Pedants insist that if you don't offer disproof of a charge then you can't be refuting it. They are incensed at the very common usage of the type *we refute any allegations of impropriety* when all that the speaker or writer is doing is declaring those allegations to be false. This is, say the sticklers, not *refuting* the charges but *denying* them. Refuting them was what the speaker or writer wished to do on being presented with them but had not yet done.

Occasionally you find that a writer is aware that there must be some distinction between *refute* and *deny* but is hazy about the exact difference. There is a temptation then to use *rebut* in the sense of *deny*. This too annoys the sticklers, who maintain that to *rebut* a charge means to offer detailed evidence against it.

Is there merit in this taxonomy of meaning? It's clear that the heart of the disputed usage is *refute*. It's a useful verb, not limited to verbal evidence. In Emily Brontë's *Wuthering Heights*, the narrator Nelly Dean recounts the state of the enfeebled Catherine Linton:

Then, the paleness of her face – its haggard aspect having vanished as she recovered flesh – and the peculiar expression arising from her mental state, though painfully suggestive of their causes, added to the touching interest which she awakened; and – invariably to me, I know, and to any person who saw her, I should think – refuted more tangible proofs of convalescence, and stamped her as one doomed to decay.

But the *deny* sense of *refute* has been around for a long time. And, as ever when you consider these fiercely contested usages, the historical evidence is more nuanced than the sticklers maintain. An early meaning of *refute*, given by the *OED*, is to *rebut*. It can be dated to Sir Thomas More in 1533, in dispute with William Tyndale: 'If Tyndale wold now refute myne obieccion of yᵉ Turkes and theyr Alcharon.'

The sense of disproving an accusation comes slightly later, as does that of proving a person to be wrong. The sense of rejecting or repudiating something is modern, and the first cited example comes from 1886. The *OED* adds that this is criticised as erroneous in usage guides in the twentieth century.

That's it. That's the evidence. It appears that what emerged as an extended meaning in the late nineteenth century was rubbished by pundits on realising its existence in the twentieth century and the condemnation has continued ever since. Contumely has had no effect; it rarely does. The extended use of *refute* is going strong. The sense is clear from the context: the point invariably overlooked by sticklers.

ridiculous, risible

These allied adjectives are an example of how words stray from their origins. Both ought etymologically to mean *laughable* yet both have acquired an extended sense of meriting mockery or derision.

Ridiculous comes from either the post-classical Latin *ridiculosus* or the classical Latin *ridiculus* meaning *laughable* or *comic*. The sense of *absurd* or *preposterous* dates early in English – at least the sixteenth century.

It's central to one of the most poignant passages in literature. In *The Age of Innocence* by Edith Wharton, there is a remarkable counterpoint between the Countess Olenska, who has left the husband who mistreated her, and Newland Archer, who loves her but is engaged to someone else. She describes as ridiculous the gift of a bouquet that she doesn't know has come from him. He dismisses as ridiculous the notion that he might marry someone other than his fiancée. Their use of the word matches each other's.

Risible, from Middle French, is more directly still concerned with the faculty of provoking laughter. It's a useful word. The makers of Monty Python did a favour to public discourse with the scene in *The Life of Brian* where Pontius Pilate, unable to pronounce the letter *r*, observes with outrage that the guards are sniggering at the name of his friend: 'What about you? Do you find it wisible when I say the name "Biggus Dickus"?'

sat, I was

Heffer says: 'One often hears the solecism "people were sat". This is grammatically impossible.'

It's grammatically possible, all right. It happens not to be the grammar of Standard English. The distinction between Standard and non-Standard English is not the same as a distinction between correct and incorrect English. No stickler could plausibly maintain that this passage from W. W. Jacobs's story 'After the Inquest' is incomprehensible: '"The news," said George, who was of slow habits and speech, "is that you was found last Tuesday week off St Katherine's Stairs, you was sat on a Friday week at the Town o' Ramsgate public-house, and buried on Monday afternoon at Lowestoft."'

My correction on this point goes to the heart of the debate on usage. It is not wrong to use non-Standard English, nor is it ungrammatical. Standard English is a dialect that children should be taught to use because it is recognisable wherever English is spoken. It remains Standard English, however, not proper English.

semi-colon; colon

Semi-colons are a matter of preference; some writers use them when a complex sentence requires a longer pause than a comma alone provides, and when the second part is too close to the meaning of the first to warrant a full stop. But the semi-colon is not even necessary in conveying meaning. George Orwell concluded that it was an unnecessary stop and resolved to write a novel without one (*Coming Up for Air*). But according to her *Times* obituary, U. A. Fanthorpe, the poet, was dedicated, in her words, 'to the cause of the unsplit infinitive and the judicious use of the semi-colon'. Only the second of those causes is defensible, and even then it isn't mandatory.

The limited but valuable use of the colon lies in signalling to the reader that something is about to be specified and that it need not be a complete clause.

sentences

Here's a sentence from a *Times* leading article:

> **It is so very much in need of revision that the Government themselves are going to utilize the Second Chamber to make good some of the numerous formal defects which have resulted from the headlong haste of its treatment in the Commons and from Mr Lloyd George's peculiar conception of statesmanship, which substitutes for thorough deliberation the process of 'squaring' deputations from day to day by a see-saw of concessions or apparent concessions.**

It will be obvious from the politician's name that this isn't a recent article. I've selected it from the *Times* archive a century on from its publication. My purpose is to point to another reason that it's obvious the article isn't recent: the sentence is seventy-three words long. Its length is far from exceptional by the standards of *Times* leaders of that era.

The style of English prose has changed even over the past generation, let alone the past century. Sentences are generally shorter. This isn't a sign that this generation has an attenuated attention span; on the contrary, it's a good thing and an aid to comprehension to punctuate sentences carefully, and the trend is now to lighter punctuation with fewer commas. Some types of writing, such as academic papers, of course tend on average to have longer sentences than newspaper articles. But it's still possible as well as desirable to make any type of article clear to read.

Perhaps surprisingly, the evidence suggests that the way to do that is not necessarily to write short sentences. A piece of prose that comprises numerous staccato sentences is dull and wearying to read owing to its monotony. It's good style instead to vary your sentence lengths. A sentence of seventy-three words carries an inherent risk of losing the reader in a succession of subordinate clauses, but a sentence of forty words followed by one of, say, six or seven, is perfectly comprehensible.

It violates no rule of style or grammar for a sentence to contain no verb. Really. But don't make a habit of it, lest you end up with a succession of fragments that breaks the flow of an argument.

See also STYLE.

shall, will

Grammarians' witticisms are dismal things. There's a traditional joke about the non-native speaker of English who fell into the river and shouted: *I will drown and nobody shall save me!*

So he drowned, as nobody saved him.

The, er, joke is that the ordinary future requires *shall* in the first person and *will* for the second and third person. But when declaring an intent, these positions are reversed: it's *will* in the first person and *shall* in the second and third. So the luckless foreigner was declaring an intention to drown and an instruction that no one save him.

It would be hard to find even the most doctrinaire among pedants who observes this distinction reliably. Nor has it been observed by noted writers. It would be invidious to list many examples, but consider Polonius' words in *Hamlet*: 'Ophelia, walk you here. Gracious, so please you, / We will bestow ourselves.'

Or the soothsayer's words to Charmian in *Antony and Cleopatra*: 'You shall be more beloving than beloved.'

Use *shall* and *will* as you wish. Or to be more precise, use *will*, because not many people use *shall* for anything any longer (I use it only occasionally and only in writing) and it may thus sound affected.

sink, sank, sunk

Pedants would have a problem with a construction like this: **As news of Douglas Carswell's defection sunk in on the streets of Clacton yesterday, affection for the former Tory MP strengthened**.

They would insist on *sank* rather than *sunk*. In fact, both *sunk* and *sank* are Standard usage as a past tense of *sink*. Here is Wilkie Collins from his novel *Antonina*: 'As she pronounced these last words, Goisvintha's manner, which had hitherto been calm and collected, began to change: she paused abruptly in her narrative, her head sunk upon her breast, her frame quivered as convulsed with violent agony.'

specious

The word comes from the Latin *speciosus*, meaning *good-looking* or *beautiful*. This meaning in English has long been superseded. If something is *specious*, it is *false* and *deceptive*, despite its attractiveness. If an argument is *specious*, it isn't only wrong: it's plausible and coherent.

In Milton's *Paradise Regained*, Jesus tells Satan: 'Thy pompous delicacies I contemn, / And count thy specious gifts no gifts, but guiles.' The modern reader might think that Jesus has uttered a tautology in referring to the specious gifts as guiles, but of course he hasn't.

Consider also this far more recent example, from P. G. Wodehouse's *Joy in the Morning*. Bertie Wooster has been persuaded by

Boko Fittleworth to pretend to be a burglar and break a scullery window at night. Bertie is terrified that he will be caught by Stilton Cheesewright, the local constable. Boko explains that this won't happen because Stilton is the type who goes to bed early and sleeps long. Bertie reflects: 'Well, that was all right, as far as it went. His reasoning was specious, and did much to reassure me.'

split infinitive

Why split infinitives should bear such stigma is mysterious. Pinker uses the term 'pluralistic ignorance' – a state where most people reject a norm but privately believe that others accept it – to explain the persistence of such notions as that split infinitives are ungrammatical.

They aren't. The very term is misleading, given that English verbs don't have an infinitive form in the way that, for example, French verbs do. *To end* is more a phrase, comprising what linguists call a subordinator and the verb *end*. There is no grammatical necessity for the words to be next to each other. The only possible objection to putting an adverb between them might be stylistic. And sometimes it's good style. It's always better to split an infinitive than to fastidiously avoid one and thereby say something clumsy or opaque.

Yet writers go to inordinate lengths to avoid being thought ignorant of the 'rule' about split infinitives. Heffer protests that in his thirty years as a professional writer 'I have yet to find a context in which the split infinitive is necessary in order to avoid ambiguity or some other obstruction to proper sense', which suggests he hasn't looked very far.

Take this sentence from the *Huffington Post*: 'Lord Feldman was forced strenuously to deny making the alleged comments after rumours swirled on the internet that he was responsible…'

Does the writer mean that Lord Feldman was subject to strenuous force? Presumably it was the denial that was strenuous, not the force, and the writer has tortured the sentence in order to keep the infinitive intact. It would be better to say that Lord Feldman had been *forced to strenuously deny*..., thereby avoiding ambiguity. By putting the adverb before *to*, the writer avoids a split infinitive at the price of clarity and idiom. It's a poor choice. Nor would it have been a solution to place the adverb after the verb, as that too would yield ambiguity: *forced to deny strenuously making the alleged comments* suggests that he was denying having made the alleged comments strenuously (as opposed to denying having made them diffidently, presumably).

How then did the prohibition on split infinitives arise? Unlike many pointless rules, this one wasn't thought of by the eighteenth-century grammarians. The first recorded objection to split infinitives appears to be a nineteenth-century piece of grammar scolding. An article in the *New England Magazine* in 1834 entitled 'Inaccuracies of Diction', signed only 'P', lamented: 'The practice of separating the prefix of the infinitive mode from the verb, by the intervention of an adverb, is not unfrequent among uneducated persons; as, "To fully understand it," instead of "to understand it fully," or "fully to understand it." This fault is not often found in print, except in some newspapers, where the editors have not had the advantage of a good education.'

And then 'P' got down to the fateful business of proscription. No one had invented a rule about the practice, and it was time someone did: 'I am not conscious, that any rule has been heretofore given in relation to this point; no treatise on grammar or rhetoric, within my knowledge, alludes to it.'

There follows, with an awful inevitability, a mistaken premise and a destructive rule (emphasis in the original): 'The practice, however, of not separating the particle from its verb, is so general and uniform among good authors, and the exceptions are so rare, that the rule which I am about to propose will, I believe, prove to be as accurate as most rules, and may be found beneficial to inexperienced writers. It is this:– *The particle,* TO, *which comes before the verb in the infinitive mode, must not be separated from it by the intervention of an adverb or any other word or phrase; but the adverb should immediately precede the particle, or immediately follow the verb.'*

From this, all manner of mischief has followed over the past two centuries. Note, again, the curious structure of the argument. There was, said 'P', no established rule forbidding the split infinitive; therefore he would invent one. Where great writers had erred (in the opinion of 'P'), they had done so because of an absence of a written rule.

I stress this not only because the rule is baloney but because it encapsulates the approach of the sticklocracy through the centuries. Instead of marvelling at the expressiveness of language and the glories of literature, they seek supposed transgressions of made-up rules. Where a great writer has adopted a particular usage frowned on by the sticklers, it is the writer who is judged to be at fault. It ought, instead, to be the rule. The apotheosis of this destructive approach to language is to *invent* a rule where none exists.

The prohibition on split infinitives is an impossible rule to defend but that doesn't stop pedants from trying. Dummett pronounces the split infinitive 'unnatural to the language'. Following him, Gwynne gives a magnificently misconceived critique in which he maintains that 'scarcely a single instance of a split infinitive is to be found in the classical authors of the last two centuries'.

The easiest way to maintain a spurious rule in the face of evidence to the contrary is to ignore that evidence. Pronouncing confidently on the practice of classical authors of the last two centuries, Gwynne demonstrates merely that he hasn't read them.

Let's take just the nineteenth century. Tom Freeman, an invaluable blogger on language, has compiled the following list:

Samuel Taylor Coleridge, 1802: 'the interest which the good people of Keswick take in the welfare of the beauty of Buttermere, has not yet suffered them to entirely subside'

Walter Scott, 1816: 'Morton left his companion, with a caution to so shade his light that no reflection might be seen'

John Keats, 1818: 'our duties there: to nightly call Vesper'

William Taylor, 1830: 'hence it is not easy to sharply characterize this Greek poet'

Lord Macaulay, 1843: 'In order to fully appreciate the character of Lord Holland'

Herbert Spencer, 1852: 'It may be easier to bear along all the qualifications of an idea and at once rightly form it when named, than to first imperfectly conceive such idea'

Anthony Trollope, 1855: 'curtains draped so as to half exclude the light'

George Eliot, 1860: 'I undertook to partially fill up the office of parish clerk'

Elizabeth Gaskell, 1865: 'being told to just step on seven miles farther'

Samuel Wilberforce, 1874: 'if we would retain that to which we had a right (the trading place upon the river bank), to continually spread the margin, and by degrees to alter the holding of that which we had reluctantly consented to receive'

Mark Twain, 1883: 'The commission's scheme to arbitrarily and permanently confine the channel'

Jerome K. Jerome, 1889: 'One never has time to really think'

Rudyard Kipling, 1890: 'which prompts a man to savagely stamp on the spider he has but half killed'

Arthur Conan Doyle, 1892: 'The observer who had thoroughly understood one link in a series of incidents should be able to accurately state all the other ones'

Thomas Hardy, 1895: 'She wants to honestly and legally marry that man'

And why stop there? Here are a few more.

Stephen Crane writes, in *Active Service*: 'they knew now that their prowess was ripe to enable them to amply revenge what was, according to their standards, an execrable deed...'

And here is Jerome K. Jerome again, from *Three Men in a Boat*: 'George said he little thought that afternoon that he should ever come to really like boating.'

In his short story 'The Sea Raiders', H. G. Wells writes: 'From the moment of the rising of the cephalopods out of the water he had been acting too swiftly to fully comprehend his actions.'

You get the point. Gwynne is talking nonsense and hasn't checked his claim. It's one thing to note that split infinitives are more common in the twenty-first century than they were in the nineteenth. To argue that this means they're wrong is a non sequitur. There is nothing ungrammatical about a split infinitive.

It's often good style too. Even Dummett grudgingly acknowledges that Milton employed a 'tacit split' in *Lycidas* – and to good effect: 'Alas! What boots it with uncessant care / To tend the homely, slighted shepherd's trade / And strictly meditate the thankless muse?'

The more sensible usage guides will acknowledge and accept the legitimacy of the split infinitive. Fowler advises using split infinitives 'sooner than be ambiguous or artificial'. But that isn't a strong enough position. It leads to such tortuous confusions as one evinced by *The Economist Style Guide*. The authors accept that the prohibition on split infinitives is pointless yet conclude feebly: 'Unfortunately, to see the rule broken is so annoying to many people that you should observe it. To never split an infinitive is quite easy.'

Yes, it's easy to never split an infinitive if you're indifferent to the speech patterns of the English language. *To boldly go where no man has gone before* is an unimprovable phrase because the positioning of the adverb puts the stress in the right place. This conforms to the natural rhythm of the language, with stressed and unstressed syllables alternating. (Though I have to give credit to Heffer for consistency. He insists he would write *to go boldly*.)

Split infinitives are important for good English. They serve clarity by ensuring that the right word is unambiguously qualified by the adverb. Yes, some readers are annoyed by split infinitives; the *Times* Letters page gets a steady stream of complaints on the issue, which aren't published and which I reply to. But the claim to be offended is no more a knockdown argument in language than it is in politics. A more fruitful response is to explain the origins of this bogus rule and thereby lift from the complainer the burden of ever following it again.

Dummett is especially scathing about 'the multiple split', by which he means the insertion of more than one word between 'to' and the infinitive. Perhaps he never came across Byron's beautiful 'Love and Death': 'Nor can I blame thee, though it be my lot / To strongly, wrongly, vainly love thee still.'

style

The oddity of most style guides is that they generally deal with a small (and largely trivial) selection of disputed usages as if they were relevant to the question how to write well. They aren't. How to write well is a separate problem. You can adopt all the preferences of the sticklers and it will provide you with a set of prejudices; it won't enhance anyone's writing style. The only sensible advice a writer can give is twofold. Find a voice; and write in a way that the intelligent general reader will understand and not feel patronised by. Everything else is either detail or futility.

Voice is individual; it can't be taught but it can be encouraged. Watching the preposterous film *Anonymous* by Roland Emmerich, which dramatises the conspiracy theory that the works of Shakespeare were written by the Earl of Oxford, I laughed at a scene where Oxford roars to Ben Jonson: 'You have no voice!'

The notion that Jonson was a mere hack is almost as absurd as the rest of the film's thesis. But the scene stays with me because 'voice' is what writers need – not only writers of columns, poems and books, but also writers of business proposals, sports reports and love letters. If young writers gain the impression that they will be helped by adopting the imagery of others, their work will atrophy. It will not be interesting.

The best advice I have ever received on writing was from James Harding, then Editor of *The Times*, when I began my career as a leader writer on the newspaper in 2008. The news each day was dominated by the collapse of the global banking system. It was a subject I knew well and I wrote numerous editorials and opinion columns on the financial crisis and its economic consequences. They weren't very good. I was struggling to explain what I knew. James told me to write what I had just said at an editorial conference – meaning, to write it as I'd said it, rather than with the elaborateness that I'd previously approached the subject with.

Writing as if you're talking seems to me the best maxim you can have for a newspaper article, a letter or most other things apart from technical journal articles and legal documents (which are dense and technical because they have to be unambiguous). It's also a way of finding your voice – because it will be derived, literally, from what you say and how you say it. Adopting someone else's voice is the problem with cliché, where a writer is by definition using the words of someone else. Once you adopt that approach, it becomes instinctive and your prose is not so much written as compiled, with one overworked phrase latched on to another. Even the most eloquent remark is wearied by repetition. And this saps an author's identity. If, in expressing a thought, we reach for phrases that have been used before and that comfort us owing to their familiarity, we are adopting someone else's language. It is a small act of plagiarism.

That's about it. Mine is different from the normal run of advice on style, largely because I think most of the usual maxims are vacuous or impractical. Michael Gove, in his time as Education Secretary, exemplified this approach when he sent a memo to his civil servants setting out his requirements on drafting letters. He dubbed these recommendations 'Gove's Golden Rules'. The guidance is well intentioned and largely either futile or destructive.

Gove wants prose to be concise. He recommends cutting unnecessary words; adopting the active rather than passive voice; and using concrete words and phrases rather than abstractions. He believes that adjectives and adverbs add little. All of these are standard recommendations in style guides. They are not rules but preferences, indeed idiosyncrasies, apart from the one about excising unnecessary words, which is useless (because you need to know which are the unnecessary words). Gove's recommendations are not essential to good writing and can easily obstruct it. The passive voice is natural and informative in such constructions as 'President Kennedy was assassinated in 1963', because the important actor is the President rather than the assassin. And if the John Lewis store were to conclude that adverbs add little information, it could presumably amend its slogan *Never Knowingly Undersold* to *Undersold* (the example is Geoffrey Pullum's).

The most pleasurable of Gove's Golden Rules is: 'Read the great writers to improve your own prose – George Orwell and Evelyn Waugh, Jane Austen and George Eliot, Matthew Parris and Christopher Hitchens.' But, except in one respect (explained below), it isn't useful. A good writer is a source of pleasure and edification, not a template for your own prose. Nor is George Eliot, for all her literary accomplishments, the model of succinctness that Mr Gove seeks.

Clarity of language is a good thing. Brevity isn't necessarily. But aversion to cliché is to be encouraged, even though it's a fine judgment whether a phrase fits that description or is merely a standard idiom. A highly enjoyable way of telling the difference and inuring oneself to cliché is to read the comic novels of P. G. Wodehouse, and especially his stories about Jeeves. This is a lesson in how to improve your own prose, in the strictly negative sense of knowing what's a fresh use of language.

Bertie Wooster, the young master, is mentally negligible (the description is Jeeves's) but his use of language is always careful. When he uses cliché, he signals that he is aware of it. Take this passage from *The Mating Season*: 'Jeeves, in speaking of Fink-Nottle, had, if you remember, described him as disgruntled, and it was plain at a glance that the passage of time had done nothing to gruntle him. The eyes behind their horn-rimmed spectacles were burning with fury and resentment and all that sort of thing. He looked like a peevish halibut.'

What makes this passage work so well is not only the description of Fink-Nottle's fishy countenance, or the neologism *gruntle*. It is the phrase *and all that sort of thing*. Bertie is using a cliché *eyes burning with fury* for effect, which he then easily betters with his reference to a peevish halibut. That is the way to write. It can't be replicated, and that's not the point of observing its style. It tells you what a voice is.

The voice is essential. The audience is its hearer. I have read (and listened to) many academics, in particular, who appear – who *are* – indifferent to the people they're addressing. There is nothing wrong with JARGON in its place: all disciplines have their shorthand terms that specialists understand. But to a general audience, such terms are deadly. I had the same problem when writing for *Times* readers about the complex financial instruments that were central to the global banking crisis. There is no rule of language that will enable a writer to hook the attention of an audience. But the best discipline I know of is to have a mental picture of the people you're writing for.

Those I write for as a newspaper columnist are intelligent general readers. They are like the people I grew up with, or went to college with, or worked with, or met socially, who went on to have different interests and professions and areas of knowledge from mine. And when I write for them, I take for granted their ability to perceive complex arguments in a subject not their own, provided these are not larded with either shorthand terms or obviously strained analogies. I try to talk neither incomprehensibly nor down to them, knowing that they know in aggregate at least as much as I do. Think of your reader or listener as yourself, but one who knows different things.

I say that clarity of language is a good thing but this isn't universally believed. Note and avoid this kind of thing, kindly sent to me by a *Times* reader as a fine though far from rare example of a type of academic discourse:

> A certain constant manner of utterance, arising in the tropological space which at once reflects and refuses the vacancy of being, finding its own rule of dispersion in the capacity of words to say the same thing in different ways or to say different things with the same words, circling back on itself to take its own modality of articulation as its signified, coming to an end as arbitrarily as it began, but leaving a verbal something in the place of the nothing that occasioned it – all this can stand for discourse as well as style ...
>
> Hayden White, *The Content of the Form: Narrative Discourse and Historical Representation* (Baltimore and London: Johns Hopkins University Press, 1987), pp. 110f.

What does it mean? Who can tell? I have a suspicion that this form of writing is more prevalent in some academic disciplines (principally, of all things, literary criticism) than others but that may simply be because I've come across it in those subjects.

See also JARGON, GOBBLEDEGOOK and SENTENCES.

subjunctive

The Fowlers described the subjunctive as 'almost meaningless to Englishmen, the thing having so nearly perished'. This was in 1906, in their book *The King's English*. Usage pundits have been predicting the death or at least terminal decline of the subjunctive ever since. It's not true, except in one limited and painless respect.

The subjunctive is not a tense but a mood. It is mainly used in clauses about things that do not (or do not yet) exist, but are requested, demanded, specified, suggested or ordered. In the present tense of the subjunctive, the verb has the same form as the infinitive (*the Editor requests that the columnist arrive on time for once*). The subjunctive mood contrasts with the indicative mood, which expresses facts (*the columnist arrives on time for once*).

Questions about when to use the subjunctive mainly arise with the verb *to be*. According to traditional grammarians, in counter-factual conditional clauses you should use *were* rather than *was*. They refer to this as the subjunctive – and, for the sake of argument, I use that term here even though recent scholars of language refer to it instead as the irrealis.

Here's an example from Jane Austen's *Pride and Prejudice*: ' "If I were as rich as Mr Darcy," cried a young Lucas who came with his sisters, "I should not care how proud I was." '

Lucas is using the subjunctive (more accurately, the irrealis) *were* in the counterfactual conditional of being as rich as Mr Darcy. That accords with the grammar of Standard English. It would also accord with the grammar of Standard English to say *if I was as rich as Mr Darcy*... Sticklers would object to *was* instead of *were* but they'd be wrong: it's just less formal.

Yet note the caution of *Merriam-Webster*: 'It should be remarked that *if* and *as if* do not always introduce an unreal condition and therefore *if* and *as if* do not necessarily call for a subjunctive.'

That's right. Here's an example of where *if* does not introduce an unreal condition: **Couples who tied the knot in the 1950s and 1970s were a third more likely to divorce if the woman were cleverer than the man, compared with the other way round.**

I'd count that ungrammatical. The subjunctive (irrealis) form *were* has been used even though the writer is not stating a hypothetical condition.

My theory is that the inaccurate use of *were* happens because sticklers spread confusion by making a shibboleth of the subjunctive. For example, Heffer insists that it's mandatory to use the subjunctive *be* as he does here: 'Though I be prejudiced, I feel my wife is beautiful.'

I don't believe that any native English speaker since about 1900 has said anything like this, apart from Heffer himself. You are highly unlikely to get tripped up by the subjunctive if you say what comes naturally to you. I cannot resist ending this entry with a letter sent to *The Times* by an irate reader who really was completely unconcerned about the indicative and subjunctive moods, and as the letter was intended for publication I see no harm in reproducing it:

Dear Sir/Madam,

I read today's Times and especially the letters page hoping to see an apology or an explanation for the AWFUL T2 front page headline 'If she <u>weren't</u> a millionaire, she...' We wonder why people can't spell or differentiate between singular and plural if the Times does this!!

supersede

The word is a transitive verb meaning *replace* or *supplant*. You sometimes find it spelt *supercede*. That is a non-Standard spelling that sticklers care about a lot. 'There is', says Cochrane simply and contemptuously, 'no such word as *supercede.*'

He's wrong. There is such a word as *supercede*; it just isn't in current use. It's wearyingly common for self-appointed usage experts not to check things in the dictionary before ululating about the state of the language. The earliest use of *supersede* that the *OED* gives (in the obsolete sense of *postpone* or *defer*) is from 1491. And guess what: it's spelt *supercede*.

A word's origin doesn't dictate its current spelling or meaning but many people mistakenly believe otherwise and *supersede* is one word whose etymology is often overlooked. It comes from the Latin verb *supersedere*, meaning *be superior to*. The *OED* notes, however, that it comes to the language by the Old French verb *superceder* – which was later spelt *superseder*.

When *supercede* crops up in modern English prose, the writer is probably assuming that it follows the same form as the verbs *accede* or *intercede*. Hence pedants with a smattering of Latin derived from style guides have their grievance. Yet the *supercede* spelling does have etymological justification and it appears in the dictionary.

My recommendation on this question is in two parts. First, do write *supersede*, because that's the modern convention of usage. Second, don't bawl out people who write it as *supercede*: their spelling is not the conventional one but it has a history and you can see in any event how this variant spelling arises.

tenses, sequence of

Tense is the form of a verb that indicates what time it refers to. When you put a verb in the present tense into the past tense, other verbs in the sentence may change their tense too. Thus *I know that the rule against split infinitives is bogus* becomes *I knew that the rule against split infinitives was bogus*. Changing the tense in that way is known as the sequence of tenses. *Merriam-Webster* sensibly advises that such locutions have been debated for centuries and you'll be happier if you don't worry about them. If the situation the sentence describes is a timeless fact, such as the bogusness of the rule against split infinitives, it would be more idiomatic not to bother changing the tense at all: *I knew that the rule against split infinitives is bogus.*

See also HISTORIC PRESENT.

testimony

A *Times* reader holding a senior judicial post wrote to me once to take exception to this sentence from a report: **In a two-page exposé, *Rochdale's Alternative Paper* set out the testimonies of boys subjected to 'medical inspection' by the local MP.**

His argument was that *testimony* is a mass noun, not a count noun, and thus that the plural form *testimonies* doesn't exist.

Well, it does. In one sense of the word (the precepts of divine law), it rarely exists outside the plural form: 'Ye shall diligently keep the commandments of the Lord your God, and his testimonies, and his statutes, which he hath commanded thee' (Deuteronomy 6:17).

The objection is an unusual example of the stickler fallacy of insisting that a usage can't be a 'real word'. It's possible for highly educated and intelligent people to go through life under this misapprehension, which could be dispelled by consulting a good dictionary. If it's in use, lexicographers record it. If it's recorded, it's a real word.

than, as

Should you say *I am not as clever as she* or *I am not as clever as her*? How about *she is cleverer than I* or *she is cleverer than me*? The eighteenth-century grammarians provided an answer that is not wrong but that became a shibboleth for determining the case of the pronoun. They determined that *as* and *than* were conjunctions, which precede a clause. They then devised the rule that there was a tacit verb after the conjunctions *than* or *as*, and that this determined the correct case of a succeeding pronoun. Thus, according to the sticklers, it must be *I am not as clever as she [is]* and *she is cleverer than I [am]*; the noun phrases that follow the conjunctions are the subject of the clause in which there is a tacit verb. Thus the pronouns need to be in the subject case: *I* not *me*, *he* not *him*, *we* not *us*.

Forget it. Both subject and object pronouns are fine in that position. Here is Satan speaking in Milton's *Paradise Lost*: 'I know thee not, nor ever saw till now / Sight more detestable than him and thee.'

The grammarians misinterpreted the grammar. They decided that *than* and *as*, being conjunctions, couldn't serve as prepositions. In fact, *than* is both a subordinating conjunction, as in *my mother is cleverer than I am*, and a preposition, as in *my mother is cleverer than me*. Both are completely acceptable usages in Standard English, never mind any other type. Modern grammarians regard *than* and *as* as prepositions that have sentences as their complements. Whether you use the subject or the object case of the pronoun is purely a question of style. Either is correct.

that, which

Heffer laments: 'It is probably not an exaggeration to say that almost everyone believes they are in most contexts interchangeable.'

Indeed. In the case of relative clauses, almost everyone does believe this and almost everyone is right. It's only usage pundits who disagree, and maintain what's known as the *that/which* rule.

Of course there are constructions in which the words are not interchangeable – but no one tries interchanging them. *That* but not *which* can introduce a noun clause (or argument clause or content clause), and *which* but not *that* can be used as a determiner with a plural noun (so *which books* but not *that books*). But it's a waste of time to worry about the choice of *that* or *which* as a relative pronoun. Your meaning will be clear with either, so long as you are careful about punctuation. Even then, your meaning will probably be clear from the context.

The rule concerns what are known as relative clauses. Take this sentence: *The article, which the columnist submitted before going to lunch, was full of mistakes.* The words between the commas form a relative clause. If you deleted them, the sentence would not only make complete grammatical sense but also convey the essential point that the article was full of mistakes. The clause provides supplementary information about the sentence's subject (namely, the article).

Now consider this sentence: *The newspaper that employs the greedy columnist has run out of blueberry muffins.* The words *that employs the greedy columnist* also form a relative clause. But here it's not just additional information: it specifically identifies which newspaper it is that has run out of blueberry muffins.

A relative clause that adds extra information, not essential to understanding the sentence, is called non-restrictive. In the sentence about the error-ridden article, it's separated from the main clause by a pair of commas. These function as a pair of brackets would do.

A relative clause that is essential to determining the reference is known as restrictive. It isn't just any newspaper that has run out of blueberry muffins: it's the one employing the greedy columnist. To denote that the clause is restrictive, there are no commas.

Here's where the *that/which* rule comes in. Sticklers insist on *that* rather than *which* in a restrictive clause, and *which* rather than *that* in a non-restrictive clause. They argue that a defining relative clause (that is, one that provides essential information about the noun it modifies) must be introduced with *that* rather than *which*. As Heffer puts it: '*That* defines; *which* is parenthetic.'

One thing you won't find in style guides that advocate the *that/which* rule is the slightest substantiation for it. You're supposed to accept it on trust, apparently. Don't bother. For centuries, great writers have used *which* instead of *that* in precisely the way that the sticklers condemn.

Matthew's Gospel in the King James Bible has Jesus say: 'Render therefore unto Caesar the things which are Caesar's; and unto God the things that are God's.' What do you know? Here are two defining relative clauses, yet the relative pronouns *that* and *which* are used interchangeably. One introduces the first clause, and the other introduces the second.

The imaginary, pointless, time-wasting rule is often attributed to Fowler. His argument is that there would be a gain 'in lucidity and in ease' if writers did adopt the convention of using *that* for defining relative clauses and *which* for non-defining ones. But he doesn't claim that such a rule actually exists; on the contrary, he says, 'it would be idle to pretend that it is the practice either of most or of the best writers'.

In fact, there are earlier examples of grammarians coming up with the *that/which* rule. Alfred Ayres, a nineteenth-century author on elocution and pronunciation, produced a book called *The English grammar of William Cobbett. Carefully revised and annotated* (1883). His careful 'corrections' included changing Cobbett's prose to make it conform to the *that/which rule*. In any event, Fowler's proposal was more moderate and has been misapplied as an inviolable rule.

they

They is the third-person plural pronoun. It is also a singular generic pronoun. The second of those characteristics prompts ferocious denials from sticklers, sometimes coupled with familiar denunciations of those barbarians who would subject language to social engineering, impose political correctness – and all the catechism of the pedants.

Heffer is typical in expostulating: 'We have no single pronoun to cover the phrases *he-or-she*, *him-or-her* and *his-or-her*. An attempt has been made in the last century or so to fill this void with *they*, *them* and *their*. I regard that as abominable and want no part in it.'

The pedants' case is that English does, in fact, have a genderless third-person singular pronoun. It is *he*. Confusion arises only because this generic pronoun is the same word as the masculine third-person singular pronoun. In Matthew's Gospel, Jesus declares: 'He that findeth his life shall lose it: and he that loseth his life for my sake shall find it.' The 'he' and 'his' in the Sermon on the Mount are generic.

The pedants are wrong on two grounds: *they* is a singular and a plural pronoun; and *he* is not any longer plausible as a generic pronoun.

Let's take them in turn. On the strict question of number, the issue about *they* is the reverse of the issue about *none*. *None* is held by the sticklers to be irrevocably singular, as a contraction of *not* and *one*. They are wrong. As we've seen, *none* can be either singular or plural. It is generally plural (*none are*) if you're considering an entire group and singular (*none is*) if you're referring to a specific member of that group.

The same is true with *they*. It is singular and it's plural. Or it can refer to neither singular nor plural but be what linguists term a placeholder – roughly a filler word, denoting something or someone whose identity is unknown (such as *wotsisface*). Pinker gives the example of this sentence: *Everyone returned to their seats*. To the sticklers, this is ungrammatical: *everyone*, they insist, means *every one*, which is singular. So there is a singular subject with a plural pronoun. It should be *everyone returned to his seat*.

The sticklers' solution ought to make you uneasy. It suggests an entire audience returning to a single seat. The reason for the unease is that *everyone* does not refer to any specific person. It is equivalent, explains Pinker, to saying, *For all X, X returned to X's seat*.

Pinker adds that the sticklers might try rewriting this 'ungrammatical' sentence: *Mary saw everyone before John noticed them*. It would be absurd to replace *them* with *him*. The pronoun is referring to a group and it should be plural.

Those examples demonstrate the legitimacy of *they* where the pedants insist there must be a singular pronoun. This is a point about language, not political correctness. The second objection to the pedants' case is, however, that if you did rewrite the sentence as *Mary saw everyone before John noticed him* you would feel that dogmatism was triumphing over common sense. So it would, and to the exclusion of any female member of the group referred to.

Now, I am sceptical of the notion (popularised by George Orwell's brilliant invention of Newspeak in *Nineteen Eighty-Four*) that language imposes on its users a particular view of the world. Scholars know this argument as the Sapir–Whorf hypothesis. It's a very common assumption that the way we use language determines, or at least shapes, the way we see the external world, including social relations, but it's highly implausible. (Pinker briskly describes such linguistic determinism as 'wrong, all wrong'.) In practice, we put names to things because they are important: things do not become important merely because we name them.

Using *he* as a generic singular pronoun doesn't condition people to regard women as second-class citizens. Changes in the social world, such as the advancement of sexual equality, shape our understanding of language, not the other way round. However, there is still exceptionally an inescapably gendered connotation to the use of *he* and *him*, which has become more noticeable as the position of women has advanced in society. The fact that in most contexts when people use *he* and *his* they do refer to someone male, and contrast this pronoun and possessive to *she* and *her*, is enough to resist broadening the concept to include both sexes.

I do not believe that there is any linguistic objection to using *they, them* and *their* as singular generic terms. Nor is anything lost in meaning. Nor is it any longer possible to argue with a straight face that the personal pronoun *he* and the generic pronoun *he* are different words that just happen to be spelt and pronounced the same way.

If, however, you're in any doubt, turn to Jane Austen, who habitually used *they, them* and *their* in precisely the way condemned by the sticklers. Examples appear in each of her completed novels.

Northanger Abbey: 'With whomsoever he was, or was likely to be connected, his own consequence always required that theirs should be great, and as his intimacy with any acquaintance grew, so regularly grew their fortune.'

Mansfield Park: 'So far from being all satisfied and all enjoying, she found everybody requiring something they had not, and giving occasion of discontent to the others. Everybody had a part either too long or too short; nobody would attend as they ought; nobody would remember on which side they were to come in; nobody but the complainer would observe any directions.'

Persuasion: 'She did not blame Lady Russell, she did not blame herself for having been guided by her; but she felt that were any young person, in similar circumstances, to apply to her for counsel, they would never receive any of such certain immediate wretchedness, such uncertain future good.'

Pride and Prejudice: 'All Meryton seemed striving to blacken the man, who, but three months before, had been almost an angel of light… Every body declared that he was the wickedest young man in the world; and every body began to find out that they had always distrusted the appearance of his goodness.'

Sense and Sensibility: 'The sudden termination of Colonel Brandon's visit at the Park, with his steadiness in concealing its cause, filled the mind, and raised the wonder, of Mrs. Jennings for two or three days: she was a great wonderer, as every one must be who takes a very lively interest in all the comings and goings of all their acquaintance.'

Emma: '[Mr. Woodhouse] was happily placed, quite at his ease, ready to talk with pleasure of what had been achieved, and advise every body to come and sit down, and not to heat themselves.'

Singular *they* is idiomatic and grammatical, and has been used extensively and to effect by the greatest writers in the language. What more evidence do the pedants need? None, of course, because evidence is not how they proceed – but that's another matter.

See also NONE and NUMBER.

till

Bryson declares trenchantly that *until* and *till* are interchangeable whereas *'til* and *'till* are 'wrong, and indeed illiterate'.

Not quite. *Till* and *until* are indeed interchangeable. They both mean *to the time that*. Some people are under the impression that the first is an illegitimate shortening of the second but this is not true. Both have been in use for something like 800 years. Though some usage guides count *till* less formal than *until*, it is appropriate in any form of writing. The contraction *'til* genuinely is a short form of *until*, and so by extension is *'till*. They're not illiterate; they're just newer, being twentieth-century coinages.

try and, try to

There is a widespread prejudice against the phrase *try and* as opposed to *try to*, as used here: **The secret is time travel, and it's up to one lowly elf, voiced by Martin Freeman, to rewind time and try and stop Santa's sleigh falling into the wrong hands.**

The reasoning is stated by Bierce: ' "I will try and see him." This plainly says that my effort to see him will succeed – which I cannot know and do not wish to affirm. "Please try and come." This colloquial slovenliness of speech is almost universal in this country, but freedom of speech is one of our most precious possessions.'

Nonsense. *Try and see* may be slightly less formal than *try to see* but there's nothing slovenly, let alone ungrammatical, about it. It's Standard English.

The idiom *try and* has a long history in English usage. It dates from at least the seventeenth century and there are many examples in English literature. 'All that Molly could do was … to try and heal up any breaches which might have occurred between him and Aimee,' writes Mrs Gaskell in *Wives and Daughters*. 'The proper aim is to try and reconstruct society on such a basis that poverty will be impossible,' writes Oscar Wilde in *The Soul of Man Under Socialism*.

Even so, critics of the phrase maintain that it lacks logic. Their argument goes like this. If you *try and stop* something, you are engaged in two different actions: trying and stopping. The lowly elf was engaged in only one action, though. He was trying to stop something, instead of trying – and then stopping something.

This reasoning lacks merit. First, even if *try and stop* were illogical, that wouldn't make it ungrammatical. Second, there are many phrases in English that conform to the same pattern as *try and stop*. Go and get me a blueberry muffin; then come and find me. These phrases don't imply two actions that are simultaneous. They imply an action that is dependent on the going, coming, trying or whatever.

Fowler sensibly observes that, 'though "try to do" can always be substituted for "try and do", the latter has a shade of meaning that justifies its existence'.

By all means insist on *try to*, if you prefer it. There is no reason, though, to regard *try and* as poor English. It's an idiomatic and entirely legitimate phrase.

unique

Sticklers maintain that *unique* is one of a group of ABSOLUTE ADJECTIVES. Being an absolute adjective, it should not be used in the comparative (*more unique*), in the superlative (*most unique*) or with an intensifier (*very unique*). As Gwynne puts it: 'Note that "unique" (meaning "the only one of its kind"), "peerless", "matchless" (both of which mean "without equal"), "infinite" and "eternal" cannot have comparatives or superlatives.'

Gwynne says that those who violate his rule this way are ignorant. Yet capable authors do, in fact, use absolute adjectives in precisely that way. What the sticklers say cannot happen, does happen.

Here is Charlotte Brontë, from *Villette*: ' "A very unique child," thought I, as I viewed her sleeping countenance by the fitful moonlight, and cautiously and softly wiped her glittering eyelids and her wet cheeks with my handkerchief.'

Here is Ayesha, the immortal sorceress, speaking in H. Rider Haggard's novel *She*: 'For thou didst forget that where they have gone there may be others even more peerless than thou art and more fit to hold a woman's love.'

Renowned writers turn out yet again not to adhere to the purported rules. Adjectives that supposedly shouldn't (or, as Gwynne maintains, 'cannot') be compared or modified, regularly are.

The adjective *unique* is regularly modified by adverbs such as *almost*, without destroying its sense of being *the only one of its kind*. Moreover, that is far from being the only definition of *unique*. The *OED* also gives definitions of its being unrivalled, especially in excellence, and – 'loosely' – unusual or remarkable. The use of an intensifier with *unique* in both these senses is fine and idiomatic.

uptalk

This useful word describes the practice of ending a clause with a rising intonation, as if it were a question. Linguists refer to it as a high-rising terminal and have traced it back to New Zealand in the 1970s. It has spread rapidly since then in English-speaking countries, especially among the young. Some pundits interpret it as defensive, even apologetic, in tone, with the speaker implicitly seeking reassurance from the listener.

One survey of senior managers in commerce indicated that uptalk would affect an employee's prospects for promotion, on the grounds that it was an indicator of underlying insecurity and diffidence. That's just prejudice. Every generation has its mannerisms and idiosyncrasies of speech. These may be confusing to others yet they are fully expressive. The manner of speech in films as recent as those of the 1950s sounds affected by the standards of today; that doesn't make it comic or ineffective.

Uptalk is a modern mannerism that is quite a polite way of drawing people into the conversation. And as it is a practice strictly of spoken English, it has no bearing at all on standards of literacy.

uxorious

A man who is *uxorious* has extreme fondness for his wife. Note, however, that to describe a married man as *uxorious* carries the pejorative implication of excessive attachment. As so often, Byron paid close attention to language when, in his epic poem *Don Juan*, he wrote: 'The same things change their names at such a rate; / For instance – Passion in a lover's glorious, / But in a husband is pronounced uxorious.'

The related term *uxorial*, incidentally, is a neutral adjective that means simply *of or pertaining to wifeliness*. There is also the phenomenon of excessive fondness of one's husband. Everyone knows the type of thing. In a memorable scene in *Asterix and the Soothsayer*, Impedimenta, the chieftain's wife, addresses her husband as Piggy-Wiggy, to the hilarity of Asterix and Obelix. There is a word for this analogue of uxoriousness: it is *maritality*. To say this is an uncommon word is to understate it.

very

Two issues of usage are raised by *very*. The first is whether it can be used to modify a participle used as an adjective. Some sticklers object to the practice but they're wrong and rarely consistent about it.

Some participles are used as adjectives. A participial adjective generally ends in -*ed* (past participle) or -*ing* (present participle). We use a past participle to describe how someone feels (for example, *bored*) and a present participle to describe what or who causes the feeling (*boring*).

The question is whether these can be modified by *very* (*very bored*) or whether they need to be modified by *much*. The intensifier *very* can't modify verbs, which is the root of the pedantic objection that they can't modify participles. We get contrasts such as that between s*he was very entertaining*, which is a possible construction and where *entertaining* is an adjective, and s*he was very entertaining the troops*, which isn't possible and where it is a verb. Similarly, consider the contrast between *she was very surprised*, where *surprised* is an adjective, and (which isn't possible) s*he has very surprised everyone*, where it is a verb.

In fact, there is nothing wrong with this practice; it depends on usage. It's fine to use *very* with a participial adjective as here in Edgar Wallace's *The Man Who Knew*: 'His beat was a lonely one, and he was a very bored man.'

It would sound not quite right, however, to say in an obituary that the deceased was *very missed*. It would be more common to say that they were *much missed*. At any moment, participles will have been accepted into usage as adjectives. There is no definitive rule about when this happens. It depends upon convention. There is no violation of grammar when they do. Words take modifiers according to their function within a sentence. *Very* modifies adjectives with appropriate meanings, including adjectives derived from participles. Hence we get *very surprising*, *very entertaining*, *very distressed*, *very frightened*, and so on.

In the case of past participles the adjectives generally have a passive meaning, and you can sometimes add the prefix *un-* when it is not possible with the basic verb. Hence we get a contrast between *the story was unreported* and (which isn't possible) *they have unreported the story*.

The second dispute about *very* concerns whether writers should use it at all. The purist advocate of omitting needless words would dispense with this intensifier altogether. But it has its uses because intensifiers allow us to economically express degrees of something. It would be hard to find a writer who had no need of *very* and a good writer can use it effectively, as James Joyce does in opening *A Portrait of the Artist as a Young Man*: 'Once upon a time and a very good time it was there was a moocow coming down along the road…'

warn

The verb *warn* is, say the sticklers, always and only transitive: it requires an object. You must warn someone of something. If not, you are *giving warning*. Heffer laments: 'We often read in newspapers that somebody has *warned* that something will happen. This is ungrammatical. The verb "warn" is transitive: it requires an object. Somebody has to be warned.'

Why sticklers should think this is far from clear. It's perfectly possible to warn in general without having anyone specific in mind. It's equivalent to *giving warning*; it's up to whoever hears it whether to heed it. Verbs of exhortation, admonition, advising and urging are all widely used intransitively. There is no reason to respect the sticklers' insistence that *warn* be transitive exclusively and for ever. Its use intransitively in a range of constructions dates from the early twentieth century.

who, whom

The term for a change of grammatical case is inflection. Only eight words in the language inflect by having different forms for the nominative (subject) and accusative (object) case. They are all pronouns.

These pronouns are *I* (*me*), *he* (*him*), *she* (*her*), *we* (*us*), *they* (*them*), *who* (*whom*), *whoever* (*whomever*) and *whosoever* (*whomsoever*). The last is archaic. Its use in the King James Bible ('for whosoever will save his life shall lose it: and whosoever will lose his life for my sake shall find it') should be realised, but I cannot think of a good reason to write it. The other pronouns, however, are indispensable. Using *whom* for the subject case is thought of by the sticklocracy as a particularly bad mistake.

Who and *whom* are known as relative (as opposed to personal) pronouns. A relative pronoun introduces a relative clause and has the same reference as an antecedent. A common construction condemned by the sticklers takes this form: **A couple of years ago, at a party, I got chatting to someone from The Times whom I presumed worked on the sports desk.**

In this sentence, the antecedent is *someone from The Times*. The case of the relative pronoun is then determined by the role that it plays in the relative clause. In this case, the pronoun is the subject of the verb *work*. So the Standard usage would be *who I presumed worked*.

The reason for non-Standard usages is almost invariably the use of parenthetical phrases. In the example I have quoted, *I presumed* is in effect a parenthetical phrase. The traditional advice is that if you are in doubt about whether to write *who* or *whom*, place brackets or commas round the parenthetical phrase, or remove it altogether, and then see how the sentence then reads. In constructions like these, traditionalists would regard *whom* as an instance of hypercorrection, the mistaken application of a non-Standard form by analogy with what is thought to be correct. The Fowlers describe this non-Standard use of *whom* as a 'gross error'.

I sometimes write *whom* in accordance with the convention that this is the form you adopt for the object case (it depends on the register I'm adopting) but I almost never use it in speech. Were *whom* to disappear from the language, its absence would cause no loss of clarity for readers while sparing confusion on the part of writers.

Edward Sapir, the American linguist, wrote a book called *Language: An Introduction to the Study of Speech* nearly a century ago, in which he advanced several reasons for doubting the usefulness and durability of *whom*. Sapir noted what is obvious in modern English: *who* is already widely used as an invariable relative pronoun (that is, it's used for both subject and object). Few people would count this wrong in written English, and I'm not among them; at worst, it's merely informal.

But even that mild criticism seems to me misplaced. There is no reason why *who* should be rejected for the object case, any more than we look askance at the use for both subject and object of the relative pronouns *which*, *what* and *that*. There's also a good reason why few people now use *whom* in speech: it sounds fussy and slows the sentence down. Where a speaker has to make a conscious effort to use *whom*, at odds with the patterns of spontaneous spoken English, there is no necessity to do it. Nor are there grounds for insisting that children learn to speak and write that way.

The non-Standard *whom* construction, which is widespread and longstanding, does have its defenders. My late and venerable colleague Philip Howard argued in his book *The State of the Language* (1986) that *whom* should be allowed 'if between the relative pronoun and its verb there are inserted two or more words, of which one is itself a verb'. Thus it would be permissible to refer to *the indolent columnist whom the Editor thinks does too little work*. Jespersen maintains that native speakers use *whom* in this type of construction 'because the speech-instinct would be bewildered by the contiguity of two nominatives, as it were two nominatives in the same clause'.[6]

My advice if you're in any doubt whether to use *who* or *whom*, however, is to stick with *who*. Nobody but a stickler will fault you for anything worse than informality, and that is no sin.

whoever, whomever

What applies to the relative pronoun *who/whom* applies also to *whoever/whomever*. The convolutions of a sentence sometimes make this difficult to spot.

A column I once wrote for the *Jewish Chronicle* included this sentence: 'Yet consider the effect his release would have on other intelligence analysts tempted to divulge information to whoever they think merits it.'

In the printed edition, *whoever* had been altered to *whomever*. I asked the Comment Editor to change it back to *whoever* in the online edition, which she immediately and graciously did.

My judgment was the one held by traditional grammarians, who would say that *whomever* in that construction is an error. Their reasoning runs like this.

Whoever governs a relative clause. Here it functions as a relative pronoun and is the subject of the relative clause. It should thus take the subject case rather than the object case. Dummett maintains: 'When "whoever" is used, the pronoun belonging to the main clause is understood (i.e. tacit). It is therefore wrong to write "whomever" just because the tacit pronoun preceding "whoever" should be in the accusative, as is nowadays commonly done.'

In my slightly ungainly sentence, *whoever* is the subject of *merits it*. Why did the sub-editors believe that the pronoun needed instead to be in the object case? Probably for two reasons. First, the pronoun is preceded by the preposition *to*, causing the sub-editors to think that it's the object of the main clause. Second, the pronoun is separated from the verb by the words *they think*. That is, however, a parenthetical phrase; it has no bearing on the case of the pronoun.

See, however, the argument in WHO, WHOM made by some grammarians that the non-Standard usage is legitimate and not an instance of hypercorrection. Exactly the same case can be made with the non-Standard use of *whomever*.

My caveat is the same as that with *whom*, however. The use of *whomever* is likely to diminish, if not die out entirely, with no ill effect on clarity or meaning. And no one will object plausibly in the meantime if you simply stop using it, which is a course I recommend.

wise

The word *wise* is now rarely used as a noun, but it does appear. It means method or manner. The phrases *in any wise* and *in no wise* are recognisably but not only biblical. The translators of the King James Bible give to Jesus, in John's Gospel, the words: 'All that the Father giveth me shall come to me; and him that cometh to me I will in no wise cast out.' The Book of Revelation describes the heavenly city: 'And there shall in no wise enter into it any thing that defileth...' Daniel Defoe notes in his *Journal of a Plague Year* that 'the shutting up of houses was in no wise to be depended upon'.

I once included the phrase *in no wise* in a *Times* leader. The sub-editors, either not recognising it or considering it an archaism, changed it to *in no way*, which was fair enough.

wrong, wrongly

Wrong is an adjective. It's also an adverb. (It's also, of course, a noun and a verb.) *Wrongly* is an adverb. Because *wrongly* exists, some people imagine that the adverbial use of *wrong* is an error. I fielded a number of complaints when this sentence appeared in *The Times*: **Denis MacShane, the former Labour minister, deliberately spelt his name wrong on bogus invoices to cover up his expenses fiddling, the Old Bailey was told yesterday.**

The gravamen of the objection was that if MacShane had spelt his name *Mr Wrong* instead of *Mr MacShane*, it was no wonder he was found out.

How witty. Except there's nothing wrong with this use of *wrong*. In the choice between *wrong* and *wrongly*, write what seems more natural. Usually, it will be *wrong*, if it comes after the verb, as in this case. And usually, it will be *wrongly* if the adverb precedes the verb, as here, from Dickens's *Bleak House*: 'Under cover of the night, the feeble-minded beadle comes flitting about Chancery Lane with his summonses, in which every Juror's name is wrongly spelt, and nothing rightly spelt but the beadle's own name...'

The rule does not always hold. *Merriam-Webster* adds a qualification that only *wrongly* will do if there is a sense of unfairness involved, whether or not the adverb precedes the adverb that it's qualifying (for example, *politicians are stigmatised wrongly for the greed of a few of them*). That sounds right (not 'rightly').

yourself, yourselves

Sticklers are incensed at the way reflexive pronouns (*myself, yourself, himself, herself, ourselves, yourselves* and *themselves*) are used in constructions that are not reflexive or not intensive (i.e. for emphasis).

Heffer asserts: 'What it emphatically is not is a synonym for the personal pronoun in any of its cases. Phrases such as "he gave it to myself" or "I see yourself there" are sheer abominations.'

That's overstating it. It is poor grammar and style to say *he gave it to myself* but reflexive pronouns have, and have had, all sorts of uses apart from that of emphasis. There are plenty of acceptable cases of a reflexive pronoun without an antecedent in the same clause.

See the entry on MYSELF for some of them. The particular value of the reflexive pronouns *yourself* and *yourselves* is that they make a distinction between singular and plural. That distinction doesn't exist with the personal pronoun *you*, which is both singular and plural. Other languages, such as French and German, distinguish between singular and plural *you*; English doesn't, and the non-emphatic use of reflexive pronouns can provide that shade of meaning.

See also MYSELF.

Acknowledgements

This book would be worse but for the advice of expert linguists in both senses of that term.

My mother, Anthea Bell, has been an inspiration to me all my life for her knowledge of languages and literature, and for much else.

Bob Borsley, professor of linguistics at Essex University, has been an invaluable and patient guide to scholarly debates about language and has saved me from many errors of fact and interpretation. Whatever mistakes remain are no fault of his.

I am fortunate to be able to expound my views on English usage regularly in *The Times*, and am grateful to John Witherow, Emma Tucker, James Harding, Keith Blackmore, Roger Alton, Simon Pearson and Ian Brunskill for their tolerance and support of 'The Pedant' column over the years.

Thanks too to the many *Times* readers who've written to me with queries, concerns and opinions about language. They are too numerous to name individually but I should mention two in particular for their illuminating comments on grammar: Dr Lindsay Hall, whose knowledge of Classics I have ransacked in various parts of this book; and Mr N. J. Dawood, translator of the Koran and works of Arabic literature into English.

Bea Hemming at Weidenfeld & Nicolson, ably assisted by Holly Harley, provided staunch encouragement and wise editorial advice in writing this book. Whenever I was minded not to heed their suggestions, I belatedly realised I was wrong. My agent, Will Francis of Janklow & Nesbit, was a believer and ally in the project from the outset. Tom Freeman (http://stroppyeditor.wordpress.com) made penetrating comments on an early draft. I have learnt much from the writings of Professor Steven Pinker and Professor James Shapiro, and am honoured to have their endorsements for this book.

I'm fortunate in the support of family, friends and colleagues including David Aaronovitch, Katherine Arora, Andrew Bailey, Gerard Baker, Martin Bell, Melissa Bell, Sharon Bell, Jessica Carsen, Tom Chivers, Michelle Chivunga, Professor Patricia Clavin, Nick Cohen, Philip Collins, Robert Crampton, Daniel Finkelstein, Jonathan Freedland, Laura Freeman, Myrto Gelati, the late Norman Geras, Francesca Gonshaw, Professor Colleen Graffy, Nigel Hankin, Gina Higgins, the late Christopher Hitchens, Sir Simon Jenkins, Alexandra Kamm, Eileen Kamm, Eleanor Kamm, Richard Kamm, Hannah Kaye, Philippe Legrain, Anna Mandoki, Beth McCann, Sarah McMahon, Robbie Millen, Alex O'Connell, Peter Oppenheimer, Agnès Poirier, Stephen Pollard, Colin Proudman, Sylvia Proudman, John Rentoul, Hugo Rifkind, Alice Thomson, Francis Wheen, Giles Whittell and Arani Yogadeva. I owe a particular debt to Dr Jeremy Nathan, Dr Annemarie O'Connor and Lord (Dennis) Stevenson.

Notes

Introduction

1. Some of the most strident campaigners against 'bad grammar' literally don't know what they're talking about. Hadley Freeman, a *Guardian* columnist and judge for a venture called the Bad Grammar Awards, congratulates herself on knowing 'the subjunctive tense'. There's no such thing: the subjunctive is a mood, not a tense. See Hadley Freeman, 'Humanity's future depends on good grammar', 2 May 2014, at: http://www.theguardian.com/books/booksblog/2014/may/02/bad-grammar-award-judge-hadley-freeman

2. An influential exposition of the reasons for this sort of linguistic change is made by Deborah Cameron in *Verbal Hygiene*, Abingdon, Oxon: Routledge Linguistics Classics, 2012, especially Chapter 4. She argues (p. 164): 'I am not claiming that the ways of using words which I criticize are "abuses" or "perversions"; I am not accusing the people I disagree with of attacking "the language" or breaking a sacred contract. I am simply reserving the right – which I must also grant to them, and to everyone else – to engage in arguments about how language ought to be used.'

Part One

1 The State of the Language

1. Henry Sweet (1845–1912) was the dominant British figure in the early twentieth century in the scientific study of language. He was a philologist (philology is the study of how language develops), who did much work on Anglo-Saxon and the history of English. He also did important work on Welsh. A photograph shows him to have borne a striking facial resemblance to Theodore Roosevelt.

2. Lynne Truss, *Eats, Shoots & Leaves*, London: Profile Books, 2003, p. 2

3. In the mid-1990s, only half of children in England reached the expected level of literacy for their age. That figure had improved to 80 per cent by 2012. According to the National Literacy Trust: 'Current literacy levels also represent a significant improvement in children's skills since the mid-20th century, since targets apply to all children, of all abilities and social classes, including those who speak English as an additional language.' See its report *Literacy: State of the Nation* (2012) at: http://www.literacytrust.org.uk/about/faqs/filter/about literacy in the uk

4. Seriously, I'm not. You can watch the debate here: http://www.intelligencesquared.com/events/between-you-and-i-the-english-language-is-going-to-the-dogs/

5. These errors may have political consequences. A pro-Israeli pressure group complained in 2003 about bias in Reuters' reporting of the Middle East. It based this claim on the number of times that journalists used the passive voice in reporting Palestinian acts of violence. Unfortunately, the study showed a ruinous inability to understand what the passive voice is. One exhibit was the headline 'New West Bank Shooting Mars Truce' – even though it is entirely in the active voice. See Geoffrey Pullum at

Language Log, 17 December 2003: http://itre.cis.upenn.edu/~myl/langua-gelog/archives/000236.html

6. One of the problems was that literature teachers believed themselves competent to pass judgment on English grammar without being aware of what scholars of language said about the subject.

7. The idea that humans have an innate faculty of language is highly influential in modern linguistics but is not held by all scholars. A contrary view is advanced by Vyvyan Evans in *The Language Myth: Why Language is Not an Instinct*, Cambridge: Cambridge University Press, 2014. Evans is a proponent of a position called cognitive linguistics, which takes the view that language is not fundamentally different from other mental capacities. Many others take the view that it is sufficiently different in its structure, functioning and acquisition to suggest that there is a distinct language faculty. I'm grateful to Bob Borsley for pointing me to this debate.

8. Melanie Phillips, *All Must Have Prizes*, London: Little, Brown, 1996, p. 69

9. N. M. Gwynne, 'Grammar worked for 3,000 years. Thanks to Gove, it will work again', *Sunday Times*, 13 April 2013

10. Gwynne is also wrong in his historical account. The abolition of grammar in English schools was due not to some progressive campaign but to longstanding criticisms advanced by literature teachers, who had no necessary grounding in the subject. 'A case could be made out for arguing that the four decades from the 1930s to the 1970s witnessed a growth of militant philistinism as a consequence of the essentially materialistic arguments put forward by the literature specialists – namely, that grammar could only be tolerated if it could empirically demonstrate that its teaching had a beneficial effect on pupils' language skills' (Richard Hudson and John Walmsley, 'The English Patient: English Grammar and Teaching in the Twentieth Century', *Journal of Linguistics*, November 2005, p. 605).

11. Kingsley Amis, 'Use and Abuse', in *The Amis Collection*, London: Penguin Books, 1990, pp. 307–8

12. Steven Pinker, *The Language Instinct*, London: Penguin Books, 1994, p. 371

13. Roger Scruton, *England: An Elegy*, London: Chatto & Windus, 2000, p. 79

14. 'Actress Emma Thompson attacks use of sloppy language', BBC News Online, 28 September 2010

15. Quoted in 'Jackson criticizes Oakland schools' "Ebonics" decision', *Los Angeles Times*, 23 December 1996

16. Quoted by Christopher Hitchens in *Unacknowledged Legislation: Writers in the Public Sphere*, London: Verso, 2000, p. 294

17. For an acute contemporary assessment of this controversy, see Geoffrey Pullum, 'Language that Dare Not Speak its Name', *Nature*, 27 March 1997, pp. 321–2, at http://www1.ucsc.edu/oncampus/currents/97-03-31/ebonics.htm

18. 'Gove: I was beaten for being cheeky to my teachers', *The Times*, 5 October 2010

19. Quoted in Tim William Machan, *What is English and Why Should We Care?*, Oxford: Oxford University Press, 2013, p. 93

20. Kingsley Amis, *The King's English: A Guide to Modern Usage*, London: HarperCollins, 1997, p. ix

2 The Errors of Pedantry

1. Cited in Gowers' introduction to 2nd edition of *Fowler's Modern English*, Oxford: Oxford University Press, 1965, p. x

2. Ibid.

3. It's in fact possible that the more linguistically informed sticklers see a precedent in the way that Latin grammar developed. Latin provides an example of a conscious policy of designing a language, which is something completely unattainable in the modern world. Between about 200 BC and

the turn of the epoch, the Latin of the educated elite underwent a radical systematisation, partly caused by the development of argument between Atticist and Asianist schools of rhetorical theory, a debate to which both Cicero and Caesar contributed in theoretical treatises and in their own rhetorical practice. The process culminated in the publication, during the reign of Tiberius (AD 14–37), of the first systematic treatise of Latin grammar, by one Remmius Palaemon, which is sadly lost to us but that apparently codified Latin grammar.

4. Cited by Noam Chomsky in *Knowledge of Language: Its Nature, Origin, and Use*, New York: Praeger, 1986, p. 1

5. Elizabeth S. Sklar, 'The Possessive Apostrophe: The Development and Decline of a Crooked Mark', *College English*, Vol. 38, No. 2 (October 1976), p. 177. I've also taken from Sklar the example of the Shakespeare Fourth Folio and the observation on the *his*-genitive form.

6. Truss, *Eats, Shoots and Leaves*, p. 44

7. The examples, cited by Sklar, come from Goold Brown, *The Grammar of English Grammars*, 1852.

8. Truss, *Eats, Shoots and Leaves*, p. 63

9. Ibid., p. 65

10. On the reform of spellings to correspond with Latin forms, I've drawn examples from David Crystal, *The Fight for English: How Language Pundits Ate, Shot and Left*, Oxford: Oxford University Press, 2006, pp. 28–9, and Edward Carney, 'Myth 5: English Spelling is Kattastroffik', in L. Bauer and P. Trudgill (eds), *Language Myths*, London: Penguin, 1998, pp. 37–8. My criticism of Truss on the use of the apostrophe follows Crystal, op. cit., pp. 135–6, though not quite as forbearingly.

11. This and the previous paragraph draw on the analysis of Edward Carney, in his magisterial *A Survey of English Spelling*, Abingdon, Oxon: Routledge, 1994, especially p. 6 on the different sounds of the final *-ed*.

12. Carol Sarler, 'Hooray for the Head who teaches correct English', *Daily Express*, 7 February 2013

13. Quoted in Fred C. Robinson, 'The History of English and its Practical Uses', *Sewanee Review*, Vol. 112, No. 3 (Summer 2004), p. 387

14. I've taken this example from Peter Trudgill, 'Myth 1: The Meanings of Words Should Not be Allowed to Vary or Change', in Bauer and Trudgill (eds), *Language Myths*, p. 2

15. John Humphrys, introduction to James Cochrane, *Between You and I: A Little Book of Bad English*, Cambridge: Icon Books, 2003, p. 3

16. Truss, *Eats, Shoots and Leaves*, p. 3

17. Daniel Hannan, *How We Invented Freedom and Why It Matters*, London: Head of Zeus, 2014, p. 29

18. See Anthony Lodge, 'Myth 4: French is a Logical Language', in Bauer and Trudgill (eds), *Language Myths*, pp. 23–31, who quotes Vaugelas, Mitterrand and others.

19. Vaugelas is well worth studying as an indication that the myth of a perfect state of language is far from unique to English speakers. See H. Nicholas Bakalar, 'The Cartesian Legacy to the Eighteenth-Century Grammarians', *Modern Language Notes*, Vol. 91, No. 4, French Issue (May 1976), p. 710: 'Vaugelas confidently informs us that the evolution of the French language which has occurred up to his own day has been a movement toward perfection, and that the French language having now attained this perfection, one can with impunity give certain rules of usage which will last forever.'

20. Winston Churchill suggested in *The Second World War* (1948–53) that one reason why the Japanese suffered a disastrous defeat in the Battle of Midway was the cumbersome nature of the Japanese language. This was not one of his more sensible pronouncements.

21. Prince Charles's comment is cited in Zoltán Kövecses, *American English: An Introduction*, Peterborough, Ontario: Broadview Press, 2000, pp. 10–11

22. The importance of Horace's principle is superbly described and applied at book length by Jack Lynch, *The Lexicographer's Dilemma: The Evolution*

of 'Proper' English, from Shakespeare to South Park, New York: Walker, 2009.
My comments in particular on Johnson's and Webster's application of the
principle of *norma loquendi* owe much to Lynch's exposition.

23. John Simon, 'Thoroughly Modern Burchfield', *New Criterion,* March
1997, p. 68, available at: http://www.newcriterion.com/articles.cfm/
modernburchfield-simon-3376

24. Otto Jespersen, *Growth and Structure of the English Language,* Garden
City, NY: Doubleday, 1938, pp. 14–15

25. Quoted in Charles C. Fries, 'The Rules of Common School Grammars', *Proceedings of the Modern Language Association,* Vol. 42, No. 1 (March
1927), p. 229

26. Quoted in Charles V. Hartung, 'Doctrines of English Usage', *English
Journal,* Vol. 45, No. 9 (December 1956), p. 520

27. Quoted in Machan, *What is English and Why Should We Care?,* p. 54

28. Fries, 'The Rules of Common School Grammars', p. 237

29. Crystal, *The Fight for English: How Language Pundits Ate, Shot, and
Left,* p. 101

30. I owe this explanation and the observation on Jespersen to Hartung,
'Doctrines of English Usage', p. 524. The examples of slang are mine.

31. *The Economist,* 1 June 2013, cited by Pullum under the wonderful title
'Economist still chicken: botches sentence rather than split infinitive' at:
http://languagelog.ldc.upenn.edu/nll/?p=4680

3 The Usage Debate

1. I draw here on Fries, 'The Rules of Common School Grammars',
pp. 221–37, and also Ivan E. Taylor, 'John Milton's Views on the Teaching of
Foreign Languages', *Modern Language Journal,* Vol. 33, No. 7 (November
1949), pp. 528–36

2. Cited in Richard L. Bushman, 'The Genteel Republic', *Wilson Quarterly*, Vol. 20, No. 4 (Autumn 1996), p. 16

3. Cited in Fries, 'The Rules of Common School Grammars', pp. 228–9

4. Ian Michael, *English Grammatical Categories and the Tradition to 1800*, Cambridge: Cambridge University Press, 1970, p. 491

5. Quoted in B. S. Monroe, 'An English Academy', *Modern Philology*, Vol. 8, No. 1 (July 1910), p. 114, who provides many useful historical references on this proposal

6. Defoe, Swift and Johnson are quoted by Crystal, *The Fight for English*, Chapter 11

7. Quoted, and termed a 'slightly silly couplet', by Henry Hitchings in *Dr Johnson's Dictionary: The Book that Defined the World*, London: John Murray, 2012, p. 198

8. This is from the preface to Johnson's *Dictionary*, quoted by Monroe, 'An English Academy', p. 120

9. Quoted by Ingrid Tieken-Boon van Ostade, 'Henry Fowler and his Eighteenth-Century Predecessors', *The Henry Sweet Society Bulletin*, Issue 51, November 2008, p. 12

10 Quoted by Ingrid Tieken-Boon van Ostade, op. cit., p. 14.

11. On Priestley, Lowth and Campbell, I've drawn on Lynch, *The Lexicographer's Dilemma*, Chapters 5 and 6

12. John Humphrys, 'I h8 txt msgs: How texting is wrecking our language', *Daily Mail*, 24 September 2007

13. David Crystal, *Txtng: The Gr8 Db8*, Oxford: Oxford University Press, 2008, pp. 162–3

14. John Dryden, 'Defence of the Epilogue', *The Collected Works*, Vol. IV, p. 217

15. On Murray and Webster, see Lynch, *The Lexicographer's Dilemma*, pp. 109–12 (Murray) and Chapter 6 (Webster). On Webster specifically, see Bruce Southard, 'Noah Webster: America's Forgotten Linguist', *American Speech*, Vol. 54, No. 1 (Spring 1979), pp. 12–22; and Tim Cassedy, ' "A

Dictionary Which We Do Not Want": Defining America against Noah Webster, 1783–1810', *William and Mary Quarterly*, Vol. 71, No. 2 (April 2014), pp. 229–54

16. I owe this point to William F. Woods, 'The Cultural Tradition of Nineteenth-Century "Traditional" Grammar Teaching', *Rhetoric Society Quarterly*, Vol. 1, No. 1 / 2 (Winter–Spring 1985), p. 7

17. I've taken these examples of Webster's orthographical reforms from Lynch, op. cit., p. 131

18. Quoted by Jim Holt, 'H.W. Fowler, the King of English', *New York Times*, 13 December 2009

19. Geoffrey Pullum, '50 Years of Stupid Grammar Advice', *Chronicle of Higher Education*, 17 April 2009, *Chronicle Review* section, B15, at http://www.lel.ed.ac.uk/~gpullum/50years.pdf

Part Two:

Usage Conundrums from A to Z

1.   http://david-crystal.blogspot.co.uk/2013/09/on-not-very-bright-grammar-test.html

2. The story is told enthrallingly in David Skinner, *The Story of Ain't: America, its Language, and the Most Controversial Dictionary Ever Published*, New York: Harper Perennial, 2013

3. Noted by Sklar, 'The Possessive Apostrophe: The Development and Decline of a Crooked Mark', p. 177

4. Geoffrey Pullum, 'A dangler in The Economist', at *Language Log*: http://languagelog.ldc.upenn.edu/nll/?p=1799

5. I owe this observation to Bob Borsley.

6. Otto Jespersen, *A Modern English Grammar on Historical Principles: Part III – Syntax*, Heidelberg: Carl Winter, Vol. 2, 1927, p. 199

Index

Words and phrases with specific discussion of usage are given in *italic* type.